DATE DUE			

Dorota Ostrowska

Reading the French New Wave

Critics, Writers and Art Cinema in France

WALLFLOWER PRESS
LONDON & NEW YORK

First published in Great Britain in 2008 by
Wallflower Press, 6 Market Place, London W1W 8AF
www.wallflowerpress.co.uk

A catalogue record for this book is available from the British Library.

ISBN 978-1-905674-57-2 (pbk)
ISBN 978-1-905674-58-9 (hbk)

Printed and bound in Poland; produced by Polskabook

Contents

Acknowledgements

I would like to thank Irena, Jan and Wojciech Ostrowscy, Ann Jefferson and Ian Christie for their support and encouragement at every stage of this project. I am thankful for the advice given to me by all my friends, in particular Graham Roberts, Robin Brown, John Orr, Eleanor Spaventa and Elizabeth Barry.

I am grateful to the Carnegie Trust whose grant allowed me to conduct research in Paris for parts of this book.

Earlier versions of chapter three were published in 'Dreaming a cinematic dream: Jean Cayrol's writings on film', *Studies in French Cinema*, 6, 1 (2006), 17–28.

To my loving parents and my brother
Kochanej Mamie, Tacie i Wojtkowi

Introduction

La Nouvelle vague, Les Cahiers du cinéma, le nouveau roman – all are among the most enduring and immediately recognisable icons of post-war Parisian culture synonymous with daring aesthetic experimentation and intellectual iconoclasm. Images of smoky cinemas with tightly-arranged rows of chairs, cine-clubs, Henri Langlois' Cinémathèque and cafés of the Quartier Latin appear as privileged sites of debates, ideas and often rapturous emotional experiences of seeing a film or reading a passage in a book. Once these films and books, acclaimed as 'art', had the power of transforming one's life if not forever then at least for a brief moment of pleasure and wonder around a café table or in front of a cinema screen. The 1950s was a time when a new way of looking at films, in particular American films which populated the screens of French cinemas after the war, was advanced. It secured a new cultural place for cinema as an art, and led to the creation of a host of new films and filmmakers, known as *la nouvelle vague*, the French New Wave.

This was a unique event in the history of European cinema because the *nouvelle vague* managed to put into practice an idea of cinema as art. This idea was first developed in the pages of a Parisian film magazine, *Les Cahiers du cinéma*. Although the *nouvelle vague* was rather short-lived – the height of its success lasted only for about three years between 1959 and 1962 – the impact it had was tremendous. In this short period about 160 filmmakers made films, many of which were débuts and a number of which became classics of world cinema – *Les quatre cents coups (The 400 Blows*, 1959), *Hiroshima, mon amour* (1959), *À bout de souffle (Breathless*, 1960), *Cléo de 5 à 7 (Cléo from 5 to 7*, 1961) to mention just a few. Even though the *nouvelle vague* was a very diverse phenomenon with so many artists participating in it, nowadays it has come to be associated with two principal groups. On the one hand are François Truffaut, Jean-Luc Godard, Claude Chabrol, Eric Rohmer and Jacques Rivette, all of them one time critics of *Cahiers du cinéma* who then became filmmakers; on the other are filmmakers who started their careers as short film and documentary directors rather than critics; this so-

called 'Left-bank' group included Alain Resnais, Chris Marker and Agnès
Varda. The guide and spiritual father of the *nouvelle vague* was André Bazin, a Catholic intellectual, a film critic and the co-founder of *Cahiers du
cinéma* who is also credited with the development of one of the most influ-
ential theories in the history of cinema – the theory of realism. Throughout
the 1950s *Cahiers du cinéma* distinguished itself as the main magazine of
French *cinéphiles* and was established as the creative and intellectual core
of the *nouvelle vague*.

Founded in 1951 *Cahiers du cinéma* was one among a number of film
magazines published in France around this time, such as *Positif, Presénce
du cinéma, Image et son, Cinéma, Arts, Gazette du cinéma, Revue du cinéma, L'Age du cinéma* and those periodicals which published film reviews
on a regular basis (*Figaro littéraire, France-Observateur, Lettres françaises,
L'Express*). A strong political affiliation was a fact of life for French film
journals and a reflection of the intellectual climate at the time. What distinguished *Cahiers du cinéma* from its main competitor *Positif* was not just
its yellow cover (*Positif*'s was black) and its role in championing American
films, but also its right-of-centre politics. While *Positif* remained under the
influence of the French Communist Party the identity of *Cahiers du cinéma*
was forged in opposition to the left-wing political militancy. According to
Antoine de Baecque, the anti-Americanism of the French Communist Party,
understood as anti-Hollywoodism when it came to cinema, was the main
reason for rupture with the progressive forces in France which occurred in
1948–50 and set up the political tone of *Cahiers du cinéma* well into the mid-
1960s (1991a: 24–5). Bazin's own participation in Catholic intellectual and
cultural life (he wrote regularly for Emmanuel Mournier's *Esprit* and contributed to the cultural Catholic periodical *Radio-Cinéma-Télévision* (later
Télérama)) and his work at the cine-clubs of the Jeunesse ouvrière chrétienne
(Christian Working Youth) were responsible for *Cahiers*' particular political
tint (see de Baecque 2003: 39). If we take a bird's-eye view of the French
cinéphilic press after the war we will see *Positif* as concerned with the political content of the films more than with aesthetic and formal questions. A
long-time *Positif* contributor, Robert Benayoun, claimed that *Positif*'s take
on cinema was 'very anti-aesthetic' because 'they wanted cinema to express
ideas which can change society and make cinema an engaged art' (quoted in
de Baecque 2003: 231). For its part *Cahiers du cinéma* was engaged in the
polemics against French cinema and in metaphysical interpretations of films.
While *Cahiers* has experienced quite a few sharp political turns and upheav-

als in its long history (one of which included the editorial of the magazine being run by a Maoist collective), *Positif* has managed to maintain an impressive continuity in its tones and attitudes. It could be that the set of liberal ideals this leftist magazine embraced at its origins have since been entrenched as the central ideological tenants of Western democracies as well as films produced and reviewed there.

In spite of its left-wing leanings *Positif* in the 1950s was in thrall to American cinema, especially its B-productions: science fiction, fantasy, erotica and thrillers (see de Baecque 2003: 230–1). This paradox indicates an important feature of French criticism at the time. Although critics were taking sides in political debates, it was the debate regarding cinema's cultural role which was of the utmost importance to them. What *Cahiers*, *Positif* and contributors to other film magazines shared was their passion for American films, some select French and European productions and a *cinéphilic* attitude towards cinema expressed in the efforts to valorise it as an artform in its own right created by individual film artists, cinema *auteurs*. De Baecque argues that the *cinéphiles* – film critics and audiences of various cine-clubs – managed to create a counter-culture of their times, which was championing the cause of cinema as an art and as a centre of cultural activities, while opposing some institutionalised sources of authority, such as universities and political parties (2003: 18–31). *Cinéphilia* was so successful because at the time cinema-going numbers were high and films were still the primary source of entertainment (this was to change soon with the advent of television which would take over from cinema as the main family entertainment). Cine-clubs were the primary source of support for critics' efforts because it was there where serious discussions between critics and cinema-going audiences were taking place. In short, cinema really mattered both in political and cultural terms and gradually became a serious rival of literature which at the beginning of the 1950s was experiencing some important new developments as well.

The 'new novelists' were a group of writers associated with the Parisian publishing house Editions de Minuit, and included Alain Robbe-Grillet, Nathalie Sarraute, Marguerite Duras, Jean Cayrol, Michel Butor, Claude Simon and later on Claude Ollier. They aimed to reinvent the novel by developing new forms of characterisation, narration and plot-development which would be radically different from the prevailing nineteenth-century novelistic norms associated primarily with the writings of Balzac. The new novelists considered their writings as a kind of laboratory, a site of a creative experiment designed to explore the particularities of the novelistic art. Just like the *Cahiers* critics who tended to downplay the achievements of the first avant-garde of the 1920s, the new novelists were more eager to contest nineteenth-century psychological realism than to see themselves as heirs of Flaubert, Proust or the American writers John Dos Passos and William Faulkner. One of the reasons for this shared attitude of the film critics and the new novel-ists was the experience of World War Two and a sense that after the war was over the artistic project of cinema and the novel not only could be but had to be started anew. As we will see later there existed obvious continu-ities between the earlier modernist projects in cinema and literature and the creative and critical practice of the *nouvelle vague/Cahiers du cinéma* and of the *nouveau roman*, yet it was a strategic decision on the part of both the film critics and new novelists to downplay these continuities in order to bring attention to their own specific projects. The new novelists managed to generate a great deal of journalistic interest in their difficult writings which made them into fashionable and high-minded literary iconoclasts, among whom Robbe-Grillet was the most vocal and prominent. Critics such as Ro-land Barthes and Jean Ricardou were among the champions of the *nouveau roman* keeping the public's interest in the new novelists' radical experiment. Robbe-Grillet's, Duras' and Cayrol's scriptwriting and directing for cinema played a decisive role in bridging the worlds of cinema and literature in the 1950s and 1960s and created an opportunity to see the cinema/literature relationship as a prism through which one could understand the dynamics of the cultural debates taking place at the time regarding the future of both cinema and literature as artforms.

During the sixty years separating us from 1950s Paris and the heyday of *Cahiers du cinéma*, the *nouvelle vague* and the *nouveau roman*, these once vibrant and fast-paced cultural phenomena have generated an overwhelm-ing number of critical responses. Those who over the years have uncovered, studied, described and analysed various aspects of the *nouvelle vague* and the *nouveau roman* have contributed to a body of work which is impressive in its richness and variety. The sheer extent of the scholarship inevitably raises the question of whether it is in fact possible to write anything new about the period when the *nouvelle vague* and the *nouveau roman* peaked. Yet, paradoxically, it is often the understanding of canonical and popular phenomena which becomes ossified and more often than not reduced to a handful of clichés repeated in classrooms, critical essays, books, on websites and during dinner table conversations. At closer inspection the scholarship of these phenomena reveals gaps and unexplored avenues of inquiry, and begs questions that this volume will hope to address.

One set of issues which has informed this interest in the *nouvelle vague* and the *nouveau roman* is the combined impact of both for the creation of the concept of art in relation to cinema and the novel. Art cinema and the art of the novel became signs put again into the cultural circulation by the critics of the *nouvelle vague* and the *nouveau roman* after World War Two. They reinvented these ideas at a time of increased interest in cinema among audiences and intellectuals and when new life was being injected into the French novel as well. Many of these ideas echoed those of the first avant-garde of the 1920s and of French modernist writers, but in the 1950s and 1960s the intellectual context was quite different than that of the recent past. It is enough to mention the impact of the experience of the concentration camps on the ideas of Jean Cayrol and the role played by semiotics and structuralism in shaping the intellectual trajectory of Robbe-Grillet, his critics, Barthes and Ricardou, and of *Cahiers'* criticism in the 1960s. The arguments of the film critics forged in the post-war intellectual climate were not forgotten like those of the first avant-garde but informed to a great degree the critical discourse and the institutional support for cinema in Europe. The concept of art cinema has been used in the ongoing battle between national cinemas of Europe and Hollywood; it has also contributed to drawing and sustaining the dichotomy between popular and art cinemas in Europe.

The intellectual project of the film critics and new novelists was possible because each had been involved in a long-standing and complex dialogue conducted through both creative and critical practice. One of the most intriguing figures of the *nouvelle vague*, Alain Resnais, collaborated with three different new novelists, Marguerite Duras, Alain Robbe-Grillet and Jean Cayrol, who wrote scripts for some of his most famous films *Hiroshima, mon amour*, *L'Année dernière à Marienbad* (*Last Year in Marienbad*, 1961) and *Muriel ou le temps d'un retour* (1963), respectively. In one of the first comprehensive studies of the *nouvelle vague*, James Monaco described these films as 'the *nouveau roman* film' which reflected the importance of the new novelists' contribution to Resnais' works:

> Parallel with *Cahiers* critics' preoccupation with genre and *auteur* and sometimes overlapping with it is the development of what, for want of a better phrase, we might call the *nouveau roman* film by Alain Resnais and those novelists who wrote screenplays for him (and later turned to

directing themselves) – notably Alain Robbe-Grillet and Marguerite Duras. (1976: 8)

In the course of their careers, Duras, Robbe-Grillet and Cayrol alternated between literary and filmic practice, thus creating a new cultural space which existed between literature and cinema. In addition to collaborative projects, the critical practice of the *nouvelle vague* filmmakers, who wrote for *Cahiers*, and of the new novelists overlapped as well. Claude Ollier became a film critic in the 1960s while Cayrol co-authored with Claude Durand a theoretical study of cinema *Le Droit du regard* (1963). Moreover, a number of the *nouveau roman* critics such as Jean Ricardou, Roland Barthes and Gérard Genette employed cinematic references in their critical writings on literature, in particular that of the new novelists.

Having identified the conceptual, creative and critical interfaces between the new novelists and the film critics the challenge is to find the most productive way to trace the developments of the concepts of the art of cinema and the art of the novel in the cinematic and literary fields. Although the creative works of the *nouvelle vague* and the *nouveau roman* have separately always attracted critics' attention, there are few studies that examine the relationship *between the two*. The ones that do propose a variety of ways to conceptualise the link between these two artistic movements. Jean-Marie Clerc's *Littérature et cinéma* (1993) examines the relationship between cinema and literature from the beginning of the twentieth century in the context of French culture. He offers a broad historical overview of processes present in the history of cinema and the novel which led to the development of particular filmic and literary forms in the 1950s and 1960s. Clerc opens his study with a claim that when such a relationship as between literature and cinema is considered, narration seems to be widely recognised as the common denominator of both arts, and the link between the *nouvelle vague* and the *nouveau roman* is a modern example of such a relationship. Lynn Higgins' study *Nouveau roman, New Wave, New Politics* (1996) identifies two ways in which the works of the *nouvelle vague* and the *nouveau roman* relate to each other: their shared approach to questions of representation, and their relation to history (1996: 5). She identifies the existence of a shared *écriture* or formal structures more generally of the *nouvelle vague* and the *nouveau roman* which allows her to consider the two artistic movements in conjunction (1996: 10). She proposes that the equivalence of cinematic and literary *écriture* as a critical and epistemological framework was established in the 1950s and remained the principle of the *nouvelle vague*'s and the *nouveau roman*'s interaction throughout the 1960s. Her definition of this *écriture* puts 'emphasis on the camera as a pen, on the development of individual authorist directorial forms of expression [and] reflected a desire to create a cinema that would not be derivative of literature but rather its equal' (ibid.). In his study *Nouveau roman, nouveau cinéma* (1998) Claude Murcia introduces a category of *nouveau cinéma* ('new cinema'), which evokes Monaco's '*nouveau roman* films' associated in particular with the oeuvre of Alain Resnais. Murcia defines *nouveau cinéma* as a product of academic criticism, distinct from the rest of the *nouvelle vague*, and linked directly with the *nouveau roman*, and also places the works of Robbe-Grillet at the centre of his analysis of the *nouveau roman* and the *nouveau cinéma*. He further examines the works of Resnais, Cayrol and Godard as belonging to the same category of *nouveau cinéma*; Murcia concentrates on the formal aspect of films and novels and identifies cinematic effects in novels and literary ones in cinema, and argues that there is a crossing between cinema and the novel in the creative works of these artists. In *Screening the Text: Intertextuality in New Wave French Cinema* (1992), T. Jefferson Kline presents French cinema's relationship with literature as one of its most important characteristics. He concentrates on 'the conscious and often unconscious relationship that the French New Wave filmmakers developed to a constituted-and-then-repressed authority: the literature(s) that subtend their films' (1992: 4–5). Kline also argues that 'one of the forms of the return of the repressed element involved self-conscious theorising' on the part of the filmmakers; as a result, 'however much they rejected any notion of borrowing their material from the novel, the new filmmakers merely ended up borrowing the *nouveau roman*'s programme' (1992: 3). In positioning his study, Kline indicates the importance of the critical discourses of the *nouvelle vague* and the *nouveau roman* which offer a new way of exploring the relationship between the two movements. These critical discourses have been the subject of separate studies conducted by both literary and film scholars but they have never been systematically explored in a comparative manner.[1] This volume is thus just such a comparative analysis, undertaken in order to establish a wider historical perspective for the development of the concepts of the art of the novel and the art of cinema.

The body of criticism generated in the context of the *nouvelle vague* and the *nouveau roman* has included critical essays written by the new novelists themselves, those written by future *nouvelle vague* filmmakers when they were still critics for *Cahiers du cinéma* in the 1950s, interviews with filmmakers and writers, critical responses to the films and novels of the *nouveau roman* and the *nouvelle vague*, and critical ideas contained in the creative works linked to their self-reflexive character. These critical discourses played a fundamental role in the development of both artistic movements and served as the arena where the dialogue between the novelists and literary critics on one side and filmmakers and film critics on the other were conducted. The examination of these discourses offers the widest and most comprehensive basis for a comparison between the *nouvelle vague* and the *nouveau roman* and serve as a prism for examining the development of the concept of art cinema and the art of the novel.

Film and literary criticism in France during the 1950s and 1960s interlocked to such a degree that they became inextricable. For this reason reading (or re-reading) the *nouvelle vague* only really makes sense in the context of literary criticism associated with the *nouveau roman*, and ideas about the art of cinema and the art of the novel developed by the critics quite often appear to be mirror-images of each other. The difference between language and text on the one hand and images and sounds on the other are blurred, creating a hybrid aesthetic structure which can bridge cinema and literature in the most surprising way evident in *nouvelle vague* film and in *nouveau roman* creative and critical practice. It is thus important to engage with the critical debates of the *nouvelle vague* and the *nouveau roman* because the concepts they developed are still with us today; art cinema, *mise-en-scène*, *montage*, cinematic style, writer-director, cinematic essay and cinematic writing are concepts which are ridden with tensions and paradoxes resulting from the complexity of the critical discourses and creative practices which generated them. These concepts also seem rather large, enigmatic and elusive. By presenting the intellectual archaeology of the concepts and the history of their creation by recreating the discursive context in which they were coined this study hopes to make these ideas more concrete and tangible.

This investigation of the criticism of the *nouvelle vague* and the *nouveau roman* concentrates on the period which began in the early 1950s and finished in the second half of the 1960s. In the early 1950s, Alain Robbe-Grillet's critical essays and book reviews could be found in *Critique* and the *Nouvelle Nouvelle Revue Française* (*NNRF*), and Nathalie Sarraute's critical essays appeared in *Les Temps modernes* and *NNRF*. In 1950 Jean Cayrol published *Lazare parmi nous*, which included 'Pour un romanesque lazaréen', a study both of prisoners' dreams and of his concept of a new type of art. In 1951, André Bazin founded a new film magazine, *Cahiers du cinéma*. The end of the period 1966–67 coincided with *Cahiers'* decision to publish a special issue, *Film et roman: problèmes du récit*, discussing the cinema/literature relationship and focusing on problems of narrative. This was also the time when preoccupations with the questions of cinema as an artform became secondary to critics' interest in ideological questions. Significantly, the cover of *Cahiers du cinéma* changed as well from yellow to red which reflected the political turn taking place at the magazine. In 1967 Robbe-Grillet made *Trans-Europ Express*, an example of self-reflexive textual film which could itself be considered a piece of criticism conducted through audio-visual practice.

Throughout the 1950s and 1960s, critical discourses of the *nouvelle vague* and the *nouveau roman* were shaped by external and internal factors which divided this period into four phases. The internal factors consisted of instances of the new novelists' creative engagement with cinema as scriptwriters and filmmakers in their own right. This practical engagement of the new novelists with the cinema of the *nouvelle vague* began to shape the concepts of cinema and novel as arts into new directions. In the period between 1951 and 1959 the successful collaboration between Resnais and Duras on *Hiroshima, mon amour* took place. In the periods between 1959 and 1961 and between 1961 and 1963, Robbe-Grillet and Cayrol worked with Resnais on *L'Année dernière à Marienbad* and *Muriel ou le temps d'un retour*, respectively. The period between 1963 and 1967 was that of Robbe-Grillet's shift into filmmaking with *Trans-Europ Express* and *L'Immortelle* (1962).

The ideas of cinema and the novel as arts were also shaped by references to critical debates of the 1920s and by critical and theoretical trends of the 1950s and 1960s, semiotics and structuralism in particular. The interests of *Cahiers du cinéma* critics and the new novelists in narrative, which constituted the basis for their discussion about cinematographic and literary writing, *écriture cinématographique* and *écriture litéraire*, could be traced to the writing of the first avant-garde, which included such artists as Jean Epstein and Marcel L'Herbier, to the self-reflexive fiction of André Gide in *Les Faux-monnayeurs* (1925) and to Jean-Paul Sartre's analysis of novelistic forms in *Situations, I* (1938). Engagement with the writings of Sartre, Jorge Luis Borges and the Surrealists was important in the periods between 1951–59 and 1959–63 because they were specifically concerned with the relationship between literary and cinematic narratives in a cultural context dominated by literary production. Sartre's and Borges' understanding of cinema was influenced by their work in both cinema and literature; the Surrealists had already brought attention to the cinematic nature of literary texts through their interest in the *ciné-roman* ('cine-novel') and through the production of literary texts inspired by their experiences as cinema spectators. In the period 1963–67, it was semiotics and structuralism which determined the critical discourse of the *nouvelle vague* and the *nouveau roman*.

During 1951–59 critics tried to develop terms with which to debate the aesthetic dimension of cinema and the novel in a historical context, and to define cinema and the novel as independent arts. Cinema became part of reflections on the art of the novel by the new novelists; this incorporation showed that the cinematic element was indispensable for defining the concepts of the novel and of the novelistic narrative attempted by the new novelists, which was modernist at its core. The definition of cinematic forms in terms of cinematographic writing, first proposed by André Bazin, Alexandre Astruc and Roger Leenhardt and then embraced by *Cahiers du cinéma* critics, was based on a paradox: the critics embedded their arguments about cinematic form in references to the literary canon, to the literary model of authorship and to literary writing while arguing for the definition of cinema which could capture this art's unique potential and features. At the same time, the *Cahiers* critics developed a particular style of writing about films which reflected their literary education firmly rooted in the French classical canon. In the 1950s cinema was the key reference for the definition of the art of the novel while literature was a model for establishing the parameters of the art of cinema.

In the period 1961–63, the Resnais/Robbe-Grillet collaboration on *L'Année dernière à Marienbad* resulted in the emergence of a new type of writing, the cine-novel, which was an example of a textual film connected with the actual film by narrative means and published as a separate work. A new kind of a cine-literary narrative was emerging, which was conceptualised in terms derived from the Surrealists and from Borges, who proposed a vision of a literary text and literary narrative which could be shared with cinema. In the period 1963–67, Robbe-Grillet's shift into filmmaking was accompanied by the rise of literary theory. Semiotics and structuralist analysis were introduced into the critical discourse of film by such critics as Roland Barthes, Jean Ricardou, Christian Metz and Noël Burch. They defined cinematic narrative, which structurally was supposed to be the same as literary narrative. Film and literary theory replacing critical writings on cinema and literature became a way of casting in new terms the cine-literary narrative which was emerging as common to both cinema and the novel.

Jean Cayrol's work on Resnais' *Muriel ou le temps d'un retour* and *Nuit et brouillard* (*Night and Fog*, 1955) took place in the period between 1950 and 1963. The critical writings of Cayrol regarding cinematic and literary criticism in this period have a special place in the account of the debates regarding the art of cinema and the art of the novel as they provide a model for the interaction between the discourses of the *nouvelle vague* and the *nouveau roman*. Cayrol showed that the critical discourse of the novel, the *romanesque lazaréen* ('Lazarean fiction'), depends on a visual element which shares many characteristics of realist cinema. In *Le Droit du regard*, Cayrol described cinematic narrative in which the verbal, synonymous with the narrative, contains and conveys the visual or cinematic. He thus uses his idea of the novel to develop the concept of the art of cinema; as a result, literary and cinematic narratives are presented as equivalent to each other and hybrid in nature – that is, cine-literary. From 1959 to 1961, formal characteristics of such cine-literary narratives made it possible for cine-novels to be treated as substitutes of films in some critical accounts. From 1963 to 1967 thus defined narrative allowed the theorists to identify the same formal structures in both films and novels.

The presence of the realist idea of cinema at the basis of Cayrol's concept of the Lazarean fiction suggests that Cayrol was also engaging with prevailing ideas about cinema. The visual, which the narrative of the Lazarean fiction was expressing, altered the realist concept of cinema, in particular the realist discourse which in the *Cahiers* context was focused on the concepts of *mise-en-scène* and *montage*. The nature of his project required Cayrol to challenge the prevailing realist concept of cinema. His role as a film critic involved in the examination of the *Cahiers* concept of cinema grew when he published *Le Droit du regard*, which could be seen as an open engagement with the concept of *mise-en-scène*. Cayrol's argument regarding the critical ideas of the 1950s *Cahiers du cinéma* critics emphasised the importance of the literary element in them; he stressed the degree to which these concepts were predicated on ideas derived from literary history and from critical discourse about the novel. From 1959 onwards, one could observe different ways in which the new novelists, like Cayrol, or the critics of the *nouveau roman* had an impact upon the critical discourse of cinema. In the course of his engagement with cinema, Robbe-Grillet expressed his ideas regarding the nature of cinema in his critical writings. Claude Ollier, another new novelist, and Jean Ricardou, the *nouveau roman* critic, also contributed to the critical discourse of cinema in *Cahiers* in the 1960s. Like Cayrol, all these literary contributors to *Cahiers*' criticism were challenging the critical line of the magazine of the 1950s by emphasising the importance of the literary element in cinema. Robbe-Grillet in particular argued that scripts were equivalent to films and his activity as a filmmaker was based on the assumption that films were equivalent to novels; Ollier emphasised the importance of scriptwriters, text and dialogue in the films he reviewed.

The arguments of Cayrol, like those of other new novelists regarding the importance of the literary element in the critical discourse of *Cahiers du cinéma* during the 1950s, initially evoked a negative reaction on the part of *Cahiers*' critics. These critics attempted to conceptualise the object of cinema by referring to literature, which was most clearly expressed in the concepts of cinematographic writing and film essays. They used examples from the literary canon, literary history and contemporary literary criticism and theory in order to define the art of cinema. This situation had two outcomes: in the first place, it defined the art of cinema in literary terms and made literature an indispensable part of the definition; secondly, since literature was part of the definition of cinema, it naturally also facilitated the engagement of literary critics and writers with cinema. In the 1950s and 1960s, the *Cahiers* critics continued to reject the input of the new novelists, but at the same time they were unable to renounce it completely, because by then the new novelists' involvement with cinema was part of the critical practice of *Cahiers* itself. Some of the most innovative filmmaking of the 1950s and 1960s was done by the directors like Alain Resnais who were collaborating with the new novelists. When the new novelists became filmmakers in their own right they were thus following an important trend in French culture whereby writers and poets, such as Jean Cocteau and André Malraux, made a successful crossing from literature to cinema. The importance of literary culture as the model for the engagement with cinema of the young critics from *Cahiers du cinéma* and of such innovative filmmakers as Chris Marker cannot therefore be stressed enough; it was not fine arts or music which served as the main reference point for the young critics and filmmakers but literature.

At their origins the concepts of art cinema, cinematic writing and visual literature as developed by the film critics of *Cahiers* were literary because they were based on models derived from literature. The *Cahiers* critics invented and described the cinema which they loved (mostly American cinema) using a conceptual framework derived from literature. Most of the *nouvelle vague* filmmakers were critics before they became filmmakers and in this sense one could argue that there almost existed a programme for literary cinema which the *nouvelle vague* filmmakers were trying to realise through their filmmaking. In this sense the term 'critic-director' might be as valid and correct as that of 'writer-director'. Paradoxically, some of the most innovative critic-directors, such as Resnais, have never published a single word on the subject and their arguments have always been conducted through innovative creative practice. The focus on the critical dimension in the definition of *auteurs* eases the bond of *auteur* with scriptwriting. Being a critic, either through the practice of writing or filmmaking, is thus made more important than authoring one's own scripts. In fact, as we shall see in the case of Resnais, collaborating with scriptwriters allowed him to make breakthroughs in his cinematic practice and push the boundaries of the cinematic form in new directions.

In this study the focus is almost exclusively on the critical and discursive part of the *nouvelle vague* experiment as it is held that it is in the pages of critical essays where the idea of art cinema was born and where analysis of films or cinematic essays were conducted. The concept of art cinema is widely recognised as synonymous with European cinema, and the strength and confidence of French filmmaking today is due in large measure to the fact that the idea of art cinema and *auteurs* was originally a French one which enjoyed an amazing pan-European success. The fact that it is in France that this idea is practised most successfully has certainly much to do with the elaborate and generous system of state subsidies and with the robustness of the French film industry in general which even today commands a greater portion of the domestic market than any other European country. As important to the success of French filmmaking is the fact that the idea of *auteur* cinema is rooted in French culture and connects its different strands – literary and visual – through the self-conscious creative and critical practice of *Cahiers du cinéma/nouvelle vague* and new novelists in the post-war period. The idea of art cinema thus resulted from an intellectual project of the community of French artists based in Paris in the 1950s and 1960s. It is because of the importance of the concept of art cinema for cinema in general that the decision was made to present critical debates on French cinema and literature drawing on texts and films which often are only known to a narrow group of French literature and French Studies specialists. This focus is also important for emphasising the specifically European and French origins of the concept of art cinema which developed a culturally-specific intellectual apparatus that was then used to engage with Hollywood films which inundated European screens in the post-war period.

The argument is presented in four parts, recreating the twists and turns of the dialogues conducted by the *Cahiers* critics and new novelists and their critics between 1951 and 1967. During this time the new terms describing contemporary cinema and the novel and the interactions between the two were invented. Chapter one examines the period between 1951 and 1959 when the critical discourses of cinema and the novel found their unique realisation and illustration in the collaboration between Resnais and Duras on *Hiroshima, mon amour*. These critical discourses focus on finding terms to describe formal aspects of cinema and of the novel in terms of *écriture*, which takes both cinema and the novel away from the constraints of the nineteenth-century realist narrative. These parallel projects reveal common features of both cinematic and literary *écriture* such as the loose essayistic architecture of films and novels, experiments with the temporal dimension of the narrative and subjective forms of narration. As literary critics, the new novelists look to cinema to help them define the art of the novel and carry out the kind of experiments they were interested in. Similarly, the *Cahiers* critics evoke the literary canon, the literary concept of authorship and literature itself to describe the art of cinema. At the same time, film critics begin to develop their own conceptual apparatus (*mise-en-scène*, *montage*, style) to help them convey the ways in which cinema expresses itself in its own formal language.

Chapter two considers the period between 1961 and 1963, when the collaboration between Resnais and Robbe-Grillet on *L'Année dernière à Marienbad* resulted in a cine-novel which was a first textual film, while the actual film was regarded as an example of literary cinema. Resnais' work was considered an open challenge to the taboo of the writer-director prevailing in *Cahiers*, and by making all of his films together with scriptwriters Resnais emphasises the fact that any inquiry regarding the cinematic form and narrative is premised on literature. His work evokes the Surrealists' focus on the idea of cinema as an expres sion of dreams and the unconscious. Resnais' films also contain references to the ideas of Borges, one-time film critic in the Argentine magazine *Sur*, for whom cinema was a visual literature, sharing its narrative structures with the novel. Both the Surrealists and Borges were thus interested in cinema as an alternative form of literature but they did not aim to eliminate the novel completely from the French cultural landscape. By evoking their arguments, Resnais is seeking to embrace literature, and to acknowledge its importance for both cinematic production and critical reflection, especially as regards narrative.

Chapter three focuses on Jean Cayrol's writings regarding both cinema and the novel. The interface between critical debates in cinema and literature concerned with the nature of visual and literary narratives is most fully realised when the crossing takes place in the critical writings of just one artist, as is the case with Cayrol. His film and literary criticism, whose sources of inspiration extend from Surrealism to existentialism, are organically interconnected in order to fulfil an artistic vision. They form a microcosm which reflects the dynamics present in the interaction of the film and literary discourses in the 1950s and 1960s whereby the film discourse is determined by the literary one. As a result the film narrative shares the characteristics of the literary narrative. However, the literary debate is itself embedded within the visual and cinematic culture and thus transformed by it in profound ways. For this reason, the *raison d'être* of the literary narrative is an attempt to express the unconscious akin to cinematic dreams. In a wider sense we could think of cinema as being the suppressed unconscious of the literary culture, which emerges at a very specific moment of cinematic history – initially at the time of the first avant-garde in the 1920s and then again in the context of the *nouvelle vague*.

Cayrol's critical writings about cinema and literature show that the inquiry into the nature of cinema grows out of the crisis of the realist novel in the context of the post-Holocaust world. He creates the theoretical basis for introducing cinema into ongoing literary debates concerning the nature of literary narrative, and also for applying the findings of these debates for the purposes of cinema. In his critical text *Lazare parmi nous* Cayrol casts the unconscious individual world resembling dreams, which the introspective novel wants to explore, in phenomenological terms of cinematic *mise-en-scène*. In this way the novel's self-referential exploration of its narrative form is premised on cinema. He then claims the equivalence between novelistic and cinematic narrative forms in his theoretical study of cinema poetics, *Le Droit du regard*, which is informed by his own cinematic practice as a documentary and experimental filmmaker. As a result, any exploration of the novel's form becomes that of cinema, and vice versa. The aesthetic discourses of both arts are interconnected because they share the object of their inquiry, which is narrative.

Chapter four covers the period between 1963 and 1967, when literary and film critics were faced with two important phenomena – Robbe-Grillet's shift into filmmaking with *L'Immortelle* and *Trans-Europ Express*, and the emergence of the literary theory associated with semiotics and structuralism. Literary critics and writers who get involved in film criticism are vehicles of new critical ideas regarding cinema; the influx of literary critics into film criticism took place at the time when new theoretical fashions, such as structuralism, semiotics and narratology, were sweeping across Paris in the mid-1960s. These intellectual trends inspired by linguistics were characterised by their applicability to all art forms, including cinema. They offered an opportunity to open the critical debate about cinema into new directions. It was the literary origins of the theoretical discourse which made film narrative a focus of this new critical inquiry. As a result the insights offered by theory resulted in redefining cinematic narrative in a way that it became a mirror image of the literary one.

The arguments of the *Cahiers du cinéma* critics developed in the pre-*nouvelle vague* period are revisited by Robbe-Grillet, a new novelist-turned-cinéaste, and given a new twist in the early 1960s. As a result of his filmmaking experiences Robbe-Grillet reinforces the aesthetic independence of cinema and the novel and comes to a surprising conclusion that the exploration of the formal aspects of both arts should be conducted independently of one another. This position questions that of Cayrol and Resnais and is theorised in semiotic terms by Jean Ricardou, who argues for the independence of cinematic and literary signs. This separation between formal inquiries into cinema and the novel is overcome by Christian Metz who reintroduces narrative as the common denominator of visual and literary arts. Noël Burch develops Metz's position and identifies shared elements of the cine-literary narratives. Metz's and Burch's findings are published in *Cahiers du cinéma* and contextualised by another new novelist, Claude Ollier, thus preparing the magazine for its subsequent engagement with theory.

While some lesser-known writers and filmmakers, such as Jean Cayrol, are very prominent in this story, the absence of other key figures such as Jean-Luc Godard may appear strange to some. The reason for this is that this study does not attempt to be comprehensive or exhaustive. It shows a slice of the cinematic and literary life of the 1950s and 1960s, with a special focus on those parts of this life where the literary and cinematic trajectories overlap or cross in both creative and critical practice. While Godard was a critic-director, his direct contacts with the new novelists were sparse, with no creative engagement with any them, which can be comparable to that of Alain Resnais. For this reason the comprehensive examination of the work of Godard does not belong to the immediate remit of this study. Marguerite Duras is not made very prominent either because she was not interested in critical writing or theory, which is the central focus here.

The focus on *Cahiers du cinéma* and the relative exclusion of its important competitor and contemporary *Positif* has to do with the concentration of the critical debates regarding the potential of cinema as an artform in the pages of *Cahiers* rather than *Positif*. The examination of the latter's interest in the genre cinema, horror and the fantastic, and its awareness of the political and ideological, would be a fascinating follow-up to this study taking it beyond the realm of literary cinema and thus offering a more comprehensive, inclusive and varied definition of cinema which will not require the label 'art' attached to it to make it worthy of attention.

I

Prehistory 1951–59

INVENTING THE ART OF CINEMA AND THE ART OF THE NOVEL

Between 1951 and 1959 young critics of *Cahiers du cinéma* and such crit-ically-minded new novelists as Alain Robbe-Grillet, Nathalie Sarraute and Michel Butor were engaged in parallel projects of defining the specificities of their respective arts. At the same time when the first issue of *Cahiers du cinéma* was published in 1951, the new novelists began to write critical es-says in which they clarified their creative objectives. Until 1959, when Alain Resnais, a filmmaker associated closely with the founder of *Cahiers*, André Bazin, made his first full-length feature, *Hiroshima, mon amour*, scripted by a new novelist, Marguerite Duras, there was little interaction between the new novelists and *Cahiers du cinéma* critics and between the worlds of cinema and literature more generally. Only two years before *Hiroshima, mon amour* was made a round-table discussion was published in *Cahiers du cinéma*, '6 personnages en quête d'*auteurs*', where Bazin and Roger Leen-hardt were emphasising the essential and historically fertile connection be-tween French literature and French cinema which was missing at the time of their debate. They argued that the input of the writers had always rejuve-nated French cinema and turned filmmaking into the personal *écriture* of the directors. Leenhardt was pointing out the crucial role that writers such as Jacques Prévert and Jean Cocteau played in the French pre-war cinema (in Bazin *et al.* 1957: 19). Bazin and Leenhardt both attributed the failure of French cinema to a break in the connection with literature, which had borne fruitful results for cinema in the past (ibid.). In 1957 French cinema was in a very good financial shape and remained popular with a wider public but was lacking in aesthetic innovation. *Tradition de la qualité* films were high-bud-get, star-studded, studio-based adaptations of literary classics co-produced with international partners by a handful of directors: Claude Autant-Lara,

Henri-Georges Clouzot and Jacques Becker. New talent was only reluctantly allowed to enter the ranks of the French industry which was hierarchical and relying on a few directors who were certain to deliver one box-office success after another. It was the absence of an analytical depth provided traditionally by a link with literature and the directors' inability to draw inspiration from contemporary French reality, which, according to Bazin, was to blame for the predictability of contemporary French cinema. The filmmakers, just like modern novelists, were reproached for creating empty and formalist works lacking the ethical dimension one should expect of serious works of art (in Bazin *et al.* 1957: 85). This criticism was a call to establish new terms to define the art of cinema, which would make it less dependent on literary collaborators. This effort to redefine what cinema could be if writers played a less important role in it meant that cinema's relationship with literature was also to be cast in new terms. This was indicated in the shift of focus of the *Cahiers* critics from post-war French cinema to American cinema of the 1940s. What is most striking about this discussion is that there is no mention of the *nouveau roman* and the consensus that there was nothing interesting happening in French literary life. The interlocutors did not mention Resnais' *Nuit et brouillard*, co-written by the new novelist Jean Cayrol, as a beacon of the much-desired collaboration between writers and filmmakers in France. The realisation of the importance of the *nouveau roman* came only with the aesthetic and cultural shock of *Hiroshima, mon amour*. The film was a provocation.

Perhaps at this stage it is important to reflect for a moment on the emphasis that the likes of Bazin and Leenhardt put on the connection between cinema and literature in the French context. In their opinion the lack of any innovative projects between filmmakers and writers was a sign that a dialogue between intelligentsia and cinema was not taking place. Literature, and writing more generally (essayistic, journalistic and scholarly), was providing the majority of cultural references for the French intelligentsia, and served as a vehicle for political debate in which the intellectuals were involved and, most importantly, was the means of expression and communication for them. The central element of Bazin's crusade as a critic and thinker was to make cinema as important for the French intelligentsia as literature. The main challenge was to find a way to engage the new generation of French intellectuals and post-war youth with cinema in the same manner that they were concerned with new developments and trends in literature, theatre, music or fine arts. In his arguments Bazin referred frequently to the times of silent cinema, especially the avant-garde of the 1920s, the proliferation of the cine-clubs and film journalism of that period. He wanted sound cinema to gener-ate the same level of excitement and debate as silent cinema did (see Bazin 1975b). The success of the avant-garde was serving as a blueprint for the plan Bazin had for sound cinema aimed at transforming the contemporary cinema aesthetically, culturally and socially. Film critics responsible for the reception of the films among cultural elites and for educating spectators, and film archivists involved in preserving the cinematic heritage and making it accessible to the public to create a greater awareness of cinematic history, were the key players in the plan of reviving cinema as envisioned by Bazin (see Bazin 1975a). Unfortunately, Bazin, who died in 1958 at the moment when the *nouvelle vague* had its first successes, lived only to see the realisa-tion of the part of his plan focused on criticism and archiving. This part of the plan was accomplished through *Cahiers du cinéma*, *Positif* and other film magazines, and the work of the Cinémathèque and cine-clubs. With the films of Alain Resnais, Chris Marker, Agnès Varda and the *Cahiers* critics-turned-filmmakers Bazin's vision was to widen to affect the very process of making films. This development was already foreshadowed by the films of Roger Leenhardt and Alexandre Astruc in the late 1940s and throughout the 1950s but was taken to a new level by filmmakers of the *nouvelle vague*. The objective of Bazin's project was to redefine and re-conceptualise the whole institution of cinema, its production, funding, exhibition, reception, criticism and preservations, in a way that would make it palatable and interesting to French intellectuals. Essentially, Bazin envisioned a cinematic turn in the predominantly literary French culture. The ambition was to engage literary elites with cinema in a way that would transform cinema itself.

The *Cahiers* critics were truly perplexed by the formal novelty of *Hi-roshima, mon amour* and struggled to come to terms with it. They loved it but did not quite know how to place it. In the round-table discussion 'Hiro-shima, notre amour' Godard claimed that for him this film created its own category and was without precedent in the history of cinema. Interestingly enough just like his interlocutors, Eric Rohmer and Pierre Kast, Godard was able to find literary (Faulkner), musical (Stravinsky) and plastic (Picasso) references in *Hiroshima, mon amour*, all of which were modernist, but no cinematic references. Rohmer argued that the film may be going even further than the Americans (American novel), Joyce and Proust. For him, Resnais, like a writer trying to write his first novel, was absorbing first the lessons of the past in order to make a step forward (in Domarchi *et al.* 1959: 10). The

Cahiers critics were not just suggesting that the literary framework might be adequate for understanding the experiment of *Hiroshima*, but that this experiment while being cinematic is also of consequence for the development of the contemporary French novel, the *nouveau roman*. In their view Resnais grasped the problems of the contemporary novel, translated them into the language of cinema and 'filmed a novel that Butor, Robbe-Grillet, Bastide and Duras were trying to write' (Godard in Domarchi *et al.* 1959: 9). According to Kast and Rohmer it was on the level of narrative where the meeting of the *nouveau roman* and Resnais' cinema took place. It was the reflexive nature of Resnais' film, which struck the familiar chord with the experiments of the *nouveau roman* (in Domarchi *et al.* 1959: 9). *Hiroshima, mon amour* was a film about filmmaking, emphasising tensions between documentary and staged sequences, present and memory, through the innovative use of *montage*. This cinematic writing did not conceal its own apparatus but revealed it and foregrounded it through the development of a new kind of narrative. Given that *Hiroshima, mon amour* was also described as the first modern sound film, recalling the modernist experiments of Sergei Eisenstein, Carl Theodor Dreyer and the German Expressionists, it is clear that sound played an important role in achieving the effect that Resnais' filmic *écriture* shared with the writings of the new novelists (Rohmer in Domarchi *et al.* 1959: 4).[2] Marguerite Duras should be credited for at least some of these effects, especially those created through the use of voice-over, in particular in flashback sequences which in time came to be recognised as Resnais' signature.

The critical reception of *Hiroshima, mon amour* in *Cahiers* was the moment when the critical discourse of cinema began to embrace some of the ideas of the new novelists and relate them to the developments taking place in cinema. Thanks to the engagement of cinema and the *nouveau roman* through *Hiroshima, mon amour* the critical discourses of both arts crossed and the critics of both cinema and literature engaged in a dialogue for the first time in the post-war period. *Hiroshima, mon amour* was an example of the exchange between filmmakers and film critics on the one hand and literary critics and novelists on the other, which was seen as vital for the health of French cinema by André Bazin and other critics of his generation. *Hiroshima, mon amour* was also a realisation of Astruc's idea of filmmaking which was akin to literary writing. In comparison to other important films from that era such as *Le Beau Serge* (*Handsome Serge*, Claude Chabrol, 1958), *Les Quatre cents coups* (François Truffaut, 1959), *À bout de souffle*

(Jean-Luc Godard, 1960) and *Paris nous appartient* (*Paris Belongs to Us*, Jacques Rivette, 1960) which were personal in terms of the story or the location, filmed with light equipment, giving full expression to the idea of the camera as a pen to capture the intimacy of personal experience, *Hiroshima, mon amour* was a type of cinematic writing which had the maturity, confidence and depth of an established art, as well as a sense of distance usually associated with age. *À bout de souffle* was a pile of notes and ideas, *Hiroshima, mon amour* was a polished argument.

This rest of this chapter further explores the evolution of Astruc's idea of cinema as personal *écriture*, which culminated in the collaboration between Resnais and Duras and led to the development of narrative as the essential expression of the art of the novel and cinema. Working independently but acknowledging critical debates taking place within their specific fields, the literary and cinema critics argued that narrative, which had the same formal characteristics in both cinema and literature, was an expression of the specificities of each and thus provided the necessary basis for defining the cinema and the novel as independent arts.

Throughout the 1950s the critical discourses of cinema and the novel were areas of intense intellectual activity. Both the literary and film critics felt that the novel and cinema respectively needed to be rehabilitated in cultural terms. There exist two elements in the evolution of the critical discourses of both arts in the 1950s, in the period leading up to the appearance of *Hiroshima, mon amour*, which serve as useful points of comparison between the two. The first element regards the references used by the critics of cinema and literature. The *Cahiers* critics developed their concepts of *mise-en-scène*, *montage* and *politique des auteurs* by weaving an intricate web of literary references. This created a paradoxical situation where the definition of pure cinematic form was based on a literary framework. Through these references cinema was implanted within the literary culture and proposed as a legitimate heir of the novel in the second half of the twentieth century. In aesthetic terms the cinematic narrative was hybrid in nature with verbal elements (voice-over, often consisting of a polyphony of two or more voices engaged in a dialogue like in *Hiroshima, mon amour* or layered asynchronically over each other like in Astruc's *Les Mauvaises rencontres* (*The Bad Liaisons*, 1955)) as important as the visual ones (camerawork, flashbacks, close-ups, and so on). New cinematic writing was born from the collision of the verbal and visual elements of the narrative. The interaction of these elements is evident in a striking film by Marcel Hanoun, *Une Histoire Simple*

(1958), where audio-visual flashbacks are layered with the voice-over of the principal character. The new novelists likewise took cinema into consideration when assessing the situation of the novel in the post-war period. They were particularly sensitive to the visual aspects of the novel, which were reminiscent of cinema. The outcome of this process is comparable to that observed in the critical discourse of cinema. The definition of the art of the novel developed by the new novelists was reflecting the cultural impact of cinema; in order to be purely literary, the novel had to in fact become hybrid – visual and textual at the same time, or cine-literary.

The second characteristic shared by the critical discourses of both arts has to do with the historical dimension of these discourses. The critical discourses of the 1950s were influenced by the debates about the art of the novel and the art of cinema conducted in the first half of the twentieth century, in particular in the 1920s. The questioning of cinema and novelistic specificity by focusing on narrative forms initiated in the 1920s served as an important subtext of the post-war debates. Modernist experiments of the 1920s were echoing in the arguments of the *Cahiers* critics and the new novelists. Jean-Paul Sartre's critical writings in *Situations, I* (first published in 1938), which contained analysis of the American modernist novel, focused on many of the arguments of cinema and literary critics concerning the arts of the novel and cinema. The evolution, which Sartre's reflection on art underwent in the period between the 1930s and 1940s, was mirrored in complex ways in the critical discourses of cinema and the novel in the post-war period. The *nouveau roman* was, in a way, a French reinvention of the American novel, while the *nouvelle vague* was a reinvention of a certain idea of the art of cinema, associated with the silent period, for the purposes of sound cinema, which had an American accent.

FROM PHOTOGENIC CINEMA AND PURE NOVEL
TO SOUND CINEMA AND *NOUVEAU ROMAN*

The tragedy of World War Two convinced many artists that a certain world order had collapsed and that the artistic project in which they were going to be involved was to be completely new (see Robbe-Grillet 1963d). There was no precedent for it in the same way as there was no precedent for the reality and aftermath of the war itself. Hence, it was the artists and critics themselves who created this vision of rupture with the past. While the new novelists were more appreciative of the efforts of their predecessors and acknowledged them occasionally, the *Cahiers* critics gave the impression that they were the first to think about questions of the cinematic form. In this sense the young *Cahiers* critics were representative of the generation, which Bazin saw as those who knew little of the history of the cinema even though they watched more films than anybody in the past (1975a: 38). The difference in the understanding of the cinematic and literary heritage was linked to the different degrees of institutionalisation of cinema and literature. While literature possessed its canon, a long tradition of academic criticism and firm cultural standing, cinema only began to gain some cultural ground in this area after World War Two with the founding of the series of cine-clubs by Bazin and the creation of filmology courses at the Sorbonne (see Lowry 1985). There was also the question of the availability of film and literary material. While novels and critical essays were published, circulated and read, the films of the first avant-garde and the writings of their critics were unavailable and therefore forgotten (see Abel 1984; Ghali 1995). It is for this reason that one cannot emphasise enough the vital role played by Henri Langlois' Cinémathèque in the preservation, presentation and unearthing of the pre-war cinematic heritage and the efforts of Bazin to revitalise film criticism in France (see, for example, Roud 1983).

An examination of *Cahiers* writings in light of those by Leenhardt, Jean Epstein and André Malraux, and the essays of the new novelists from the perspective of those of Sartre and André Gide reveals profound continuities between the projects of the literary and film critics in the 1920s, 1930s, 1940s and 1950s (see Epstein 1924 and 1974; Gide 1925; Leenhardt 1936; Sartre 1947a–d; Malraux 1996). World War Two only lessened the intensity of their research without changing its direction. Not only were the interests of film critics related across time but they also coincided with the concerns of the literary critics who were their contemporaries. For this reason similar issues and concerns echo in the projects of Sartre or Gide to those of Leenhardt, Epstein, Malraux and Astruc (see Astruc 1992b). They shared the desire to discern the specific features of their respective arts and offered similar strategies to achieve this goal. Owing to the parallels in the projects of their predecessors, the critical discourses of the *nouveau roman* and *Cahiers du cinéma* critics were also related.

Epstein and Gide defined the formal characteristics of their respective arts called *photogénie* in cinema and *roman pur* ('pure novel') in literature. Epstein described *photogénie* as 'an element of all things, beings and souls, which emphasises their moral quality by the means of cinematographic reproductions' (1924: 6).[3] *Photogénie* revealed itself in non-narrative cinema, which liberated films from the constraints of realism determining the mode of representation offered by the cinema of continuity editing (Epstein 1974: 87). Echoes of Epstein's argument are found in Bazin's essays regarding the ontology of the cinematic image and non-narrative neo-realist Italian cinema, which foreshadowed the questioning of the limits of storytelling in *Cahiers'* debates about *mise-en-scène* and *montage* (see Bazin 1997f).[4] Epstein's concerns also coincided with those of André Gide who regarded narration and plot as very problematic aspects of the novel which strived to achieve the quality of *roman pur* – the novel reduced to its form only (1925: 58–9). For Gide, the way in which events were arranged in order to create the plot was marked by a high degree of artifice. He wanted to replace this artifice of plot with an arrangement of the events issuing from themselves and the reality of which they are part and not from the order imposed by the narrator (1925: 18). His project was the same as Epstein's who argued that

> There are no stories. There have never been any stories. There are only situations, without the head or the tail, without the beginning, middle and end … with no limits imposed by the past or the future. These stories are present. (1974: 87)

Both Epstein and Gide searched for a new mode of artistic expression and urged the development of a modern aesthetic which was focused on form at the expense of storytelling and representation. The objectives of the critical discourses of cinema and the novel coincided.

One of the reasons for the rapprochement between the film and literary discourses is found in the efforts of the critics of both arts to associate them with other arts. André Malraux presented the history of cinema in the context of painting and photography. The representation of fiction and the obsession for ever-greater realism were inherent to the history of visual art in the West. Unfortunately, the development of painting and photography was hindered at the same point when their inability to represent movement became apparent. Neither of these arts could develop beyond this point because it was no longer a question of artists' creativity but of the technological limits of painting and photography. It was cinema which allowed Western visual arts to overcome this impasse (Malraux 1996: 4–10). Gide's vision of the history of art had a quite different emphasis from that of Malraux. Gide argued that by eliminating 'foreign elements' the novel joins painting and music in their progress towards purity (1925: 57). Cinema and the phonograph, which developed later than the novel, would absorb the elements which Gide believed to be superfluous, in the same way that photography supposedly absorbed some elements of painting when the latter was growing more abstract (1925: 78). He argued that 'the external factors, accidents, traumas belong to cinema' and for this reason it is necessary that 'the novel leaves them to cinema' (ibid.). First writing in 1950 Nathalie Sarraute endorsed Gide's view and argued that cinema would absorb narrative elements of the novel when the latter became preoccupied with purely formal experiments (1956b: 78).

Gide's definition of novelistic form also revealed a certain negative dynamic present in the comparison of the novel with other arts. Arts such as cinema absorb elements of the novel which are no longer needed in the novel's progress towards purity. As the novel strives towards formal 'purity', cinema becomes a rubbish bin full of discarded elements the novel no longer needs or wants. In Gide's view such cinema is necessary for the novel to reach the next step in its development. If there had been no cinema which could take over the role of the storyteller, the 'pure novel' would not have emerged. In cinema, the same dynamics could be detected between popular/ genre filmmaking and what came to be known as art cinema, which makes processes leading to the emergence of the 'pure novel' and art cinema very much alike. In both cases they presupposed that cinema and the novel would be discharging themselves of plot and characterisation, and other constraints imposed by realist representation.

Sartre's and Gide's definition of the art of the novel equates it with narrative. The arguments of the new novelists and *Cahiers* critics in the 1950s made the same comparison. Sartre's and Gide's analyses focus on defining and describing formal aspects of literary narrative emerging in the process of abstracting from storytelling elements. Gide argued that in the 'pure novel' there would be no extended dialogues, dramatic developments, unnecessary digressions and character descriptions (1925: 78). In *Situations, I* Sartre attacked the omniscient point of view adopted by the narrator of François Mauriac's *La Fin de la nuit* (1947c: 52). Sartre and Gide agreed that, instead, events should be narrated from different points of view by characters who participated in them. The existence of the story would thus depend on a reader who would piece it together from the available accounts (Sartre 1947c: 42–3; Gide 1925: 28). The same formal characteristics were present in the new novelists' definition of their project. Talking about cinema Malraux was convinced that editing and continuity achieved through sound enhanced cinema's narrative capabilities and made cinema more like a modern novel (1996: 14–17). Usually the film's structure could have been fragmented with sound providing a degree of narrative cohesion. Editing in sound cinema also offered film directors exciting and varied means of expression and transformed the filmmakers from cameramen into artists creating their own films comparable to novels (1996: 9–10).

Malraux's arguments are important not only because they sketch the direction for the development of the art of cinema after the advent of sound but also because they are coming from a critic who was both a writer and a filmmaker. His own films are seen as an expression of cinematographic writing, a combination of writing and filming. Bazin believed that Malraux was among those contemporary writers who spoke best of cinema because there existed deep affinities between his style of literary writing and the language of his cinematographic expression achieved through the use of ellipses. While in literature ellipses introduced gaps, which could be filled quite easily by a reader, they presented a much greater challenge for a spectator (1983: 157). It was sound, in particular the voice-over, which allowed the spectators to negotiate the presence of ellipses in Malraux's films. Intertitles in *L'Espoir* (1945) for example fulfil a similar role to ellipsis, providing a sense of continuity in a narrative which is moving between different temporal and spatial levels. As a result, cinema's main rival was no longer theatre but the novel (Malraux 1996: 74–5). In other words, sound cinema was closely related to literary writing which in turn became the source of increased tensions between cinema and literature. Sound cinema as envisioned and practised by Malraux could not be reduced to a worthless invention whose origins were novelistic.

Malraux's view openly contested Gide's and later also Sarraute's account of the evolution of cinematic art. They all agreed that in the course of its history, cinema was struggling to become more like a novel. For Malraux, this process did not stop at the moment when the novel became reflexive and self-referential. Rather, cinema followed the novel in the same direction and struggled to gain a better understanding of its narrative techniques and of its forms. Cinema wanted to join the novel rather than absorb the techniques discarded by the novelists as suggested by Gide and Sarraute. The objectives of the film and literary critics were in conflict indicating that the coexistence of both arts was marked by serious tensions. In the 1950s, the *Cahiers* critics will argue that cinema should take over the place of the novel altogether while the new novelists will have to build up a whole defence against this cinematic assault. The result will be a compromise: the development of the narrative form, which could be shared by both arts.

The dismissive attitude of literary critics such as Gide and Sarraute towards cinema is surprising given the importance of cinema and of other arts, such as music, for shaping literature's formal project. Sarraute compares the effects of her novels on their readers to the workings of a slow-motion silent film (1956e: 8–9). Alain Robbe-Grillet (1963b) refers to cinema in order to tackle questions of subjectivity in his novels. Gide's and Sartre's discussions regarding the novelistic art involved comparisons of the narrative aspects of writing with music. In *La Nausée*, Roquentin reveals that he would like the events of the story of his life to be arranged like the notes of a ragtime piece he has heard played in a café. He is interested in the formal side of music, particularly in its ability to create its own time independent of the time in which listeners live. He also focuses on the fact that progress and irreversibility in time mark musical composition (Sartre 1938: 37, 58). In Gide's *Les Faux-monnayeurs*, Edouard compares the novel he would like to write to Bach's fugue (1925: 187–8). The interest in the impact of music on literary narrative continues in the writings of the new novelists. In his critical work on Proust, Michel Butor (1964b) makes a claim that musical pieces included in the text of *A la recherche du temps perdu* (*Remembrance of Things Past*, 1913–27) can be seen as the elements determining the novel's composition. Butor also reveals that the music of Webern was a source of inspiration for his writings and suggests that the structure of the novel, like that of a poem, may be parallel to that of a musical piece (1964a: 97; 1992a: 16; 1992b: 48).

These remarks about music and cinema show that references to other arts are an indispensable part of literary critical discourse. They are also an important feature of film criticism in which the main reference point is literature when cinematic forms are defined in terms of narrative. In the case of the critical discourse of cinema the comparison of the art of the novel and cinema is based on a paradox. While the critics attempt to define the specificity of cinema, they do it by referring to the literary canon, and try to model the concept of cinema after that of the novel. As we will see, in the long run, this paradox of the critical discourse of cinema will become a way of bridging it with the critical discourse of the novel. In other words, the hybrid nature of the critical discourse of cinema will relate the art of cinema to the art of the novel.

The signs of bridging the two discourses were already present in the pre-*Cahiers* period when film critics defined cinema in narrative terms, and the novel was the prime example of narrative art at that time. It was not enough for film critics to say that cinema was narrative but an argument had to be presented to contextualise and support such a claim. For this reason the critics referred to Hollywood cinema and the literary canon. Roger Leenhardt, another early film critic, based his concept of cinematic form, the cinematic rhythm, on narrative cinema whose best examples could be found in Hollywood films. Cinematic rhythm was associated with a type of invisible and continuous film editing which was perfected in Hollywood cinema (1936: 630). Leenhardt's criticism shows that some French critics referred to Hollywood cinema if they wanted to focus their argument on the question of cinematic narrative. Malraux presented John Ford's *Stagecoach* (1939) as an example of classical film narrative (1996: 16). According to Bazin (1997a), just like William Wyler's *Jezebel* (1938) and Marcel Carné's *Le Jour se lève* (1939), Ford's film was an example of cinema which found the perfect balance between dramatic and moral themes. Bazin was also bringing out literary examples in order to illustrate the formal innovations of the cinema he was describing. He referred to the fiction of William Faulkner, Ernest Hemingway and John Dos Passos writing about the aesthetics of neo-realist Italian cinema (1997c: 274). The efforts of Malraux and Bazin to fashion film history after the literary canon were also a feature of *Cahiers du cinéma* criticism especially pronounced in the writings of Eric Rohmer (1955a, 1955b, 1955c, 1955d, 1955e).

From Epstein to Bazin, from Gide to Sartre, it is evident that the project of *Cahiers du cinéma* and that of the new novelists to define the specificity of their respective arts and to discern their formal characteristics had many predecessors in the French context in the pre-war period. The writings of Epstein, Leenhardt, Gide, Sartre, Malraux and Bazin highlight the dynamics of the literary and cinematic critical discourses which will be also evident in the critical writings of *Cahiers du cinéma* and of the new novelists.

ERIC ROHMER AND CINEMA AS A VISUAL NOVEL

From the inception of *Cahiers du cinéma* in 1951, the critics of the magazine were involved in the project of defining the place of cinema in the French cultural context, which historically was dominated by literary production. Their passionate engagement with cinema could be seen as a reflection of wider trends and tendencies which became apparent in French culture after World War Two. The popularity of cinema was increasing among the general public. Intellectuals, such as Jean-Paul Sartre, who developed the concept of *littérature engagée* ('engaged literature') as applicable to all the arts and not just literature, were becoming interested in cinema as a vehicle of political change and a way of mobilising and organising the cinema-going masses (see Chateau 2005). It was in this climate of excitement regarding the redrawing of the French cultural map that Eric Rohmer, one of the leading *Cahiers* critics in the 1950s, was able to advance his definition of the art of cinema as a classical art. Rohmer, just like other *Cahiers* critics, wanted cinema to be an art comparable to the individual arts of the novel, music and painting. Rohmer's and his fellow critics' efforts led to the development of the critical category of the *mise-en-scène*, which was used to found the *politique des auteurs*. Rohmer envisioned cinema as replacing the novel by becoming an example of new visual literature. Only cinema independent from any literary input could become visual literature. This was one of the reasons that the *Cahiers* critics promoted American Hollywood cinema rather than French films, which were characterised by contributions from writers.[5] The desire to distance themselves from literature was also associated with a particular vision of the art of cinema as popular that *Cahiers* critics like Rohmer were advancing. At the origins of this attitude we can find *Cahiers* and post-war critics' complex and conflicted attitude towards the works of the silent avant-garde. From twenty years' distance the critics were looking with jealousy at the network of cine-clubs and an effusion of cinema at that period. At the same time, they were very weary of the elitist stigma of the films and their limited appeal to audiences. Bazin argued that 'cinema needs an elite but this elite can only have any influence if it realistically understands all the sociological pressures of the seventh art' (1975b: 72). It was Bazin who captured best the nature of the critical project of the 1950s – cinema should be the art of elites but it should not be elitist. Obviously, this view itself was full of tensions but proved to be a good starting point for a magazine such as *Cahiers du cinéma*. It allowed it to engage more openly with popular cinema, such as that of Hollywood, and champion American filmmakers as artists and *auteurs*. It also led the magazine to speak of cinema as an art and draw from the legacy of the first avant-garde.

The novel of the post-war period created by the new novelists was seen as going down the same road as the avant-garde cinema of the 1920s and becoming increasingly isolated, formalist, with no wider appeal. This elitism of the *nouveau roman* shaped the attitudes of critics like Eric Rohmer and Jacques Rivette who presented a view of cinema as distant from any

direct literary influences and claimed that the cinema they were championing could actually pick up where the novel had left off. The best films of the
1950s were seen as continuing the tradition of the nineteenth-century novel
and were described as classical by *Cahiers* critics. The desire for a distance
from literature of the twentieth century also led to the film critics' disregard
for developments in literary criticism where the new novelists were trying to
find new terms for conceptualising the novel. Initially, it was quite easy for
the *Cahiers* critics to ignore the critical writings of the new novelists because
their reflections were developing independently. The *Cahiers* critics were directly confronted with the new novelists' ideas when Resnais began his collaboration with the new novelists such as Duras, Cayrol and Robbe-Grillet
and later on when they became directors of their own films. It was only in
this later period that the view of cinema as a classical visual novel had to be
radically reviewed. In the 1950s Rohmer was busy conceptualising it.

Eric Rohmer was one of the leading and oldest critics of *Cahiers du
cinéma* (see de Vincenti 1980; de Baecque 1991a: 220–8). He was associated with *Cahiers* from its inception and, after Bazin's death, became its
chief editor. He held this position from 1958 to 1963 when, according to de
Baecque, '*Cahiers* achieved its greatest coherence at the risk of certain dull-
ing' (1991a: 224). In his five-part article from 1955, 'Le Celluloïd et le marbre', Rohmer distanced cinema from literature in order to present it as a new
visual novel, which indicated a major shift in the cinema's relationship to literature. In 'Le Celluloïd et le marbre' Rohmer argued that the modern novel
failed to make its formal experiments indicative of any deeper philosophical
or scientific meaning; there was no philosophy and no faith behind any of the
contemporary writing (1955c: 3–4). In the same breath Rohmer claimed that
the clock of literary history stopped with Balzac, when literature reached its
artistic peak and the novel achieved its expressive limits (1955c: 4). He proposed cinema as a new medium of artistic expression capable of incarnating
and conveying Balzacian ideals based on the constancy of human nature and
desires (1955b: 15). Cinema was a new art which would take on the role of
the bearer of moral values thus far fulfilled by the novel. It was due to its inherent modernity that cinema could become the privileged means of artistic
expression in the twentieth century, capable of transmitting ancient beliefs
and convictions by the means of its medium (1955c: 7). Essentially, Rohmer
made the crisis of the novel in the twentieth century the condition for the development of cinema into the most important contemporary art form (1955a).
In fact, Rohmer's programme for cinema seemed quite plausible given the

growing popularity of cinema among the French public and leading intellectuals such as Jean-Paul Sartre. Rohmer's conviction regarding the weak position of the novel further strengthened his ambitions for cinema.

It was the debate '6 personnages en quête d'auteurs' in 1957 which reflected a widespread disappointment among the critics of *Cahiers du cinéma* with the filmmakers who at first seemed to be able to rejuvenate French cinema. The participants of the debate referred to the hopes they vested, after the Liberation, in Robert Bresson, Jacques Becker, Henri-Georges Clouzot and René Clément who were supposed to launch a new school of French cinema (Doniol-Valcroze in Bazin *et al.* 1957: 19; Rivette in Bazin *et al.* 1957: 24).[6] They were believed to be a new avant-garde whose birth was announced by Alexandre Astruc in the late 1940s (1992b). Since these hopes were not realised throughout the 1950s, American productions of the 1940s captured the imagination and interest of the young *Cahiers* critics and satisfied their growing appetite for cinema. Many American films had not been available in Paris at the time of their original release because of the ban imposed by the Germans during World War Two. In 'Le Celluloïd et le marbre' Rohmer pointed to the American films of Alfred Hitchcock (*I Confess* (1953)), Fritz Lang (*The Big Heat* (1953)) and Howard Hawks (*The Big Sky* (1952) and *Monkey Business* (1952)) as the best pictures of the time. The only European exceptions were Jean Renoir's Italian-made *The Golden Coach* (1952) and Roberto Rossellini's *Europa 51* (1951) (1955a: 34). Hence, it was Hollywood which after the Liberation gradually became the source of inspiration for the *politique des auteurs*, the springboard for exploration of formal aspects of the cinema, and the establishment of cinema as an important art in France. This cinema became central to developing the key concept of *Cahiers du cinéma*, *mise-en-scène*, which was seen as the expression of the aesthetic value of films. One of the distinguishing characteristics of Hollywood films was an absence of any literary contribution comparable to the historically strong presence of literary figures in French cinema. This independence of American cinema from the impact of writers encouraged the *Cahiers* critics in their claim that cinema can openly compete with the novel as an equal and even take over the novel's cultural place.

The reflections on cinema of such *Cahiers* critics as Rohmer were linked to their ideas about the novel. Rohmer subscribed to the view that the nature of art was constant and unchanging. For him art was not 'a reflection, a thermometer of the civilisation, [or] an outcome of a certain worldview, of a sensibility which was changing day by day' (1955b: 14). Rather art was 'an autonomous organism growing by itself in the same way that a living human being has its childhood, the time when it is mature and when it ages' and 'it is justifiable to give preferential treatment to the period of maturity, the classical period' (1955b: 14–5). For him, cinema was characterised by constancy and was an expression of an eighteenth-century harmony of form. His focus on American film allowed him to think about the development of cinema as a closed system free from French local contingencies, like the relationship between the literary and cinematic worlds, because he had virtually no connection to and little understanding of the context in which American films were made.[7] In other words, Rohmer's argument regarding the nature of cinematic art might have been quite different if he had focused on the French case. Cinema's relationship with literature would be of crucial importance for creating an understanding of cinema in a wider historical context. While the material was American, the conceptual apparatus *Cahiers* critics developed was exclusively French and deeply rooted in French thinking about art and literature in particular. *Politique des auteurs, mise-en-scène* and eventually the *nouvelle vague* were born of the meeting of the French mind and American Hollywood cinema in the particular moment of French intellectual and cultural history.

Eventually, Rohmer came to believe that cinema would become a leading art, taking the cultural place of the novel. Such high hopes were naturally linked to the increased popularity of cinema in the post-war period. Antoine de Baecque's *La Nouvelle vague: Portrait d'une jeunesse* (1998) presents a fascinating portrait of cinema-goers at the time while Noël Burch (1996) connects *cinéphilia* with the explosion of cinematic critical activity in the post-war period. Rohmer and his young friends from *Cahiers du cinéma* shared their fascination with the silver screen with a great number of *cinéphiles* who were discovering old and new films on the screens of cine-clubs and Henri Langlois' Cinémathèque. His generation 'had for cinema the same respect as for the heavy monuments of the past' (1955a: 33). Rohmer also condemned the 1930s critic René Clair and the critics of the first avant-garde. While presenting his critical stance as highly sophisticated and cultured he also praised the tastes of the public, which in the past had rejected avant-garde films such as cinematographic poems (1955b: 10). He also declared his desire to employ his critical skills in order to explore a commercial and popular, mostly Hollywood, cinema which gained wide public appeal. Rohmer's views are part and parcel of the process by which cinema's relationship with literature was shifting in a new direction. This shift was partly because Rohmer was redirecting the attention of his readers from French to American cinema and from purely formal concerns to the question of a relationship between formal and ethical dimensions of cinema, which found its full expression in the book on Hitchcock he co-authored with Claude Chabrol (1957).

Rohmer's view of cinema disregarded any critical developments taking place in the literary camp, where the new novelists were as intent as the *Cahiers* critics on finding some remedies to challenges of their times. In their critical texts, Nathalie Sarraute and Alain Robbe-Grillet were attempting a critical assessment of the condition of the novel in order to redefine its boundaries and to indicate the direction of its future development. Sarraute pointed out that in light of the events of World War Two, such as the horrors of the Nazi concentration camps or the carnage of the battle of Stalingrad, it was no longer possible to use nineteenth-century models of fiction in contemporary prose. When it came to relating the experience of these events, a good monograph was able to provide a much richer and more powerful experience for the reader than a novel full of characters and plots (1956d: 69). The new novelists argued that the form of the novel had to change, because the global system of morals and beliefs had been transformed by the impact of World War Two. Naturally, they were determined to reform the novel rather than let cinema or anybody else take over its place in French culture. Their creative and critical activity focused on this reform. Due to the growing cultural importance of cinema, first manifested critically and eventually creatively, the changes envisioned by the new novelists actually brought the novel and cinema closer together with new novelists becoming scriptwriters, directors and film critics.

The position embraced by Rohmer in the 1950s seemed to be very much conditioned by the historical moment in which it was shaped. That period was characterised by the weak performance of French cinema, the insularity of contemporary novelistic writing, the growing popularity of American cinema in France, the focus of critics on the American cinema, and the conviction that cinema was the incarnation of a set of morals and values that Rohmer felt was responsible for France's spiritual rebirth after World War Two. In an interview in 1983, with Jean Narboni, he admitted that, in comparison with his past convictions, he 'no longer considers cinema as a saviour of all arts, opening a new era, the same way that Jesus Christ marked the beginning of the era of Christianity' (1984c: 10). Rohmer himself acknowledged that his position was dated and for this reason he decided not to include the set of 'Le Celluloïd et le marbre' essays in the collection of his critical writings *Le Goût de la beauté*. He said that in 'Le Celluloïd et le marbre' 'there are too many things which seem ... monstrously naïve' (ibid.). Given how perceptive the essays were, the judgement of the author seems rather overcritical. There is little doubt that Rohmer's position regarding the novel in the 1950s was extreme not only because of the magnitude of his claim, but also because it was highly polemical. These essays, as with all the writings in *Cahiers* at that time, were an expression of the *politique* and quite a hard-line one for that. The scale of the *Cahiers* critics' assault on the novel should be seen in the context of the great hopes Rohmer had for cinema and a self-doubt expressed by the new novelists themselves. Rohmer's concept of cinema as a visual literature indicated a shift in the cinema's relationship with literature on the part of film critics while they underestimated the deeply experimental nature of the *nouveau roman* writing. The new novelists were engaged in a type of critical reflection similar to the one taking place in *Cahiers du cinéma*. Their efforts to get involved with cinema posed a serious challenge to the ideas about it developed by *Cahiers* critics based on distancing it from literature. Rohmer did not envision the results of a fruitful co-operation between the modern writer and filmmaker in a way that could transform both arts. The first such co-operation was *Hiroshima, mon amour*. But before the creation of that film the cultural landscape was reshaped by the new novelists in their critical essays.

THE NEW NOVELISTS, CINEMA AND JEAN-PAUL SARTRE

The critics of the *nouveau roman* had to position their creative and critical project in a cultural reality, which was dominated by mass culture of which cinema was an integral part (Gracq 1950: 41–2). The new novelists' task was not easy. Throughout the 1950s, Alain Robbe-Grillet emerged as a spokesman for the *nouveau roman*. Unlike Michel Butor and Nathalie Sarraute, he was making statements not just about his own novels but also about the works of other new novelists. Exemplary in this respect is his review of Sarraute's *L'Ere du soupçon* (1956). Robbe-Grillet emphasised how alienated the new novelists were in their project to rescue the novel and to ensure its development in the post-war period:

> From 1945, what has happened in France? Sartre did politics, Camus was preoccupied with moral questions; and literature, who did it? It was the

nouveau roman which did. And it is because of that it is important. Us, with a clenched fist, us – believing in literature. Us, Simon, Pinget, Sarraute and others. (1963h: 3)

In his view the new novelists revitalised the French literary tradition by being concerned exclusively with the problems of the novel. In the 1950s the dominant model of fiction did not challenge readers and diverted the novel from the sphere of art into that of entertainment:

Ten, fifteen years ago, the French public did not need us. Nobody had a physical need to read the *nouveau roman*. French publishing was doing very well turning out traditional fare but nobody had faith in it. It is likely that everybody was awaiting something without even realising it. (Ibid.)

Robbe-Grillet's critique of popular literature was also a way of reproaching cinema which enjoyed the popular appeal of mass entertainment. The lack of such appeal on the part of the *nouveau roman* called into question the very survival of more experimental kinds of writing. Consequently, unlike the emergence of a new film criticism which was supported by cinema's continuing popularity, the literary criticism written by the new novelists was more like an attempt to rescue their novels from a sea of misunderstanding on the part of critics and readers. It was a matter of urgency for the new novelists to identify the reasons for the lack of popularity of their writings. Cinema played an important part in their analysis, and its cultural role was carefully considered.

Sarraute referred to cinema as a threat when assessing the condition of the novel before the appearance of the *nouveau roman*. Critics were warning the docile literary community that if they do not propose something new, inject some new blood into French literature, the battle for minds will be won by cinema, 'the novel's best armed-rival' (Sarraute 1956b 60). The new novelists recognised cinema as an important and powerful means of expression and pointed to its growing popularity as a motivation for the project of the *nouveau roman*. Robbe-Grillet showed how Sarraute's urgent search for a new novelistic mode was in part informed by these concerns:

It is all about demonstrating that a contemporary [literary] form is possible, that it is necessary and that it will revalorise the art which others tried to substitute with cinema, reportage and cartoons. (1956: 695–6)

The strong position enjoyed by cinema in the French context influenced the development of the *nouveau roman*. The writings of the new novelists regarding the condition of the novel read like a direct response to *Cahiers'* criticism, in particular to Rohmer's conviction that cinema would be a new visual literature capable of transmitting nineteenth-century values by means of a new medium. The new novelists' recognition of the importance of cinema was also evident in their critical activity and in their relationship with the literary projects of the past, in particular Sartre's writings in the 1930s about the American novel. Most importantly, the new novelists appeared to be familiar with the arguments of Sartre's post-war critic, Claude-Edmonde Magny, for whom the formal innovations of the American novelists described by Sartre were influenced by cinema. On their part the new novelists attempted to absorb some of the formal innovations introduced by cinema into the narrative of the American novel analysed by Sartre. The new novelists turned to cinema to find some solutions to formal problems that they wished to address in their own writing. This not only shows that cinema was important for the new novelists' definition of the novel but also that, by default, the new novelists developed some understanding of the art of cinema. For this reason, their definition of the art of the novel also revealed a certain concept of cinema.

Sartre's writings on the American novel show how important cinema was in fact for the definition of the art of the novel advanced by the new novelists. In their critical essays we can find numerous references to Sartre's writings and to the fiction of the American novelists. These two clues allow us to identify some aspects of the new novelists' concept of cinema and the novel's relationship with cinema. In order to draw parallels between the critical discourses of the *nouveau roman* and the arguments of the *Cahiers* critics, it will be helpful to understand the crucial role played by criticism in the whole phenomenon of the *nouveau roman*, which was one of the movement's distinctive characteristics. It is clear that the character of the critical discourse of the *nouveau roman* was different from that associated with *Cahiers du cinéma* and the *nouvelle vague*. The films of the *nouvelle vague* grew out of *Cahiers'* criticism while the new novelists wrote literary criticism to clarify the creative aims realised in their novelistic writings. *L'Ere du soupçon*, a collection of critical articles by Nathalie Sarraute, some of which had appeared earlier in *Les Temps modernes* and the *Nouvelle Nouvelle Revue Française* (*NNRF*), was published in 1956.[8] A series of articles written by Robbe-Grillet appeared in the popular magazine *L'Express* between November 1955 and March 1956. He also published a number of critical essays in the *NNRF* and literary reviews in *Critique* starting in 1951. A selection of these essays appeared in the volume *Pour un nouveau roman* in 1963. Michel Butor also wrote several critical essays which came out in his first volume of criticism, *Répertoire*, in 1960. Butor pointed out that 'novelists live in an environment which is increasingly "reflective", increasingly critical' (1960: 5). Such a critically-conscious environment began to develop in France in the nineteenth century; Robbe-Grillet referred to Gustave Flaubert, André Gide, Franz Kafka and James Joyce as predecessors of the *nouveau roman* who reflected on some of the problems posed by their creative writing (1963a: 11). Marcel Proust was another important writer who was mentioned and written about by all of the new novelists. Robbe-Grillet claimed that until the emergence of the *nouveau roman*, 'the very experience of Proust had not been followed' (in Bourin 1959: 4). He described Proust's novels as 'filled with stories ... which dissolve and then are restructured in order to create a mental architecture of time' (1963c: 32). Sarraute defined her central concept of 'tropismes' in light of Proust's ideas concerning psychology and the novel (1956a: 16; 1956c: 85–6). Cinema became the twentieth century's most important addition to this critically buoyant literary world. Hence, the new novelists' critical activity was as much a continuation of a certain analytical tradition in France as it was a response to the critical activity of the contemporary film commentators.

Robbe-Grillet blamed readers' and critics' lack of understanding of the purpose of the *nouveau roman* on the dominance of the nineteenth-century model of fiction. He was not condemning the novels of Balzac; after all he emphasised that Stendhal and Balzac each wrote the *nouveau roman* of their times and the new novelists did the same in the second half of the twentieth century. Robbe-Grillet envisioned a future when the narrative of the *nouveau roman* would be acknowledged by the critics as an accepted element in the general framework of literary references (1963a: 10). He was critical towards the writings of those who 'do' Balzac and who believe that this conception of writing is the best or even the only one (in Bourin 1959: 4). Arthur Babcock argues that 'Robbe-Grillet saw himself to be working in a critical climate that had not yet understood the lessons of the modernists, and he was writing against a much earlier tradition, that of Balzac and nineteenth-century realism. This is the tradition that modernism opposed as well, and Robbe-Grillet today is often thought of as a modernist despite his radical stance, which in the context of the 1950s we would normally call postmodernist' (1997: 12).

Rohmer's deepest desire for cinema in the 1950s was 'to "do" Balzac'. The new novelists' rejection of psychological analysis, plot, characterisation and omniscient point of view was dismissing all classic cinema of the *mise-en-scène* supported by Rohmer. This dismissal also establishes an important link between the narrative of the *nouveau roman* and those film narratives which challenge Rohmer's view of cinema. One of the most striking examples of such new film narrative related to those of the *nouveau roman* was Resnais' *Hiroshima, mon amour*. Given the importance of *montage* for Resnais' films, Sarraute's arguments about cinema foreshadow the challenge posed by the narrative of *Hiroshima, mon amour* to Rohmer's conception of cinematic narrative, which associated it closely with the Balzac model. Sarraute pointed out how the modern cinema of *montage* took cinematic art beyond the classical moment, which was privileged by Rohmer. As a result, cinema was experiencing the same 'suspicion', which was transforming the novel:

> It seems that cinema is threatened as well. The suspicion experienced by the novel reaches cinema as well. Otherwise, how does one explain the anxiety of certain directors which makes them make films in the first person by introducing a witnessing eye or a narrative voice. (1956b: 78)

This view indicates that the evolution of cinema was subject to the same processes as the art of the novel. Sarraute was making a claim about the existence of modern cinema different from the one described by Rohmer before the *Cahiers* critics recognised the achievement of Alain Resnais or Ingmar Bergman, who became key representatives of modern European cinema. For Sarraute, such cinema was not taking the place of the nineteenth-century novel; rather its evolution was putting it on a par with the modern novel. The challenge to Rohmer's argument, which we can infer from Sarraute's critical writings, highlights two important aspects of the relationship between cinema and the novel in the French context. Firstly, it shows how this relationship can be reconstructed and described on the basis of the references present in the critical discourses of cinema and the novel. Hence, the parallel critical discourses of cinema and the novel define the art of cinema and the art of the novel respectively. Secondly, Sarraute's argument demonstrates that the level on which the critical discourses of both arts can be related and most successfully compared is that of the development of narrative forms. These are the elements of cinema and the novel on which the critical discourses of both focus. A true parity between the developments in modern cinema and the novel could be achieved only if the form of the novel was marked by cinema in some more definite way and not just through critical discourses of both arts.

For such writers as Robbe-Grillet cinema contributed directly to solving the problems they encountered in their writings. Robbe-Grillet found there answers to the questions of objectivity and subjectivity. The cinematic image expressed some of the effects he was trying to achieve in his novels; he was fascinated by the fact that 'around us, things simply *are*' (1963b: 18). He argued that it is cinema, which makes it possible to 'relive at will this strange experience' (1963b: 19). By examining the objectivity of cinematic representation the novel was becoming more aware of the power of commentary in relation to the image. As a result, it was able to render more successfully images in writing (ibid.). In the 1950s, when the critical discourses of cinema and the novel ran along without crossing, the impact of film on formal developments in the novel was rather limited. In order to understand the full impact of cinema on the growth of the novelistic form to which the *nouveau roman* contributed, it is worth examining the arguments of the *nouveau roman*'s important predecessor in the exploration of the novelistic form – Jean-Paul Sartre. It is necessary first to consider briefly the *nouveau roman*'s complex relationship with Sartre's essays on the American novel and the reaction of the new novelists to the shift of Sartre's interests towards *littérature engagée* in the post-war period.

In his *L'Age du roman américain* (1948), analysing the position of Sartre from *Situations, I*, Claude-Edmonde Magny argued that cinema inspired the narrative techniques of William Faulkner, John Dos Passos, Ernest Hemingway and John Steinbeck and thus was the most important source of formal innovations in their novels. In Magny's view the American novel shows that cinema and the novel are linked because they are both narrative arts. The fact that 'both were *narratives*' constitutes 'the deepest relations between the novel and film, an *aesthetic* relationship, on which other, more superficial similarities, psychological and sociological ones, are founded' (1948: 30). Magny suggested that such impact of film techniques on literary narrative was a characteristic of not only the American but also the French novel. This is an important moment in Magny's argument because it explicitly connects the narrative forms of the American novel discussed by Sartre and that of the *nouveau roman* fictions. Magny points to the effort on the part of the American novelists and the new novelists to imitate the effects of cinematic forms in fiction writing which become 'the common origins of the transformations undergone by the American and French novel' (1948: 11). This suggests that the narrative techniques of the *nouveau roman*, like those of the American novelists, were influenced by cinema. Magny's study also contributed to the formulation of a new critical language which was used in drawing a critical response to the *nouveau roman*.

The new novelists themselves saw modern American novelists as their forefathers and stressed the importance of their novels for the evolution of their creative project. According to Robbe-Grillet, the *nouveau roman* appeared in the period when the formal revolution brought about by the writings of the Americans had been largely forgotten (in Bourin 1959: 4). Some literary critics in France were not able to comprehend the novelty of the *nouveau roman* because in the past they had disregarded the innovations of the American novel (1963c: 26). He and his fellow new novelists were deeply indebted to the American novelists whose works were introduced to the French public by Sartre. The link between the narrative forms of the American novel analysed by Sartre and those of the *nouveau roman* was best expressed by Betty Rahv who wrote that 'the technical handling of person and of tense first proposed by Sartre has evolved in the most creatively meaningful way to give rise to the aesthetic formulations of the new novel in all their variety' (1974: 6). For Sarraute, American novels were important because they had instigated the break with the French tradition of psychological introspection in novels and given new energy to her own writing (1956a: 18). In light of the writings of the Americans she even came to wonder whether any kind of psychological analysis, which was key to her writing, was still possible (1956b: 65). Both Sarraute and Robbe-Grillet stressed the importance of Faulkner's experiment regarding the portrayal of characters in *The Sound and the Fury* (1929): Faulkner introduced ambiguity in his narrative by giving the same name to two characters. For Sarraute, this experiment with the pronouns challenged the readers who could not trust the narrator's guidance in the way they did in the traditional novel. Instead, they had to recognise the characters by the description of their internal lives. As a result, the readers' position approached that of the writer as far as the intensity of his or her engagement with the characters was concerned (1956b: 75–6). This view could be associated with Magny's argument regarding the objective form of narration present in American novels. These novels were examples of the ways in which cinematic techniques influenced narrative forms of the novel. Magny associated the objective style of these novels' narration with conventions of cinematic art and the presentation of different points of view on the same event or character with the freedom of a filmmaker 'to put his camera where he pleases, to change its position, in order to show us the life of the characters in the unexpected moment' (1948: 49–50). The new novelists' close affiliation with the American novel supports the view that the formal aspects of the *nouveau roman* were affiliated to cinema. Due to its cinematic roots, the developments of the modernist novel and cinema are related.

Although the new novelists recognised the impact of the American novel on the *nouveau roman* form, and thus by default that of cinema, they failed to credit Sartre for this in any way. They did not regard him as a literary critic who advanced the understanding of the modern novel and created a critical framework for some of their formal experiments. For them, Sartre was first and foremost a philosopher of existentialism and a prophet of *littérature engagée* from whom most of them wanted to distance themselves.[9] Sarraute rejected the concept of *littérature engagée* because it was encouraging the usage of outdated novelistic techniques 'whose only aim was to turn writing into a revolutionary weapon' (1956d: 147). For Robbe-Grillet, art could serve no other ends but its own and for this reason 'art could not be reduced to serve the cause, which it was going to surpass' (1963c: 35). Robbe-Grillet's rejection of Sartre's role as the prophet of the *littérature engagée* could be linked to Sartre's support for the more social and political type of cinema and indicates Robbe-Grillet's interest in film, and more generally art, which was more radical from a formal perspective.[10] Cinema, 'l'art des foules' ('art of the crowds'), was crucial for shaping Sartre's idea of the social function of art.[11]

Sartre's life was marked by fascination with cinema. He gave expression of this in his autobiography *Les Mots* where he said 'we were the same mental age: I was seven years old and knew how to read; it [cinema] was twelve years old and did not talk. They said that it was only starting and that it is going to progress; I thought that we would grow up together' (1964: 100). We can identify two different attitudes towards cinema embraced by Sartre during his lifetime. As we have seen, according to Magny, in the 1930s, when Sartre's interests focused on the formal aspects of the American novel, he looked into cinematic techniques in order to illustrate the formal experiments of American novelists. In the post-war period, his interest in cinema took a different form, following a more general shift in his reflection about art. His vision of literature as politically engaged also changed his perspective on cinema, which was important not because of its form but as a potential tool for political and social action.

Among the new novelists Sarraute had the closest and most personal relationship with Sartre in spite of her criticism of *littérature engagée*. She was his contemporary and the first collection of her stories, *Tropismes*, was published in 1939, only a year after *La Nausée*. In the early 1950s, her critical essays appeared in Sartre's *Les Temps modernes*. In 1947, Sartre wrote a preface to Sarraute's *Portrait d'un inconnu* (*Portrait of a Man Unknown*) in which he acknowledged the novelty of her achievement. Sartre recognised that the concerns of Sarraute were very close to his own explorations concerning point of view in the novel (1956: 8). As a result, she was the only new novelist whose writing was endorsed by Sartre as far as its formal aspects were concerned. At the same time, Sarraute believed that cinema was using the discarded elements of the realist novel. Hence, cinema was an heir of the novel whose development towards abstraction should follow that of the novel and other arts and be similar to theirs. For her, cinema was the younger and thus lower form of art. It would make little sense for her to engage with cinema in order to address creative problems she encountered in her novelistic work. Sarraute's idea of cinema as the art which follows literary development agreed with Sartre's vision of cinema as an instrument of political and social action which should be controlled by writers as it gradually grows to resemble the novel. Sarraute's concept of cinema was thus in tune with Sartre's vision of cinema as a political tool.

CAHIERS DU CINÉMA, *POLITIQUE DES AUTEURS*
AND LITERARY TRADITION

One of the important characteristics of *Cahiers'* criticism in the 1950s was a rejection of literary cinema, in particular that associated with *tradition de la qualité* and a focus on films in which the presence of literature, defined in terms of film adaptations of literary texts and the contribution of scriptwriters, was limited. In his now notorious article 'Une Certaine tendance du cinéma français', written in 1954, François Truffaut attacked the practice of literary adaptation popular in the French cinema of the time. He focused his criticism on two scriptwriters, Jean Aurenche and Pierre Bost, who developed a practice of creating 'cinematic equivalences' of literary classics. Aurenche and Bost judged some parts of literary works unfilmable and for this reason were inventing whole scenes and dialogue for the purposes of the film. Truffaut was opposed to the cinema of equivalences because he saw it as a betrayal of literary works, as an expression of the attitude which was underestimating the creative potential of cinema to capture and convey the complexity of literature, and as a reflection of the political views of the scriptwriters with which he disagreed. In Truffaut's view the cinema of equivalences aimed at inventing parts of the literary work which an author would write if s/he were responsible for generating the script. Obviously, the scriptwriter responsible for the adaptation had no way of knowing the potential intentions of the author and for this reason Truffaut believed that people like Aurenche and Bost should stay as close to the original source as possible. In his view the creative practice of these scriptwriters was compromising the value of not only literature but also of cinema itself. To claim that some passages of a literary text were not cinematic meant that there were some aspects of literary works that cinema simply was not able to convey on screen. Such a view was an overt and blatant underestimation of the creative potential of cinema which was so dear to all the *Cahiers du cinéma* critics. In Truffaut's view the cinema of equivalences and the studio practice on which *tradition de la qualité* was based had a limited aesthetic range and did not possess a formal apparatus to create films which would capture the often subtle formal distinctions existing between different literary works. Truffaut was so adamant about the cinema of equivalences because he judged it dangerous not only on aesthetic but also on political grounds. He argued that by creating cinematic equivalences Aurenche and Bost were transmitting some of their leftist and anti-clerical ideas into the films whose literary counterparts expressed a much more conservative attitude.

'Une Certaine tendance du cinéma français' was a passionate and polemical piece of writing in which the author was defending his two great loves, cinema and literature, and in the spirit of the times was launching not only an aesthetic but also political critique of the prevailing practices. In many ways the cinema of equivalences was a cinema of scriptwriters rather than filmmakers; apart from some rare exceptions (for example, Jean Renoir) directors were there to provide an audio-visual illustration of the scripts and from Truffaut's point of view they did not have full creative control over the films. Truffaut described these directors as '*metteurs-en-scène*' as opposed to '*auteurs*'; Jean Cocteau, Jacques Becker, Abel Gance, Jacques Tati, Roger Leenhardt, who invented stories of their films, wrote dialogue and directed their own scripts. The impulse for *Cahiers*' belief that filmmakers are just like literary authors came from Alexandre Astruc's article in which he compared the camera to a pen and a filmmaker to a writer. For him 'a filmmaker was somebody who tells a story with images in the same way that a writer writes with words' (1992a: 269). He argued that the difference between a scriptwriter and a director was to be obliterated as the act of directing came to resemble the act of writing a novel or an essay in conveying thoughts and emotions by the means of cinematic language (ibid.). *Auteur* cinema, present on the margins of French production in the 1950s, was creating a counterbalance to the cinema of literary adaptations and was seen as a source of much needed aesthetic innovation.

It is important to note that Truffaut was directing his attack at a particular kind of literary adaptation associated with the French *tradition de la qualité*. In fact, among the *auteurs* of cinema he mentioned we can find artists such as Robert Bresson who was also involved in a range of projects based on literary sources (1987a: 216–17). This was the case with Bresson's *Le Journal d'un curé de campagne* (1951), which was an adaptation of Georges Bernanos' novel bearing the same title. In this film the literary source did not limit the expressive power of cinema and the creative talents of the filmmaker. On the contrary, according to André Bazin (1997d), it only enhanced and supported them, making the film one of the earliest and most accomplished expressions of *écriture cinématographique*. His achievement depended on the ways in which he treated Bernanos' literary text by visual means. Also during his career as a filmmaker Truffaut, just like his *nouvelle vague* friends Rivette and Chabrol, made a number of films based on literary sources; Michel Marie noted that the *nouvelle vague* filmmakers made almost as many adaptations as the directors of the *tradition de la qualité* (2002). But the *nouvelle vague*'s method of re-working a literary text for the purposes of a film was quite different from the cinema of equivalences practised by Aurenche and Bost. Apart from the fact that in the 1960s young directors embraced the *auteur*ist ethos championed by *Cahiers* in the 1950s, a group of new scriptwriters appeared who were replacing the older generation of the *tradition de la qualité* and whose state of mind regarding literature and cinema was much more in tune with that of the *auteur* directors.

Truffaut's article was a significant turning-point in *Cahiers*' efforts in championing the cause of cinema as an art comparable to the individual arts of the novel, music and painting. The arguments regarding the relationship between cinema and literature were at the heart of these critical efforts, but for cinema to become an art did not depend solely on limiting literary contributions to cinema or changing their character. The burning question of cinema as an art went beyond these concerns. For cinema can only come into its own as an art when it manages to transcend its material base and achieve an aesthetic effect referred to on the pages of *Cahiers* as *mise-en-scène*. The term itself was derived from theatre and meant 'to put on stage'. It was very effective in capturing the Jekyll and Hyde nature of cinema which required a complex creative, industrial and economic base, mobilised in the process of filmmaking (actors, crew, lights, stage design, costumes, audio-recordings, editing, scripts and locations), to create an intangible and fleeting aesthetic effect as its final result. All these various material elements of cinema had to be pulled together during filming and filtered through the *auteur*'s creative consciousness. Once recorded, the cinematic building blocks were turned into cinematic forms whose interplay on screen could create the filmic *mise-en-scène* – the most desired end result for any film and the way to achieve the status of a cinematic artwork. This *mise-en-scène* differed from one *auteur* to another making films an expression of the *auteur*'s individual style. In the view of *Cahiers* critics the more elements of the filmmaking process were controlled by the filmmaker the greater the chance of creating a work of art. For this reason, a writer-director was a model promoted by *Cahiers*. Such versatile *auteurs* just like writers, painters and music composers remained in full control of their creative apparatus. *Cahiers* argued for a change in the conditions in which a film was made to open cinema's aesthetic potential. The magazine also believed that the cinematic medium possessed some unique features which supported cinema's claim to become an independent artform.

Eric Rohmer was criticising the ways of thinking about cinema which linked it too closely to the history of literature and painting and thus obscured cinema's inherent and unique ability to record and reproduce the real in a manner that no other art could (1984b). He focused on questioning literary underpinnings of the *mise-en-scène* in order to show it as an essentially cinematic characteristic and the basis of cinematic art (1984a: 27). The most telling in this respect was Rohmer's rejection of Malraux's argument regarding the historical evolution of cinematic language. According to Malraux, the first step towards the development of a cinematic language was the introduction of 'la succession des plans' or editing which created the possibility of narrative in film and affiliated cinema more closely with the novel (1996: 9). But for Rohmer, editing was important for entirely different reasons than forging cinema's links with literature or developing a narrative. It enhanced the expressive power of cinematic space thus making it into a significant element of cinematic art (1984a: 27). By developing such an important technique as editing cinema was coming into its own. Unfortunately, historically these crucial steps taken by filmmakers on the way to emancipate cinema as an artform were entangled with the debates about literature and other arts. For this reason one of Rohmer's objectives was to chisel out aspects of pure cinema from the historical medley of cinematic practices often involving writers and painters. It is to break cinema's links with literature that Rohmer condemned the experiments with cinematic space in Luis Buñuel and Salvador Dalí's *Un chien andalou* (*An Andalucian Dog*, 1929) and Jean Cocteau's *Le Sang d'un poète* (*The Blood of the Poet*, 1932). He believed that these experiments were too dependent on the contemporary avant-garde conceptions of literature and cinema (1984a: 28). Rohmer's strategy was based on distancing his vision of cinematic art from the critical discourses of other arts. In spite of his radical position, throughout the 1950s literature and its discourses were coming back in the arguments of *Cahiers* critics.

The literary framework proved to be indispensable for conceptualising critics' ideas of the art of cinema and for systematising the history of cinema. Cinema was becoming the visual literature dreamt by Rohmer not only because it was supposed to replace the novel in French culture but also because its definition was based on literary references. Cinema was claiming the place of literature both through practice and criticism. The first was evident in the filmmaking of Alexandre Astruc, Marcel Hanoun, Alain Resnais and a host of *nouvelle vague* filmmakers who adapted para-literary techniques in their films. The latter happened by the process of designating filmmakers as *auteurs* on the basis of the personal style of their works, the establishment of a cinematic canon according to the literary one, by displaying a great reverence for literary tradition, and by the critics' acknowledgement of their literary culture. Clearly, *politique des auteurs*, a strategy to promote and support *auteur*ist film practice, was a way of shaping the history of cinema according to the model derived from literature.

Every filmmaker whose achievement was recognised by *Cahiers* critics underwent a process of 'authorification'. His/her films were discussed in *Cahiers* by the critic who liked a given film most. The interviews conducted with filmmakers were the expression of the critics' desire to get to know their favourite artists better and to achieve a certain degree of intimacy with them. That happened through a direct interaction or through the emotional and emphatic engagement with their work expressed in sympathetic film reviews. After a filmmaker was recognised as an *auteur*, his/her subsequent films received special treatment from the *Cahiers* critics because they were seen as bearing marks of the *auteur*'s personal style. It was believed that the fullest understanding of an *auteur*'s art was possible through the examination of the style of his/her films in terms of *mise-en-scène*; such designation of the *auteur*'s personal style was an integral part of the *politique des auteurs*.[12] Importantly, *mise-en-scène* as a marker of the personal style of an *auteur* had an equivalent in literature where style was defined in formal terms by Roland Barthes in his *Le Degré zéro de l'écriture* (1953). Style was an individual expression of *écriture*, which reflected a relationship between society and the writer.[13] The ideological implications of the cinematic forms were of some importance to the *Cahiers* critics (but much less so than for those writing for *Positif*). It is enough to recall Truffaut's attack on Aurenche's and Bost's cinema of equivalences as an expression of their political convictions. In the long term, throughout the 1950s, these ideological concerns were suppressed and politics was a rare guest on the pages of *Cahiers* whose critics claimed that the only politics they embraced were the *politique des auteurs*. The promotion of artistic concerns at the expense of ideological ones is one of the reasons that the creative relationship between the *nouvelle vague* and the *nouveau roman* could actually be established, thus further opening literary discourses to cinematic ones and vice versa.

In his article 'Le Cinéma, art de l'espace' Rohmer argued that the expressive powers of cinematic space were unique and for this reason the transformation of cinematic space lay at the source of the language of cinema and formed the basis of *mise-en-scène* (1984a: 29). The key aspect of Rohmer's conception was the way in which gestures and movements were arranged in this space to reveal a meaning, which was purely cinematic. Rohmer was convinced that cinema is able to connect two attitudes which are often believed to be contradictory – the representation of reality and self-reflection regarding cinematic forms (see Magny 1986: 14). Cinema becomes an art when filmmakers begin to employ cinematic apparatus in a self-conscious way, which express their creative consciousness. In his view of cinema as an art Rohmer privileged the expressive qualities of the cinematic space and made it the central tenet of *mise-en-scène*. As noted, for him cinema was a classic art and his focus on space, the place of characters and gestures corresponded to a certain notion of harmony of cinematic forms which he embraced. For Godard it was *montage* and the temporal dimension of cinema which were central for his understanding of film as an art which was not classical but modern.

In 'Montage, mon beau souci' Godard argued that in films, *montage* enhances the effect created by *mise-en-scène* and suggested that cinematic specificity was the end product of the tension between the effects of *montage* and *mise-en-scène*, as each of them brought quite different dynamics into the cinematic structure (1989a).[14] Time rendered through *montage* was that of a profound continuity in the characters' emotions and reflections because it conveyed the shocks, haphazardness and coincidence of our emotional life (1989a: 78–9). *Mise-en-scène* was linked with observation, calculation and rationalisation, in other words, the abilities associated with intelligence and reflection. *Mise-en-scène* was about structuring events and carrying out whatever plot there was in a film, while *montage* created the flow, the birth and death of emotions as they emerged in the course of the narrative (1989a: 79). *Mise-en-scène* was associated with the characters' movement in space, which was the reality of the body; *montage* was linked with the movement of their emotions, which was the reality of the mind. The time of *mise-en-scène* was needed for the successive progress of the narrative, while that of *montage* interrupted the narrative, introducing an order, which was not based on cause and effect. Most importantly, the characteristics of both *mise-en-scène* and *montage* were defined through their relationship with narrative – not only cinematic but also literary. *Mise-en-scène*, in its focus on continuity and flow, emulated the narrative effect that classical cinema and nineteenth-century literature shared. That is why in Rohmer's view cinema could become visual literature if it was centred on the expressive effect of *mise-en-scène*. However, such visual novels bore little relationship to modernist literary experiments. It was the introspective and subjective nature of *montage* which was key for affiliating cinema with the modernist novel. These associations served as entry points for a crossing between literary and cinematic forms realised by the *nouvelle vague* filmmakers and new novelists. The collaboration between the new novelists and Alain Resnais and the shift of the new novelists into filmmaking initiated a very long debate regarding the character of narrative in cinema. This debate opened with the critical reception of *Hiroshima, mon amour* and continued until the mid-1960s when the advent of theory reaffirmed the hybrid nature of narrative not only in cinema but also in the novel. Before that happened, in the 1950s, the critics of *Cahiers du cinéma* added another element – an account of cinematic history – into the discussion of cinema as an artform, which emphasised its paradoxical and hybrid nature because this account yet again revealed the embedding of cinematic discourses in literary ones.

The transformation of space and time relating to *mise-en-scène* and *montage* respectively, were two poles around which the *Cahiers* critics focused their discussion of the two moments in the history of cinema – classical and modern. The debate regarding the Hollywood cinema of the 1940s and 1950s was centred on the question of *mise-en-scène*, and resulted in a definition of the classic epoch in the history of cinema. The discussion of the post-war European cinema of Ingmar Bergman, Roberto Rossellini, Jean Renoir and, most importantly, Alain Resnais was an attempt to come to terms with the challenge these films presented to classical *mise-en-scène*. This second stage in *Cahiers'* version of cinematic history was designated as 'modern'. The *Cahiers* critics were forging an account of the history of cinema by drawing an analogy with the history of literature. They compared the works of Howard Hawks to those of Molière, Corneille and Balzac; those of Jean Renoir to Stendhal; and those of Rossellini and Bergman to the novels of Proust and Gide (see Rivette 1955: 20; Godard 1958: 137). Such a 'taxonomy' of cinema based on references to literary classics and figures made it part of literary culture. Importantly, the *Cahiers* critics and the new novelists used the same set of literary references in their arguments about the specificity of their respective arts. Rohmer and Sarraute both mentioned Jean Genet as an example of a modern writer. Sarraute and Robbe-Grillet also referred to the modernist literature of Proust, Woolf and Joyce, American writers such as Dos Passos and Faulkner, and French contemporaries, Gide, Sartre and Camus. This shared set of literary references brought the discourses of the *nouveau roman* and *Cahiers* closer together and was a step in the process of the crossing of both critical discourses.

NARRATIVES IN CINEMA AND LITERATURE

In view of the poor fortunes of French post-war cinema and the critical immersion of the *Cahiers* critics in Hollywood, it is surprising that in 1959 it was a film by a French filmmaker, Alain Resnais, *Hiroshima, mon amour*, which won the greatest praise of the *Cahiers* critics. *Hiroshima, mon amour* was recognised as a definite break with classical cinema and the beginning of modernity in cinematic history. According to Truffaut, this break was expressed through liberating film from the constraints of storytelling:

> If our objective is to free cinema from the necessity of telling stories, there is still a lot to be done and with *Hiroshima, mon amour*, the film

without a plot, strictly poetic and emotional, Alain Resnais has just made
a great step forward in the right direction. (1987c: 14)

Such critical acclaim of the film in *Cahiers du cinéma* is striking, given the
fact that the film compromised one of the key premises of the *politique des
auteurs*. Resnais, film *auteur*, did not write the script of the film himself,
but asked a new novelist, Marguerite Duras, to do this for him. The participants of *Cahiers'* debate 'Hiroshima, notre amour' emphasised the fact that
although the film had every chance of being 'literary' due to Duras' contribution and, as a result, of compromising its cinematic specificity, it ended
up demonstrating a uniquely cinematic quality. *Cahiers'* acceptance of *Hiroshima, mon amour* shows that the formal experiment of the film invites
an interpretation that employs the magazine's critical categories of *mise-en-
scène* and *montage*.

Reviews of *Hiroshima, mon amour* imply that the film successfully realised Rohmer's project of creating visual literature with cinematic means.
Godard argued that Resnais filmed 'the novel that all young French directors, people like Butor, Robbe-Grillet, Bastide and also Marguerite Duras
are trying to write'; for this reason, 'cinema has managed to express something which was believed to belong exclusively to the literary domain' (in
Domarchi *et al.* 1959: 9). Resnais gave the modern literary narrative a visual
form and made cinema modern. In support of Godard's point, Rohmer also
argued that Resnais absorbed the lessons of Faulkner and Dos Passos regarding the narrative 'even though this happens thanks to Marguerite Duras' (in
Domarchi *et al.* 1959: 4). In his review of the film, Jean Douchet also compared it to the works of the modernist Faulkner and Picasso (1959: 4). The
references to American novels show that the narrative of *Hiroshima, mon
amour* incorporated the most radical narrative devices used in these novels,
which in turn were related to those of the *nouveau roman*. This absorption
took place because of the critical reflection regarding cinematic and literary narrative undertaken in the period preceding the making of *Hiroshima,
mon amour* by Sartre in literature and by the *Cahiers* critics in relation to
cinema. The cinematic narrative emerging out of the critical discourse of
cinema in *Cahiers* in the 1950s had the same formal features as literary narrative defined by Sartre in his analysis of American novels in the 1930s. The
focus was on formal experimentations regarding plot, characterisation, composition and time which clearly departed from the norms of the nineteenth-
century realist novel. The successful collaboration of Resnais and Duras was

thus possible because of the historical developments regarding the reflection on the narrative in the critical discourses of cinema and the novel.

In Sartre's critical essay about Nathalie Sarraute's *Portrait d'un inconnu* he argued that this novel belongs among 'these completely negative works which could be called the anti-novels' in literature (1956: 7). For him, Sarraute's work was an attempt to explore novelistic specificity by altering the conventions of a detective story and by experimenting with characterisation. The same formal concerns were also identified by Jacques Rivette in Fritz Lang's *Beyond a Reasonable Doubt* (1956), which was one of the key *Cahiers* examples of classic Hollywood cinema. For him this film was an expression of cinematic specificity, 'a completely objective *mise-en-scène*', achieved by the exploration of the limits of the detective story and by proposing new forms of characterisation (1957: 50). A comparison between the narrative techniques of Dos Passos and Faulkner, discussed by Sartre in *Situations, I*, and the elements of narrative in Rossellini's *Viaggio in Italia* (*Journey to Italy*, 1953) and in Bergman's *Sommaren med Monika* (*Summer with Monika*, 1952), examined by Godard and Rivette as examples of modern cinema, reveals some striking parallels (Godard 1958; Rivette 1959).[15] According to the critics, these filmmakers and novelists rejected the importance of storytelling and chronology in their works. They also aimed at producing a different sort of characterisation, which was not based on detailed presentation of outer features. In this they continued the exploration of formal aspects of narrative initiated in reviews of Sarraute and classic Hollywood cinema. Sartre's exploration of the modernist American novel was used by the new novelists in evaluating formal aspects of their own fictions. This continuous preoccupation with the modern American novel also echoes in the *Cahiers* reviews of modern cinema in the period preceding the new novelists' active engagement with film.

In Hollywood cinema, strict and detailed *mise-en-scène* was an expression of a very coherent narrative (Rivette 1953: 19). The reviews of Lang's *Beyond a Reasonable Doubt* and Sarraute's *Portrait d'un inconnu* show that such narrative possesses elements of a detective story, which are sabotaged in various ways. Sartre describes Sarraute's novel as 'a parody of a crime novel' where the detective is not able to build up a case and, as a result, abandons the investigation completely, only to turn out at the end of the novel to be the perpetrator of the crime himself (1956: 8). Any reader familiar with the rules of the detective genre as developed for example by Agatha Christie is bound to be confused when faced with Sarraute's *policier*. Rivette ob-

serves that Lang also refers to the conventions of the classic detective story
and, like Sarraute, emphasises the effect of surprise and confusion achieved
by providing conflicting information about the crime and by introducing
unexpected twists into the story. As a result, Lang's film becomes an exploration of the limits of the genre, which dominated American production in
the 1940s in a similar way that Sarraute tests the limitations of the detective
novel (1957: 50).

The novelty of modern cinema lay in the way in which *mise-en-scène*
was created through the relaxation of cinematic space. There was a sense
of the expansion of cinematic space which also became more fluid. Rossellini was among the modern filmmakers whose *mise-en-scène* was different
from that known in classical films, in particular that of Hollywood cinema;
the different quality of his *mise-en-scène* also introduced a major change
in the composition of his films, which critics such as Rivette no longer described as a narrative but as an essay. According to Rivette, Rossellini gave
the impression of opening up and relaxing cinematic space by presenting it
in a fluid and asymmetrical manner. This resulted in a composition which
gave a sense of much greater freedom (1955: 16). In Rossellini's film where
the plot is suppressed 'one no longer knows what is going to happen, where
and how; the event is hurried but it no longer progresses' (1955: 19). According to Sartre, narrative in the novels of Faulkner and Dos Passos also
underwent a dramatic transformation; the writers' experiments altered the
nature of facts, which made up the events of their stories, and made them
into the novel's formal material. The events in their novels usually belonged
to the past and were recalled in the course of narration; this meant a lack
of dramatic development or suspense. As a result, the structure of narrative
was not linear; rather it was created by listing these events recalled from the
past, or by what Sartre calls 'adding' (1947b: 17; 1947d: 67). The effect of
halting the narrative observed in modern cinema was also present in modernist American novels. Both in modern cinema and in the modern novel the
transformation of the traditional narrative structure brought about new types
of characterisation.

Lang's characters were presented in a very abstract way. There were no
real-life details which would help to place them or to understand their particular condition. In other words, Lang's characters lost their individuality
and became 'human concepts' (Rivette 1957: 49). Sarraute's characters underwent a similar process of losing their individual identity. Sartre argued
that 'a man for her is not a character, neither the story, nor a network of

habits: it is a ceaseless and limp to-and-fro movement between the particular and the general' (1956: 13). The arguments of Sartre and the *Cahiers* critics suggest that this process of abstracting characters was taken one step further in Resnais' *Hiroshima, mon amour* and in Dos Passos's novels. Rivette suggests a conflation between the film's account of Emmanuelle Riva's efforts to reconstruct her fractured self and the presentation of the struggle of the city of Hiroshima to rebuild after nuclear disaster (Domarchi *et al.* 1959: 8). For this reason, the film could be seen as a documentary about the city and about the main female character (ibid.). Rivette went so far as to suggest that *Hiroshima, mon amour* was a documentary about the city of Hiroshima with commentaries by Riva (Domarchi *et al.* 1959: 12). Such fusion between urban documentary and psychological introspection, between the collective and personal, the objective/factual and the subjective can also be found in Dos Passos's characterisation, which presents a human being who is 'a hybrid being, internal-external'; we can follow 'his/her uncertain individual consciousness [until] suddenly, it gives in, weakens, and dissolves in the collective consciousness' (Sartre 1947b: 23). Dos Passos emphasises the tension between the external and internal by presenting the thoughts of his characters in the form of a news report (1947b: 20). The exploration of the characterisation follows the same lines in cinematic and literary narrative bridging both types of narratives.

Challenges to plot and traditional characterisation changed the role of time in cinematic and literary narratives. Time, which was no longer chronological, became an incentive for the exploration of the workings of memory in both films and novels. In *Viaggio in Italia*, time exercised immense pressure upon the elements of the *mise-en-scène*, which traditionally had been linked to the plot. Gestures, looks and the most banal events lasted for ever without giving an impression of working towards any definite resolution (Rivette 1955: 19). But it was really the use of flashback which seemed to bring the action to a complete halt, ultimately making the narrative inconclusive; it was a reflection of the characters' minds and emotions in a specific moment in time. Bergman emphasised flashback as a tool in exploring the workings and the nature of memory. He was fascinated by the ways in which film gradually transformed a present moment into a past one. He wanted to 'capture in the present moment that which was the most fleeting in it and extend it to make it feel like eternity' (Godard 1989b: 147). Dos Passos was also interested in memories and for this reason in his novels narrative is an account of somebody remembering the past; he was also exploring ways of resolving the tension between the past and present in his novels (Sartre 1947b: 16). In other words, he struggled to capture the moment when the present became the past and could be interpreted. The exploration of the nature of time led cinema and the novel to create new narrative structures different from the nineteenth-century realist narratives.

The enthusiastic reception of *Hiroshima, mon amour* showed that the contribution of a scriptwriter could have a vital importance for film's form. It was possible because historically the artistic objectives of the modernist novel and cinema coincided. There were not two different narratives in cinema and the novel but one type, which displayed the same characteristics irrespective of the medium. The existence of such shared narrative had important consequences for the critical discourse of cinema and implied some shifts in it. Namely, the film critics had to acknowledge the fact that literary narrative was developing in parallel with cinematic narrative in a way which made it impossible for cinema to usurp the cultural place of the novel. Instead, the narrative form was defined by the critics of both arts in a way that allowed them to use the same definition of narrative in discussions of cinema and the novel. The existence of such narrative was made possible by the successful collaboration of Resnais and Duras on *Hiroshima, mon amour.* It would be a constant feature of subsequent critical debates as Resnais continued his collaboration with two other new novelists, Alain Robbe-Grillet and Jean Cayrol.

Rohmer challenged the novel on moral grounds and argued that cinema should take its place and become a visual novel. This assertion was based on the assumption that the novel would disappear, that there would be no *nouveau roman* emerging. The new novelists responded to the challenge of film critics and to the questioning of the validity of their formal project. It was this response on the part of the new novelists which put the *Cahiers* critics in a very curious situation as they continued along the lines sketched out by Rohmer and defined the specificity of cinema according to a literary framework, as though cinema was actually going to become this new type of literature – a novel in visual form. The arguments of the new novelists were fuelled by Sartre's analysis of the modern American novelists in the 1930s. It was the shift in the position of Sartre – from formal and aesthetic interests when writing about the American novelists in the 1930s to the ideas of art as engaged in the post-war period – which was ultimately responsible for linking the critical discourses of *Cahiers du cinéma* and the new novelists in the 1950s. Those discourses were related not because they coincided chronologically but because of Sartre's different reflections on the novel and other arts. The position of Rohmer, who drew on the Sartre of the post-war period, was certainly linked to Sartre's arguments in the 1930s to which the new novelists referred. After all, Rohmer, just like the new novelists with regard to the novel, wanted to define formal elements of the art of cinema. Hence, to relate the parallel discourses of cinema and the novel in the 1950s essentially meant creating a connection between the two moments of Sartre's intellectual life. This dependence on Sartre in the arguments of the critics of both arts reveals an important characteristic of the critical discourses of cinema and the novel not just in the 1950s, but also in the 1960s. As we will see in the next chapter, the collaboration of Resnais with Robbe-Grillet would create a new kind of narrative, and new critical terms to describe formal aspects of this narrative became embedded in the arguments of Surrealists and Jorge Luis Borges concerning the nature of narrative in the twentieth century.

II

Revisions: 1959–61

In the short period between 1959 and 1961 the critical discourses of *Cahiers du cinéma* and of the *nouveau roman* underwent significant transformations. The combined success of *Hiroshima, mon amour, Les Quatre cents coups, À bout de souffle* and *Les Cousins* (1959) marked the beginning of the *nouvelle vague* and a shift of such *Cahiers* critics as Jean-Luc Godard, Jacques Rivette, Claude Chabrol and François Truffaut into filmmaking. After their departure *Cahiers* was radically transformed for the first time in a decade. The remaining critics of the magazine began to change their approach to cinema from the *cinéphilic* one, which led their predecessors to embrace the *politique des auteurs*, to a more analytical one. It was the first time in the magazine's history that the object of the critics' passion, cinema, was put at a distance and examined with a still loving but more critical eye (see de Baecque 1991b: 14–15). The magazine, which in the 1950s was focused on American cinema and dismissive towards most of the French productions, had to find a way to respond to the phenomenal increase in the number of local films. The matter was complicated by the fact that some of the most successful of the *nouvelle vague* films were made by the former *Cahiers* critics with whom the remaining *Cahiers* staff were long-standing friends. In the period in question Eric Rohmer acted as the magazine's chief editor. He provided continuity between *Cahiers* before and after the *nouvelle vague* but was also torn between his love of classical cinema and his affection towards his former *Cahiers* friends and the films they made.

Cahiers critics were not just alarmed by the possibility of replacing *politique des auteurs* with the *politique de l'amitié* ('politics of friendship') because of these personal relationships; their concerns were also very pragmatic. The problem was that the first successful film of an emerging *nouvelle vague* director was then often followed by a less accomplished work. For instance, Truffaut's *Les Quatre cents coups*, awarded the prize for best direction at Cannes, was superior and more popular with audiences than his next film *Tirez sur le pianiste* (*Shoot the Piano Player*, 1960). This uneven output of the *nouvelle vague* directors made it very difficult for the *Cahiers* critics to pass a firm judgement regarding the nascent filmmaker. Moreover, the *nouvelle vague* presented such a diversity of cinematic styles and experiments in such a short period of time that attempts to evaluate and systematise them presented a huge challenge to the critics. In short, the increasing number of the *nouvelle vague* films and directors, commercial failure of many films and confusion of genres and styles were the reasons why *Cahiers'* criticism found itself in disarray (see de Baecque 1991b: 17).

Along with Jean Douchet, Luc Moullet and Michel Mourlet, Rohmer remained the advocate of classic cinema on the *Cahiers* staff and overall rather sceptical towards the *nouvelle vague*. Only very gradually, *Cahiers* moved from the position of frontal attack on French cinema initiated by Truffaut's criticism of the *tradition de la qualité* to a hesitant support of the *nouvelle vague*, from the focus on American cinema to the exploration of young European filmmakers. The shift of *Cahiers* towards modern cinema accomplished by the mid-1960s was a result of the pressure that young *Cahiers* critics, including François Weyergans, André S. Labarthe and Michel Delahaye, were exerting on Rohmer and more traditionally-minded *Cahiers* critics. Weyergans and Delahaye, who joined the magazine in 1960, were the new voices of *Cahiers*; Labarthe had been on the staff of *Cahiers* since 1956. The three of them became champions of modern cinema and the progressive line of *Cahiers*. They were not tied up by any personal allegiances to the *Cahiers* critics-turned-*nouvelle vague* directors, but were curious about new trends in European cinema and new intellectual fashions. Delahaye passionately argued the case for the *nouvelle vague* and was a great enthusiast of structuralism and Claude Lévi-Strauss. Labarthe was described by Antoine de Baecque as 'the most persistent indicator of modernity' in *Cahiers* which is most evident in his writings on French and European beacons of this modernity: Godard, Antonioni, Resnais and Buñuel (1991b: 72). Weyergans was interested in the exploration of the director's subconscious mind and was the first to refer to Lacan on the pages of *Cahiers*. His texts were very intellectual and peppered with references to a variety of philosophical and theoretical writings, and were quite different in style from the *cinéphilic* texts of the 1950s. Weyergans, Labarthe and Delahaye were developing a new critical discourse which was distinct from the 1950s critical line founded on the *politique des auteurs*, the critical category of the *mise-en-scène* and a parity of cinematic and literary narratives. The young critics underplayed the question of adaptation, literary references and authorship which were central to their predecessors' arguments about the art of cinema. But in the final count these critics did not so much challenge the critical line of *Cahiers* from the 1950s but extended and enriched it. Their arguments were powered by the fact that the *nouvelle vague* films they were writing about were seen by their creators as a way of conducting critical activity through creative means.

L'Année dernière à Marienbad was one of the most self-conscious pieces of filmmaking appearing at the time. The narrative of Resnais' film was radical and posed interpretative difficulties for the new generation of *Cahiers* critics who turned to its filmmaker to search for some critical clues. Resnais evoked Surrealism and critical works by Jorge Luis Borges to discuss the narrative of his film and the place of cinema in a French culture dominated by literary production. The strength of Resnais' arguments lay in the character of his references, which allowed him to bridge the literary discourses of cinema and the novel. Both the Surrealists and Borges were active as filmmakers, scriptwriters, writers and film and literary critics. The variety of their engagements resulted in definitions of narrative and culture which were hybrid or cine-literary in nature. It is for this reason that Resnais' vision could be seen as an elaboration and development of the *Cahiers* criticism of the 1950s which saw narrative as something that cinema shared with the novel. In other words, the character of Resnais' references emphasised the literary aspect of the critical discourse of cinema and once again opened an exchange with the critical discourse of the novel. This interchange could develop for yet another reason. The critical ideas of Resnais were most successfully expressed by his scriptwriter, Alain Robbe-Grillet. This initiated a shift of some new novelists into film criticism, including Claude Ollier. Robbe-Grillet argued that the narrative of films was equivalent to the scripts on which the films were based. The literary critic Gérard Genette, who evaluated the script of *L'Année dernière à Marienbad*, used critical categories developed by *Cahiers* criticism of the 1950s in his essay 'Vertige fixé', first published in 1962. In the period between 1959 and 1961, we can thus observe a process by which discourses of cinematic and literary critics cross and engage in an exchange. For the first time in history, the traffic was not only from literature into the discourse of cinema but also the other way round. This strengthened the 1950s arguments about the existence of narrative, shared by both arts, and with the same formal elements, irrespective of the medium. This shift indicated the transformation of French culture from purely literary into cine-literary.

The shift of the former *Cahiers du cinéma* critics into filmmaking as part of the *nouvelle vague* in the beginning of the 1960s shed a new light on a group of filmmakers who lacked critical apprenticeship in *Cahiers* and whose background was instead in short films and documentary filmmaking: Agnès Varda, Chris Marker, Jacques Demy, Jean Rouch, Georges Franju and perhaps most significantly, because of his connections with new novelists, Alain Resnais. Their early films were contemporary to the *Cahiers* criticism of the 1950s and possessed an analytical dimension which made them into early examples of modern cinema which was aware of the medium's formal dimension. For this reason these documentary and short films were seen as being on an equal footing with the critical essays written by the *Cahiers* group. This was made apparent in the publications which sought to systematise the *nouvelle vague* phenomenon from the early 1960s onwards. 'Repères chronologiques du nouveau cinéma', published in *Cahiers du cinéma*'s special issue on the *nouvelle vague*, Bazin's 'Ontologie de l'image photographique', Astruc's 'Naissance d'une nouvelle avant-garde: la caméra-stylo' and Truffaut's 'Une Certaine tendance du cinéma français' are mentioned alongside Resnais' *Van Gogh* (1948), *Guernica* (1950–51), *Nuit et brouillard* (*Night and Fog,* 1955), Franju's *Le Sang des bêtes* (*Blood of Animals*, 1949), Rouch's *La Circoncision* (1950–51) and *Les Maîtres fous* (*The Mad Masters*, 1953–54), Varda's *La Pointe courte* (1954), Marker's *Dimanche à Pékin* (*Sunday in Peking*, 1956), *Lettre de Sibérie* (*Letter from Siberia*, 1956) and *Les Statues meurent aussi* (*Statues Also Die*, 1953), the film he made made with Resnais. As early as 1960, in *Essai sur le jeune cinéma français*, Labarthe mentions the same names and films to show the roots of the *nouvelle vague* which were to be found in documentary and short filmmaking as well as in critical writing. In this group of short and documentary filmmakers Resnais played a particularly important role. Roger Leenhardt, one of the critics close to Bazin, suggested that Resnais was a filmmaker who managed to take cinema back to its beginnings and to rethink it with disregard for its history (see *Roger Leenhardt ou le dernier humaniste*, directed by André S. Labarthe, 1965). Resnais' creative project thus evoked the critical one of *Cahiers* in the 1950s.

In Resnais' own understanding, his work as a filmmaker overlapped with his critical activity. According to him, it was the filmmaker's role as the first spectator of the film which mirrored his critical interests:

> I often recall the words of Marcel L'Herbier, who said that 'the director is
> the first spectator of a film', which means that in a film there is ... a poetic
> linking and I have to be the one who grasps this linking before him (the
> spectator). (in d'Allones 1967: 128)

The critical attitude reflected in this role as the first spectator of his films
was associated with an interest in the abstract effect of his films. He claimed
that it was necessary to speak about 'formalist realism' because in order to
'communicate something one has to pass through forms'; for this reason he
has 'never lost the view of the whole, the totality which is the film itself' (in
Rasking 1967: 98). It is this focus on the formal aspect of the work which is
found at the origins of Resnais' critical attitude. This made his case similar
to that of many of the *nouvelle vague* filmmakers even though for them critical engagement with cinema preceded creative endeavour.

Although Resnais' critical ideas were related to those of the *Cahiers* writers in the 1950s, in his films he developed this critical reflection further.
Resnais' attitude towards his literary collaborators was a way of exercising
his new critical ideas. He did not regard himself as a film *auteur* in the way
initially proposed by *Cahiers* for at least three reasons. Firstly, his short films
were commissioned which made him believe that he 'should not be considered somebody ... who had a message to deliver to the world' (in Delahaye
1959: 5). Secondly, he emphasised the fact that his training was in film editing, not in directing, and claimed that the reason he made films was due to
the fact that he could not find work in editing (ibid.). Given the tremendous
strides made by Resnais in cinema, the circumstances which pushed him
towards film directing were most fortunate. Resnais' background in editing
is visible in the daring *montage* sequences of his features, *Hiroshima, mon
amour*, *L'Année dernière à Marienbad* and *Muriel ou le temps d'un retour*,
which are recognised as the director's signature. It is also significant for a
formal and critical bridging between the worlds of cinema and literature. It is
enough at this stage to recall André Malraux's view that it was editing which
gave cinema a narrative dimension, the one it shares more closely with literature. For Resnais himself it was not just his experience as a film editor but
also his admitted inability to write his own scripts that prevented him from
considering himself an *auteur*. He said that he 'regrets the fact that he cannot
write, that he is not at all a writer' (in d'Allones 1967: 123). At the same time,

he believed that film directing was the only way in which a filmmaker can attain his/her artistic goals fully. Thirdly, he stressed the collective aspect of filmmaking by saying that 'he has always collaborated with others, but it is always his name which is kept [in relation to the film] not that of other collaborators' (in Delahaye 1959: 5). He emphasised the role of the writers in the creative process of filmmaking:

> Obviously, one could ask whether the narrative is not created thanks to the writer, the primordial element of the films on which I collaborate with others. At the same time, I don't believe that we are dealing here with 'literary' cinema. Most of the authors of my films are not just *writers*, they are also *people of show business*. (in d'Allones 1967: 124)

Scripts were not less important than films themselves; rather they constituted an integral part of Resnais' conception of cinema. While working so closely with scriptwriters, Resnais insisted on scripts being written especially for his films, because 'one cannot film a book', which is 'a finished, complete work unlike a script' (ibid.). The nature of Resnais' relationship with his collaborators had an impact upon the director's critical ideas, which were inspired by the Surrealists' and Borges' experience of the medium. Resnais' debt to Surrealism was evident in his choice of literary collaborators for his short films. The commentaries for *Le Chant du styrène* (1958) and *Guernica* were written by Raymond Queneau and Paul Éluard respectively, both of whom had been associated at one time with the Surrealist movement. The collaborators on Resnais' feature films also had complex connections with Surrealism, such as Jean Cayrol, scriptwriter for Resnais' *Nuit et brouillard* and *Muriel ou le temps d'un retour*. Some of Resnais' views of his films overlapped with those of the Surrealists. For instance, while making his films he wanted 'to preserve the instinctive side, make films a bit like automatic writing' and remained guided 'by internal images' (in d'Allones 1967: 127). This goal was evocative of the aims of the Surrealists, who developed 'the poetic, frantic criticism, which was interested in all which was invisible, of the whole mystery of film' (Torok 1964: 82). The Surrealists' engagement with cinema was just like that of Resnais, both critical and creative.

Next to the cultural identity of his literary collaborators, references found in Resnais' films are another way of tracing ideas which shaped his vision of cinema. His films are clearly marked by the influence of Borges. According to Edgardo Cozarinsky, it was thanks to the films of Resnais and Rivette that the Borgesian sign gained visibility in the French context in particular with films such as *L'Année dernière à Marienbad* and *Paris nous appartient* (1975: 106). This visibility should be understood quite literally as in *Paris nous appartient* where the shot of Borges' *Enquêtes* (1957) appears because a member of the crew was reading it (1975: 118). Sylvia Molloy opens her survey of Borges' entry on the literary scene by quoting a number of films, which in one way or another refer to Borges and his stories such as Godard's *Une Femme mariée* (1964) and *Alphaville* (1965) (1972: 194). Her list also includes most of Resnais' productions.

The director's interest in Borges' ideas was linked to the writer's efforts to incorporate cinema in his reflections on the nature of literary narrative. The presence of Borges' trope in cinema is another manifestation of the writer's impact on French culture. John King in his book about the magazine *Sur* and Sylvia Molloy in *La Diffusion de la littérature hispano-américaine en France au XXe siècle* point to three historical factors which shaped Borges' status in France and preceded the embrace of his ideas by filmmakers like Resnais. The cultural elites of Argentina, headed by people like Borges and Victoria Ocampo, wanted to inscribe literary developments in Argentina onto the intellectual and artistic trends of Europe, particularly of France. This led to the visits of Ocampo to establish personal links with the main figures of the cultural world in France, such as André Gide, and the journeys of various well-known French literary figures, such as Drieu la Rochelle and André Breton, to Argentina. Official recognition of these Franco-Argentinian contacts occurred on two occasions in the post-war period. In 1946, Gide addressed a homage to Ocampo during her stay in France, calling her the 'mythe argentin' ('Argentine myth') (in King 1986: 103). In 1962, the French government, following a suggestion from André Malraux, decorated Ocampo and Borges with the *cravate de commandeur de l'ordre des Lettres et des Arts* (see Molloy 1972: 229). However, the key importance in bringing Borges onto the French stage, apart from these cultural and personal links, had to do with World War Two, which had forced a number of French intellectuals to remain in exile in Argentina. During this period one of them, Roger Caillois, founded the magazine *Les Lettres françaises* which appeared both in Buenos Aires and in Paris. In 1944, he published his translation of Borges' two stories 'The Babylon Lottery' and 'The Library of Babel' under the title 'Assyriennes'. Borges' work as a film critic in *Sur*, which was founded by Ocampo, led him to include film in his investigation of questions regarding the novel. He calls film 'le roman spectaculaire' ('spectacular novel'), and refers to the process of watching a film as reading. In his view, cinema not only partakes in the culture dominated by literature but also moulds this culture; this idea was embraced and explored by Resnais who envisioned cinema as making a significant contribution to French literary culture. Such a contribution completely transformed the nature of literary culture by making it, at least in part, visual. As we will see, narrative will offer a common language for this process of integrating cinema into literary culture and in turn changing this culture's status.

Resnais was not the first filmmaker to use ideas developed by writers to conceptualise his understanding of cinema. In his book *Le Cinéma ou l'homme imaginaire* (1956) Edgar Morin, sociologist and film theoretician, referred to Adolfo Bioy Casarès' novel, *L'Invention de Morel* (1973), significantly prefaced by Borges, to support his argument about cinematic form. In his book Morin tried to fathom the mysterious attraction that cinema holds for its spectators. He focused on the exploration of the imaginary of cinema because 'image is a strict reflection of reality but its objectivity contradicts the imaginary extravagance [of the image]' (1956: 83). Bioy Casarès' novel is an account of the workings of a certain machine, invented by Morel, which is able to record people and events in a very special way. When the images recorded by Morel's machine are played and replayed, they become inseparable from the environment in which they are projected.[16] In the course of his argument, Morin referred to Bioy Casarès' novel in order to illustrate a certain ideal which, in his opinion, cinema struggles to attain. This ideal is the total myth of cinema which is the realisation of the greatest human desire – the desire for immortality:

> *L'Invention de Morel* offers us an ultimate cinematographic myth: the absorption of the man in the split universe … if the myth of cinema signifies immortality, the total cinema is in itself a variation on the imaginary immortality. Isn't then an image, a reflection, a shadow, the first and final refuge from death? (1956: 51)

Morin makes it clear that the story in *L'Invention de Morel* presents us with an ideal of cinema which is impossible to reach. In fact, he says that

> the evolution of cinema will be over when cinema will be able to present to us the characters in colour, maybe fragrant, when the characters free themselves from the screen and darkness of cinema halls to walk in

public places and enter private spaces: just like the men and women from Morel's islands... (1956: 9)

Morin points out that it is the constant transformation of the cinema which brings it closer to its ideal state. This transformation happens through strengthening the intrinsic effect of cinema which is 'doubling'. This consists of the cinema's ability to evoke the spectators's identification with whatever is happening on the screen. The sources of identification are various cinematic techniques such as 'the transformation of time and space, the camera work and changes in point of view' (1956: 104). Since all these elements contribute to the development of cinematic narrative, it is narrative that creates the possibility of identification which is synonymous with achieving a realist effect. The fact that such a concept of cinema was first outlined in a novel means that, thus understood, cinematic narrative is a fantasy developed by a writer which could also be shared by a filmmaker.

Morin's argument signals an important duality of cinema which in the 1950s was articulated by Godard while being a commonplace much earlier. The idea is that cinema consists of two core elements – one derived from Georges Méliès and the other one from the Lumière brothers; the flip side of cinematic realism is fantasy or magic (Collet *et al.* 1999: 207). This view highlights two important aspects of Resnais' endeavour. Firstly, it emphasises his link with *Cahiers du cinéma*, which professed the realist idea of cinema or the ontological myth of cinema. Secondly, the fact that this double nature of cinema is so well captured by a writer like Bioy Casarès shows the importance of writers for the development of any conception of cinema in the French context, including Resnais' works. Film critics' view of cinema possesses a literary dimension, which allowed literary critics to draw extensively on cinema in their arguments concerning literature. Critical treatment received by Resnais' works, especially *L'Année dernière à Marienbad*, reflected these dynamics present in both literary and film criticism.

Between 1959 and 1961 a new venue of exchange was opened between the critical discourses of the cinema and the novel, which blurred differences between cinematic and literary narratives. It was manifested on three different levels. Firstly, the literary element in the critical discourse of cinema was defined in Surrealist and Borgesian terms. These arguments about cinema and literature helped bridge the discourses of both arts. Secondly, new novelists such as Robbe-Grillet and Ollier became involved in film criticism and defined the cine-novel as a film in written form; thus the cine-novel became a new manifestation of a narrative form shared by cinema and the novel. Thirdly, some elements of the critical discourse of the 1950s about film were found in the literary critical discourse; this meant that a new channel of communication was created between the two, previously more remote, critical discourses.

BEYOND *MISE-EN-SCÈNE*: THE *NOUVELLE VAGUE* IN *CAHIERS DU CINÉMA*

The shift of the most important critics of *Cahiers du cinéma* into filmmaking temporarily weakened the critical potential of the magazine and created a challenge for the generation of critics who replaced them. They strove to develop new critical categories to evaluate the creative output of the *nouvelle vague* filmmakers who made 'films which contradicted the theories they advanced as critics' (Hoveyda 1960: 34). Inspired by structuralist ideas, the new generation of *Cahiers* critics searched for a critical discourse which would break with the ontological myth of cinema and the belief that the camera is in some way innocent in its process of filming. It was essential to emphasise the fact that even 'the presence of the camera transforms the setting' rather than to perpetuate the view that the camera just records reality without altering it in any way (Hoveyda 1960: 39). *Cahiers* began to shift from the phenomenological to the linguistic understanding of cinema. There still existed a number of critics called MacMahonians, led by Michel Mourlet, who continued to use the category of *mise-en-scène* in the best *Cahiers* tradition in regard to a selected number of Hollywood filmmakers: Fritz Lang, Otto Preminger and Raoul Walsh. MacMahonians were named after the Cinema Mac-Mahon located at 5, avenue Mac-Mahon, near place de l'Etoile, which in the post-war period boasted a programme of Hollywood films particularly dear to the *Cahiers* critics of the 1950s. As a result in their criticism in the 1960s the MacMahonians took the position of *Cahiers* of the 1950s to its limits. The effort of the critics such as Weyergans, Labarthe and Delahaye to break from the ontological line of criticism was signalled by the treatment an important critic of the previous period, Roger Leenhardt, received in the television series *La Nouvelle vague par elle-même* which Labarthe made in collaboration with Janine Bazin, the wife of André.

Leenhardt perceived his engagement with cinema as an extension of his interest in the novel. The link between cinema and literature and the literary quality of his cinema was noticed by André Bazin when Leenhardt's *Les Dernières vacances* was released in 1947 (see Bazin 1948). In the documentary *Roger Leenhardt ou le dernier humaniste* (1965) Leenhardt himself recalls that, just like Alexandre Astruc and the former *Cahiers* critics who became *nouvelle vague* filmmakers, he was one of the young *gars* ('lads') who came to Paris from the provinces dreaming of writing their first novel. In the capital they discovered cinema and ended up using 'a camera like a pen' to write their version of a poetic story of a childhood or a lost paradise, told in a manner inspired by Impressionist painting. For Leenhardt, it was his *Les Dernières vacances* which incarnated this ideal. He also recalled how he became an apprentice in the art of cinema working as a film critic and only later moved into filmmaking, thus presenting himself as a role-model for the *nouvelle vague* filmmakers (see Leenhardt 1986). Leenhardt features so prominently in the series *Cinéastes de notre temps* (1964–), a series of television programmes about cinema launched by André Labarthes and Janine Bazin featuring a film director or movement, because the new critics recognised his importance for the formulation of the *politique des auteurs*. At the same time, they wanted to depart from this position which is indicated in the final shot of the programme where instead of '*fin*' ('the end') we find an inscription which refers to Leenhardt as 'a filmmaker of other times', which contrasts with the title of the series *Filmmakers of our Times*. The new generation of film critics drew on the literary critical paradigm proposed by *Cahiers* critics-turned-filmmakers in the 1950s while trying to develop this position further. To this end they began to engage with the writings of literary critics such as Roland Barthes who was a representative of new criticism in literature which was inspired by structuralist thinking. They also searched the *nouvelle vague* films themselves for the critical ideas the filmmakers claimed that their cinematic works contained; the self-conscious engagement with cinematic forms was thus the expression of this critical position on the part of *nouvelle vague* filmmakers. The literary criticism and critical ideas contained in the *nouvelle vague* films were the way of developing a new mode of thinking about cinematic narrative, its relationship to novelistic narrative and about cinema's function as an art.

In his review of Godard's *Une Femme est une femme* (*A Woman is a Woman*, 1961) Labarthe referred to the new type of narrative which had been jointly proposed by literary and film critics in the 1950s. He argued that until the emergence of the *nouveau roman*, the novelistic genre was in a deep crisis which had been initiated by Paul Valéry, whose critique of the genre was used by André Breton to denounce the novel in the pages of the *First Surrealist Manifesto* (see Labarthe 1961: 53; Breton 1988: 313–14). According to Labarthe, it was the new concept of the novel advanced by the *nouveau roman* which offered a way of overcoming the impasse in which the genre found itself. The new goal that the novel had constructed for itself brought it closer to cinema. The novelists rejected the *passé simple* ('past tense') and began to employ the present tense in their works which, according to Labarthe, was the tense favoured by cinema. The goals of filmmakers and writers coincided as they tried to develop new ways of conveying verisimilitude. As a result, the *nouveau roman* was seen in cinematic terms:

> If the past tense is the tense of knowing, the present tense is by definition the tense of consciousness, that is the tense of the gaze ... the novel is attached to the same root as cinema – which is that of Lumière. (1961: 54)

Labarthe argues that although this common ground is established between the *nouveau roman* and cinema, the latter is infinitely better equipped to achieve the end it shares with the novel. The reason for this is linked to cinema's unique quality which for him is based on 'the automatic recording of the real' something that 'no other art can do in the same way' (ibid.). The importance of the visual element in the development of narrative makes cinema better equipped to convey the real thus expressed. Interestingly enough, this view also foreshadows some of the developments in the arguments of such literary critics as Gérard Genette, who used the terms derived from film criticism of the 1950s to discuss the features of the cine-novel, *L'Année dernière à Marienbad*. This was at least in part conditioned by the evolution of the novelistic forms in ways which made them closer to cinematic forms.

According to Labarthe, *Zazie dans le metro* (1960), Louis Malle's adaptation of Raymond Queneau's novel of the same title, is a perfect illustration of the process of going beyond the *Cahiers* framework of the 1950s. The *Cahiers* critic argued that if Malle's film was just a translation of literary narrative into cinema then it should be possible to adopt Barthes' argument concerning the form of the literary narrative for the purposes of film – *Zazie dans le metro* 'embraces Literature in the same way that Literature embraces the real' – and reformulate it for the purposes of the film in the following way:

> If Malle's film is really an equivalent of Queneau's novel, [then] *Zazie* embraces cinema in the same way that cinema embraces the real. (1960a: 58)

By using the term 'equivalent' Labarthe was referring to the central concept developed by *Cahiers'* critics in the 1950s. Unlike his precursors, he argued that it would be impossible to achieve such an equivalence of literary and cinematic formal language. In Labarthe's view there existed a certain surplus in the cinematic form which could not be contained by its literary equivalent. For this reason, 'faithfulness to the plot is not enough to resolve the problem of the critique of the language that Malle believed to establish as his central goal' (1960a: 58–9). It was not possible to account for this surplus by comparing cinematic narrative to literary narrative as it had been in the 1950s. There was a need for a new critical language and a new set of references to account for the developments in cinema. The film practice of the *nouvelle vague*, which revealed a heightened awareness of the medium, offered a new sense of confidence to the film critics while becoming a serious challenge.

In his review of *Paris nous appartient* Michel Delahaye emphasises the fact that the film surpasses any literary work to which it might be compared (1962: 42). The most telling example of this lack of references to literature is François Weyergans' review of *L'Année dernière à Marienbad* (1961b). The scriptwriter, Robbe-Grillet, does not receive any mention in this review, apart from a vague reference which can be inferred from the review's title, *'Dans le dédale'*, which brings to mind Robbe-Grillet's *Dans le labyrinthe* (1959a). The only other literary reference to be found in Weyergans' review is to Adolfo Bioy Casarès' *L'Invention de Morel*, whose French translation was reviewed by Robbe-Grillet (see Weyergans 1961b: 26; Robbe-Grillet 1953a). Weyergans suggests that it is possible to offer a reading of the film emphasising its narrative structures, but this is not the path he follows in his review. Instead, he compares the film to a painting by Baldung Grien, *La Mort donnant baiser à une femme nue devant un tombeau ouvert* (1517). The comparison of cinema to painting emphasises its visuality rather than its narrative element. This is a way of describing cinematic form which goes beyond its narrative structures and literary heritage. It is also an attempt on the part of Weyergans to relate his line of thinking about cinema to the reflection on it which took place at its conception, in particular the argument which presented cinema as the synthesis of all arts (see Canudo 1995). Weyergans searched for a framework which highlighted cinema's visuality and not its ability to tell stories.

A new element emphasised by the critics along with the visual aspect, or in conjunction with the visual aspect, is the self-reflexive nature of the *nouvelle vague* films. Weyergans argues that *L'Année dernière à Marienbad* is unique because 'criticism is included in the work itself' (1961b: 22). Labarthe sees Godard's *Une Femme est une femme* as both 'the spectacle and the charm of spectacle' which can also be interpreted as privileging the self-reflexive element of the film (1961: 56). The existence of this element in Rivette's work as well is implied by Delahaye, who argued that 'Rivette reinvented cinema' (1962: 42). This self-reflexive element present in the films of the *nouvelle vague* resulted from the past critical practice of such filmmakers as Godard. This also explains the link between the visual and the critical elements; by becoming filmmakers and engaging with the visual medium, they continued their reflections on cinematic form, as was the case with Godard who said:

> I consider myself a critic and in a way I am one more now than before. Instead of writing criticism, I make a film and introduce a critical dimension into it. I think of myself as an essayist. I write essays in the form of a novel or novels in the forms of essays; simply I film instead of writing. (in Collet *et al.* 1999: 193)

The *nouvelle vague* filmmakers indicated their desire to continue to contribute to reflections about cinema after shifting into filmmaking, an initiative which had an important outcome. Due to the continuation between the *Cahiers'* ideas of the 1950s and the *nouvelle vague's* critical reflections, the roots of the *nouvelle vague* ideas expressed creatively could often be traced back and found in the earlier *Cahiers* criticism. In other words, the *nouvelle vague* films did not require a new critical framework but rather the readjustment and expansion of the existing one, established in the 1950s.

For Weyergans, the temporal dimension of film is the area in which a film's self-reflection takes place and where a film's unique visual dimension comes most forcefully into play. For him, film's internal chronology ends up being nothing more than 'this duration [*durée*] contained by it [the chronology]: the time of the projection' (1961b: 23). Weyergans disregards the fact that this strictly cinematic temporal dimension of film had become visible only because of the nature of the film's narrative. In *L'Année dernière à Marienbad*, the time of the story and of the film overlap. The exploration of the temporal dimension of the film is possible because of the nature of the narrative and not in spite of it. Although Weyergans admits the importance of the time of the narrative, he does not mention that the chronology of the film is the same as that of its narrative. In other words, in the case of *L'Année dernière à Marienbad* there is no way of exploring the film's temporal dimension outside of the narrative structure because the time of the narrative and of the film are the same.

The indispensability of the literary framework and the critical ideas of the 1950s are also evident in the case of *Paris nous appartient*, which, according to Delahaye, is an exploration of authorship. The problem of the film is indicated in his article's title, 'L'Idée maîtresse ou le complot sans maître' ('Master idea or a plot without a master') (1962), which asks whether the film is the filmmaker's creation or the reflection of a conspiracy which involves the actors and the crew and could possibly be aimed at sabotaging the director's efforts. Delahaye argues that the best illustration of Rivette's and the film's position regarding the question of authorship can be found in the *mise-en-abyme* of the film – the play *Pericles* which a theatre director, Gérard Lenz, Rivette's alter ego – attempts to stage (1962: 43). Lenz's reflection about art that accompanies the rehearsals and is inspired by the play mirrors the main argument of the film regarding authorship. Staging a play or making a film is an effort in manipulating and ordering the elements with which the director is faced by chance or by coincidence (1962: 42). For another critic of the film, Weyergans, 'Paris, which belongs to us, is Paris contaminated by the plot which Rivette uses to threaten us' (1961a: 23). By calling the film *Paris nous appartient* the director suggests that this city, which is so full of dangers and uncanny coincidences, has been contained and then shaped by the very process of filmmaking and by the exercise of his authorial control over the film. It is only by drawing a parallel with the role of the theatre director that *Paris nous appartient* manages to convey its argument regarding film authorship. In other words, the evocation of a literary framework and literary references is necessary to initiate the debate regarding cinematic form.

The reviews of *nouvelle vague* films show the involvement of the new *Cahiers* critics with issues which deeply concerned their predecessors, such as the importance of adaptation, literary references and authorship. The new critics' interest in these problems was an attempt to develop a critical discourse of cinema, which emphasises the visual element of films without referring to literary discourse. This explains the emphasis they put on the temporal dimension of cinema, film's ability to capture and to convey the present, and those cinematic elements which are absent from the literary work found at the origins of the film. However, these film critics were not successful in defining cinematic form outside of the literary discourse. It was the self-reflexive or critical elements present in the films of the *nouvelle vague* which were of key importance in this process. These critical elements reflected some of the concepts developed by *Cahiers* critics in the 1950s. The presence of literature was fundamental to this process and clearly visible; when evaluating the films of the *nouvelle vague* the new critics could not ignore this literary element.

Even though the critics of the 1950s greatly appreciated Resnais' contribution to the development of their critical ideas it was clear that the filmmaker was going against the grain of the *politique des auteurs*. Moreover, he emphasised the crucial importance of scriptwriters in the composition of his cinematic narratives and revealed that he always co-operated with them because he was not capable of writing his own stories (in d'Allones 1967: 123). By collaborating with different scriptwriters, Resnais focused on the place of narrative and literary frameworks in his films. At the same time, he delegated the literary aspects of the film to the writers which allowed him to concentrate on the visual part of his work. For this reason, an examination of the ways in which Resnais engages with literature provides answers regarding the differences, if any, between cinematic and literary narratives, and the ways of conceptualising cinematic form which addresses cinema's visual character more directly.

ALAIN RESNAIS, THE SURREALISTS AND JORGE LUIS BORGES

From the beginning of his career as a filmmaker shortly after the end of World War Two, Resnais had close links with the *Cahiers du cinéma* critics of the 1950s and with André Bazin (Benayoun 1980: 46). In 1957 he edited Jacques Doniol-Valcroze's film, *L'Oeil du maître*, but even ten years earlier Bazin had made an appearance in Resnais' documentary about the gardens of Paris, *Les Jardins de Paris* (1947–48). Indeed, Dudley Andrew suggests that it was under the wing of Bazin that Resnais' transformation from a *cinéphile* into a filmmaker took place (1990: 95; see also Fleischer 1989). Bazin and Resnais shared the same conception of cinema which was recognised by the *Cahiers* critics. In a review of Truffaut's *Les Quatre cents coups* Doniol-Valcroze explained that, had Bazin been alive, Truffaut's film would have been dedicated to Resnais (1959: 42). In a review of Resnais' *du styrène* Godard connected Resnais' creative oeuvre, represented by his documentaries, to the theoretical work of Bazin:

Beginning with *Van Gogh*, one had an impression that it was not just the movement of the camera, but also the research into the secret of this movement [which was important to Resnais]. It was an amazing coincidence that this is the secret that another solitary researcher, who was also starting from zero, André Bazin, discovered, at the same time but with different means. (1959: 37)

Godard suggests that the critical thrust of Resnais' documentaries, apparent in their self-reflexive character, put this filmmaker on an equal footing with Bazin. In other words, Resnais was a critic of cinema just like Bazin, although Resnais' medium of expression was documentary and short filmmaking rather than essay and article writing. Moreover, for his part, Resnais emphasised his conceptual links with the *Cahiers* critics by pointing to the literary references in his understanding of the art of cinema. René Prédal remarked that Resnais' films, such as *L'Année dernière à Marienbad*, evoked more comparisons with literary works (Lovecraft, Julien Gracq, Borges, Bioy Casarès, W. Jensen), than they did with cinema (Cocteau, Buñuel) (1968: 6). Apart from emphasising a literary dimension of Resnais' oeuvre, this set of references also brings to mind the *Cahiers* tradition of comparing films to novels in order to create parallel canons in cinema and in literature, and shows affinity between Resnais and the *Cahiers* group.

Literary collaborations did not limit Resnais' creativity; rather they helped him to focus on the formal aspects of his films and to open new ways of exploring cinematic specificity. This is made evident in the comparison Bazin drew between Resnais' art films and Robert Bresson's film adaptations, and in the framework developed by Resnais to examine filmic form. Resnais evoked Surrealism in order to frame his experiments with cinematic form through *montage* in terms of dreams, and as an exploration of the unconscious. The references to Borges not only redefined cinema's cultural role but also emphasised its affiliation with literature. The seeds of such ways of defining cinematic form are also found in the writings of the *Cahiers* critics of the 1950s. There were affinities between Surrealism and *Cahiers'* critical practice, and also between *Cahiers'* and Borges' respective visions of the relationship between literary and cinematic narrative. These links strengthened the relationship between the critical line of Resnais and that developed by the *Cahiers* critics in the 1950s.

Bazin drew a comparison between Bresson's adaptations of Georges Bernanos' novel and Resnais' art films (1997f). Resnais' work on art films was revealing as far as his relationship with scriptwriters, scripts and wider literature was concerned. Bazin argued that what interested Resnais 'wasn't the subject of the painting but the painting itself', which means that the director's foremost concerns were with questions of form rather than those of representation (1997d: 126). For Bazin, Resnais managed to reveal aspects of the painting which were not accessible without the movement of camera. It was 'by distorting the work, by breaking its frame, by attacking the very essence of the film that film is forced to reveal some of its secret potential' (1997f: 192). This fragmentation and deformation of painting, which characterised its representation in cinema, amounted to art criticism for Bazin; there exists 'literary criticism which is also a recreation, like that of Baudelaire on Delacroix, of Valéry on Baudelaire and of Malraux on Greco' (ibid.). He argued that these were examples of criticism which creates a new work of art. Similarly, disclosing by means of cinema an otherwise inaccessible layer of the literary script and providing a critical reading of the script are ways by which Resnais established his relationship with his scriptwriters.

Resnais considered editing one of his principal activities as a filmmaker. He said that in cinema 'the real tension does not spring from the script, but from image and sound which impose themselves on the eye and the ear' (in Anon. 1961b: 9); cinema was about moulding reality 'by manipulating images and sounds' (in Rasking 1967: 97). His interest in *montage* was long-lived and was first revealed in *Van Gogh*. With *montage* he was trying to convey the imaginary universe of painting:

> It was about finding out whether the painted trees, characters and houses, could by the means of the cinematographic *montage*, fulfil the role of real objects, and if so, would it be possible to substitute the artist's internal world with the photographed world? (1948: 2)

Montage is the primary means of artistic expression for a filmmaker because it faciliates 'the passage from the real to the imaginary' (in Rasking 1967: 97). Such a view of *montage* emphasised the role of the filmmaker in achieving a level of abstraction in his work. The result of this drive towards abstraction was a development of cinematic narrative whose equivalent was found in the literary narrative of the film script created by Resnais' literary collaborators. He related Eisenstein's experiments with *montage* to the Surrealist encounter 'of an umbrella and a sewing machine on the dissection table', and revealed that he himself is very responsive to the efforts of the Surrealists but 'feels even closer to Eisenstein's ideas' (in Labarthe & Rivette 1961: 8). It is through his study and practice of *montage*, inspired by Eisenstein's experiments, that Resnais managed to convey in his films the level of consciousness privileged by Surrealists – the sphere of dreams.

Resnais compared his method of shooting to *écriture automatique* ('automatic writing') in order to demonstrate the importance of the Surrealist tradition for him. He emphasised spontaneity and the lack of self-censorship in his creative work (in d'Allones 1967: 127). Resnais also shared the Surrealist desire to see cinema not just as the reflection of dreams but also as the expression of the workings of thought. *L'Année dernière à Marienbad* was not only a dream-like film, but also 'an attempt to convey the complexity and mechanism of thought' (in Roumette 1961: 46). Ado Kyrou, a film critic associated with the Surrealist movement, argued that the purpose of cinema is to give access to surreality which, as Breton himself said, 'relies on the belief in the existence of higher forms of reality consisting of neglected associations, and (on the belief) in the power of the dream' (Breton in Kyrou 1963: 10). Kyrou's understanding of cinema explains why it was possible for Resnais to frame his experiments with cinematic form in Surrealist terms. Kyrou's ideas about cinema were inspired by the findings of the Surrealist movement, which in their origins were mostly literary; he thus adapted the Surrealist vision of literature for the needs of cinema. From the point of view of Resnais, this interface between cinema and literature present in the Surrealist movement was crucial for establishing the equal relationship between the narrative of his films and that of the literary scripts on which they were based.

Resnais' description of cinematic form in Surrealist terms also revealed the presence of Surrealism in the critical method of *Cahiers* in the 1950s centred on the arguments about *mise-en-scène*. The *mise-en-scène* of a film was a cinematic experience which was not tangible and could only be revealed as the narrative of the film was unfolding on the screen, gradually transcending the material limitations of the cinematic apparatus which had been mobilised in the process of filmmaking. This triumph of spirit or imagination over matter and reason was evoked by the experience of surreality described by Kyrou as 'the liberation of a man through research and discovery of the "real workings of thought" and the destruction of senile Cartesian ideas' (1963: 10). Some of the earliest films of the *nouvelle vague* contained direct references to Surrealist cinema; it is enough to mention the tribute to Jean Vigo's *Zéro de conduite* (*Zero for Conduct*, 1933) in Truffaut's *Les Quatre cents coups* and both the ominous and enigmatic atmosphere of *Paris nous appartient*.

Evidence of how deeply the Surrealist experience was ingrained in the consciousness of the 1950s critics of cinema is also apparent in the recognition of Surrealist filmmakers as the beacons of the *nouvelle vague*. It is not without reason that André S. Labarthe chose to initiate his television series *Cinéastes de notre temps* with programmes about Luis Buñuel and Jean Vigo. The critical method of the *Cahiers* critics bore some resemblances to the practice of the Surrealists: they shared the belief that it is not necessary to write about a whole film, or even to write about it in its totality – it was enough to focus on fragments of the film because it was details, a few unique elements of the work, which touched spectators and made them pass judgement on the film. Kyrou's idea that 'often a short film scene is the film' could be seen as crystallising into the category of *mise-en-scène* which was evoked by the *Cahiers* critics in their enthusiastic response to American and European films in the 1950s and early 1960s (1963: 225). In the same way the Surrealist fetishising of film stars is comparable to the *Cahiers* critics' obsession with some filmmakers. Geneviève Sellier gives a powerful description of *Cahiers' cinéphiles'* fetishisation of American filmmakers, and also places this phenomenon in its historical context (1998: 203).

Resnais was using Surrealist methods in his works, which explored numerous themes inspired by Borges. According to Cozarinsky, Resnais shared his fascination with libraries and labyrinths with many film critics of *Cahiers du cinéma*, *Positif* and *Présence du cinéma*, who in the early 1960s 'fought their guerrilla wars while regularly engaging with Borges' (1975: 105). The reason why Borges attracted so much attention among film critics and filmmakers was linked to his interest in film. King argues that the style of Borges' stories was developed in the literary and film reviews he wrote for *Sur* in the 1930s, 'the *Nouvelle Revue Française* of Latin America' (1986: 45). His literary production carried the seeds of his earlier reflections on Hollywood, Soviet and Argentine cinema. According to Borges, cinematic products were comparable to literature. Through the interaction of sound and image, cinema was able to create cultural products which were equal to those generated for centuries by literature. He outlines this position in a review which is an attack on dubbing:

The Greeks created Chimera, a monster with the head of a lion, dragon and goat; theologians of the second century – Trinity, inside which are present the Father, the Son and the Spirit ... Hollywood has just added to this vain teratological museum; thanks to dubbing, it offers us monsters which combine the celebrated features of Greta Garbo and the voice of Aldonza Lorenzo. How can one not express one's surprise before this appalling wonder, before these up-and-coming phonetico-visual anomalies? (1975: 88)

Although the example is rather negative and Borges is clearly critical of Garbo's voice being replaced with that of a Spanish actress, he nevertheless implies here that cinematic product can be considered a continuation of a certain literary tradition. Borges also indicates that this product undergoes a specific transformation. Although its origins are literary, its cinematic incarnation enriches it with new visual and aural elements. Such an evolution of chimera could be seen as standing for the transformation literary culture underwent as a result of cinema's impact on it.

Like the *Cahiers* critics of the 1950s, Borges identified narrative as the common denominator of the cinema and the novel which allowed him to compare and relate them. According to Cozarinsky, for Borges, 'the narrative apparatus is the same in written and cinematographic fiction' (1975: 19). The review of King Vidor's *Street Scene* (1931) outlining Borges' vision of Hollywood centred on narrative was published in the same issue of *Sur* where his essay 'El arte narrativo y la magica' ('Narrative Art and Magic') appeared. In this article, Borges presented characteristics common to the narrative techniques of the novel and of film (1961: 8) and he includes film in his investigation of the functioning of the novel. In his view, narrative cinema not only follows the principles of a culture dominated by literature but is moulding it in the same way literature does. Resnais' documentaries and, later, his feature films supported and developed this idea. Robert Benayoun suggests that every Resnais' documentary has a corresponding feature film: *Toute la mémoire du monde* (*All the Memory of the World*, 1956) and *L'Année dernière à Marienbad*; *Nuit et brouillard* and *Hiroshima, mon amour*; *Le Styrène* and *Muriel ou le temps d'un retour*; *Les Statues meurent aussi* and *Stavisky* (1974) (1980: 45).

One of Resnais' works marked by the Borgesian influence was *Toute la mémoire du monde*. Weyergans argued that in that film Resnais explored the unconscious and saluted literary culture, represented in the form of the Bibliothèque nationale, thus showing that 'imagination and culture are no strangers to each other' (1961b: 27). The library space represents the collective imaginary, the collective unconscious which is being explored by the filmmaker. The link between memory and audio-visual culture is established in the opening sequence of the film where we see a microphone gliding slowly along a corridor followed closely by the camera. The voice-over explains that the weakness and unreliability of memory are the justification for the existence of such libraries. With that Resnais wanted to emphasise 'the very important notion of the usefulness of books and to show the infinity of memory' (in Baby 1957: 6). Resnais was also fascinated by the idea that in such a library 'close to six million books could interact without any ideas being censored' (ibid.). According to Doniol-Valcroze, represented by cinematic means the National Library is a place of freedom rather than 'the place where all books are imprisoned from birth' (1957: 59). Hence, it is not only the filmmaker's commitment to the idea of freedom and his respect for cultural heritage which are behind this project concerning the library, but also his desire to contribute to literary culture by expanding and liberating it through visual means. For Resnais, cinema offers a new medium for representing literary culture. The filmmaker creates visual libraries not only by making films about actual libraries, as was the case with *Toute la mémoire du monde*, but also by making films which express literary culture by cinematic methods. This new representation does not leave the literary culture unchanged but transforms it in a fundamental way; it is no longer a literary culture alone once it comes to include cinema as well. The source of Resnais' conception of cinema as a library was Borges' belief that the library is the most complete embodiment of culture and its workings (see Benayoun 1980: 54).

Resnais' critics suggest that the filmmaker's projects, which are often considered intellectual and elitist, were not the ones the artist himself was most interested in. Jean-Paul Torok argues that it is the films Resnais did not manage to make rather than those he made which say most about the filmmaker (in Prédal 1996: 86). It is from these projects that we can learn the most about Resnais' view of cinema because they can be treated as subtext to the narratives of the films Resnais did manage to make. Prédal suggests that each film made by Resnais can be coupled with another one which he did not manage to realise; Tintin's adventures instead of *Hiroshima, mon amour*; Queneau's *Pierrot mon ami* (1942) and not *L'Année dernière à Marienbad*; *Fantômas* instead of *Muriel ou le temps d'un retour*; and *Les Aventures de Harry Dickson* (1962) rather than *La Geurre est finie* (*The War is Over*, 1966) (1996: 86). Resnais' official projects are considered literary, high-brow and associated with the dominant literary culture. But it is both the films he made and their imaginary subtext which express fully the concept of cinema for Resnais. It is the relationship between the project Resnais realised and his imaginary filmography which mirrors contemporary culture for him. The literary projects, which can be either films or their equivalent cine-novels, are accompanied by imaginary cinema. It is Resnais' desire to adapt *Les Aventures de Harry Dickson* which best conveys this side of 'the unknown Resnais, close to Feuillade and Lovecraft' (Prédal 1996: 87)

In the story, Georgette Cuvelier is a femme fatale trying to kill the detective Harry Dickson in an act of revenge to which she is obligated by her father. In the course of her brief encounters with Dickson she falls in love with him, and becomes a poignant and tragic figure. Dickson is chasing her, aware of both her plans and of her feelings towards him. It is this project, among those mentioned by Torok, which was taken most seriously not only by Resnais, but also by cinema critics and producers. The critical interest evoked by his unrealised films suggests that a wider and more complex concept of culture proposed by Resnais was accepted by his contemporary critics. Clearly his conception is one which mirrored more general transformations which French culture was undergoing at the time.

Délphine Seyrig, the female star of *L'Année dernière à Marienbad* and *Muriel ou le temps d'un retour*, reveals that she was approached by Resnais for the first time in New York with an offer of the role of Georgette Cuvelier in *Les Aventures de Harry Dickson* (1967: 65). A reference to the film also appears in the autobiography of Anatole Dauman, which reproduces the originals of numerous documents, letters and scripts linked to the films he produced (1989: 93). The reference is in the form of a dedication Resnais wrote to Dauman in the album *Repérages*, which included a selection of photographs taken by Resnais in preparation for shooting the film. The commentary to the photographs presented by Jorge Semprun shows that they should be taken as an expression of Resnais' creative process (see Resnais & Semprun 1974: 10). Resnais himself mentions *Les Aventures de Harry Dickson* when he speaks about the difference between this film and his fourth feature film, *Je t'aime je t'aime* (1968–69); he discusses his desire to have more music in his future projects (in Rasking 1967: 102). These numerous references to *Les Aventures de Harry Dickson* imply that this project and the vision of cinema it conveyed did not belong to the sphere of imagination and fantasy only but was seriously considered by Resnais and the critics of his films. The film's more popular source, the comic strip, which is very different from the highly literary sources of Resnais' other films, raises questions regarding the transformation of his concept of cinema as a result of engaging with such a popular source.

The formal links between his other projects and *Les Aventures de Harry Dickson* demonstrate that cinema can preserve its formal integrity and independence whether it is based on a highly literary or a popular culture source. Pierre Samson, writing for *L'Arc*, stresses how *Les Aventures de Harry Dickson* was supposed to assemble all the archetypes of Resnais' other films; for instance, the representation of space as a labyrinth and a character as an eternal traveller (Samson 1967: 106, 109). The script of the film includes flashbacks and a voice-over, which are evocative of *Hiroshima, mon amour* and *L'Année dernière à Marienbad*. Temporal and spatial changes could be conveyed through the type of *montage* used in *Muriel ou le temps d'un retour* which Resnais was filming at the time of writing the script of *Les Aventures de Harry Dickson* (de Towarnicki 1967: 23). The character of Harry Dickson appears as the director's alter ego and his philosophy of work is close to that of Resnais; indeed, as we have noted, the director's vision of cinema is integral to all his films. The detective believed that 'to look does not mean to see' (Resnais & de Towarnicki 1962: 3). It is 'the fantastic ballet of the images, the finale which seems to embrace the whole existence of Harry Dickson' (1962: 31). From time to time 'he abandons the frantic activity, stops the fight and gives himself to love' (1962: 33). The imaginary filmography of Resnais possesses the same characteristics as the films; it is the filmmaker's concept of cinema and his personality which connect all his projects. The coherence of Resnais' creative output, which ranges from the projects counted among literary cinema to attempts to film comic strips, is indicative of the character of contemporary French culture. It lost its exclusively literary character as literary works found full expression in films. As the same time, it expanded as filmmakers like Resnais envisioned adaptations of comic strips which could create a completely new cultural product.

SCRIPTWRITERS AND NOVELISTS AS FILM CRITICS

The environment in which Resnais made his films and elaborated his critical ideas had two important characteristics. Firstly, *Cahiers du cinéma*'s criticism displayed signs of crisis because the critics of the second generation replacing those who shifted into filmmaking had problems with developing an alternative critical framework to that of the *politique des auteurs* and *mise-en-scène*. Resnais' reflections on the art of cinema present in his films was seen as filling this critical gap. Secondly, Resnais' creative work marked a departure from the *Cahiers* criticism of the 1950s which had impact upon his critical ideas; collaboration with scriptwriters allowed him to focus on the formal aspects of his films, which he then conceptualised in terms borrowed from both the Surrealists' and Borges' reflections on cinema. As we have seen above, although Resnais' critical ideas were innovative and different from the *Cahiers* criticism of the 1950s, they could be inferred from his films and reconstructed on the basis of his interviews. This silence on the part of the director and the ineffectiveness of the critical discourse of *Cahiers* empowered a new set of actors on the French critical stage – the scriptwriters of Resnais' films.

The credits of *L'Année dernière à Marienbad* must be striking to anybody who has ever read Truffaut's 'Une Certaine tendance du cinéma français' or Astruc's 'La Caméra-stylo' and consequently has come to believe that directors could be, just like writers, *auteurs* of films. *L'Année dernière à Marienbad* opens with the information that Alain Robbe-Grillet, the scriptwriter, is the *auteur* of 'the original script and of the dialogue of the film'. The name of Alain Resnais, who was the director, the *réalisateur*, comes only second after that of the scriptwriter. Furthermore, Robbe-Grillet appropriated Resnais' film by inserting still shots of Resnais' *L'Année dernière à Marienbad* into the text of the cine-novel, which for him was 'the description of an imaginary film' (1961b: 9); when Resnais made *L'Année dernière à Marienbad* 'he created it for the second time' (ibid). The prominent position of the scriptwriter is alarming in light of the film criticism of the 1950s. The term '*auteur*' became so heavily charged in the context of that criticism that it was impossible to designate a scriptwriter an *auteur* of a film without compromising the role of the film director.

Historically, scriptwriters published their scripts in order to mark their impact on films or even to maintain creative control over them. The very process of filmmaking could alter the script so substantially that writers feared losing their original contribution (see Virmaux & Virmaux 1983: 69). This hypothesis does not really account for the case of the cine-novel *L'Année dernière à Marienbad*, where Robbe-Grillet claimed that he and Resnais were in total agreement over all elements of the film and for this reason they decided 'to sign the whole film together without separating the script and the *mise-en-scène*' (1961a: 12). Rather it seems that Resnais accepted Robbe-Grillet's ideas of the equivalence between script and film and scriptwriter and filmmaker.

The scriptwriter and the filmmaker were jointly interviewed by Rivette and Labarthe in *Cahiers du cinéma*. Although such interviews of film creators belonged to the logic of the *politique des auteurs* and were a common practice of *Cahiers*, the case of *L'Année dernière à Marienbad* was different in at least two ways. Firstly, *Cahiers* critics decided to interview both the scriptwriter and the director; this was a change from the *politique des auteurs* which, as we know, privileged directors at the expense of all other contributors to the film. Secondly, traditionally, the interviews with *auteurs* were treated as something special in *Cahiers* and were accompanied by a whole range of reviews written independently of the interview; in the case of *L'Année dernière à Marienbad* the lack of a decisive critical response to the film was a sign of a certain critical weakness or conceptual vacuum on the part of the second generation of film critics – they were clearly interested in the film, but did not quite know how to deal with it.

Robbe-Grillet's decision to publish the cine-novel, and to present his ideas about the film and the cine-novel in the introduction, was part of the process of developing a critical framework to compensate for the conceptual shortcomings of *Cahiers*. As discussed, it was not just Robbe-Grillet, but also new novelists such as Claude Ollier who became film critics and began to shape the debate about cinematic form (see Ollier 1961a and 1961b). These writers-turned-critics developed the ideas of the *Cahiers* critics of the 1950s, keeping their focus on questions of narrative; using this element as an entry point into the critical debates of cinema was only natural for these writers and also happened to coincide with the views of the film critics which were heavily marked by literature. It is for these reasons that the textual film of Robbe-Grillet, his cine-novel, was a creative realisation of the critical ideas of the previous decade.

L'Année dernière à Marienbad appeared in a different critical environment from that of *Hiroshima, mon amour*, which was reflected in Marguerite Duras' relationship with the film and with its director. Duras also decided to publish the script of the film but she did not stress her role in the development of the film to the same degree that Robbe-Grillet did. In the credits of *Hiroshima, mon amour* we find Resnais, in first place, credited with the direction (*réalisation*) of the film, and in second place Duras, as the author of the script and dialogue (*scénario et dialogues*). In the *avant-propos* to the script she explains that, for her, the text of *Hiroshima, mon amour* is an account of her collaboration with Resnais in which her role was 'to realise the elements on the basis of which Resnais made his films' (1960: 19). The primacy given to the director by the scriptwriter was an incarnation of Truffaut's ideal regarding the collaboration between a scriptwriter and a film-maker. If a director decided to use a scriptwriter, the script should be just a springboard for the creative project. Duras emphasised Resnais' creative contribution to the writing of the script; this exchange with the director was of great importance to Duras' work on the film, and she regretted that the conversations she had with Resnais in the course of making the film were not part of the published script (1960: 19–20). By claiming that 'Resnais works like a novelist', she designated the director as the film *auteur* and stressed the importance of the film over the script (1959: 36). She also did not attempt to frame the critical discourse regarding the film which, for her, was the job of film critics. Robbe-Grillet's position in relation to Resnais' was completely different from that of Duras; this is reflected in his concept of the script's narrative which is independent of the film and equal to it.

Robbe-Grillet believed that it would be possible to recreate filmic narrative in the written mode of the cine-novel. To disregard the formal aspects of the film would make the writing of the *découpage* as inconceivable as creating a novel without using grammatical tenses; for this reason, 'it is in the form where one should look for the true content' (1961a: 12). The creative realisation of Robbe-Grillet's idea of literary narration in the style of the cine-novel was new and original. It complemented the creative project of Resnais in cinema and was an expression of an idea of cinema in the written method. Thanks to the cine-novel, the one-way traffic of ideas from literature into cinema began to flow in the other direction as well, as films were being realised in written form first.

Robbe-Grillet found strong support for his ideas in the critical work of Claude Ollier. For this writer, the narrative of *L'Année dernière à Marienbad* was related to that of *Dans le labyrinthe*, and more widely to the *nouveau roman*, and associated with its critical reflection on the art of the novel and literary narrative (see Ollier 1961a: 711; 1961b: 908). Ollier's argument about the narrative of *L'Année dernière à Marienbad* focused on the same elements as Robbe-Grillet's analysis of the cine-novel. This is particularly evident in the role both assigned to the voice-over. For Ollier, the voice of X is 'a thread leading us through the maze of obsessions; that's the connection between all the linguistic, sound and visual elements [of the film]' (1961a: 716). In the same way, Robbe-Grillet argues that X dominates the narrative of the film by imposing order upon the universe of the film with his storytelling powers (1961a: 14).

The traffic of ideas between literary and cinematic worlds was also apparent in the terms in which the narrative was conceptualised. Ollier shows the ways in which a focus on narrative can also become a way of exploring cinematic form. He argues that time is the formal element of narrative, which is film's central concern. This element of the film, the film as a sign of plot development, was put under tremendous pressure from the modernist experiments (1961a: 715). The attack on chronological time, causality and linearity of the events resulted in the representation of a different reality, 'that of the mental processes ... referred to by André Breton as "the real functioning of the thought"' (1961a: 715–16). As we have already seen, challenging the conventions of verisimilitude in narrative was a way of exploring cinematic form. The use of the Surrealist frame to conceptualise this departure from realist narrative links Ollier's argument with Resnais' vision of cinematic form. It is the scriptwriter and the writer-turned-critic who express the vision of a filmmaker by verbalising it. Although already implied in Resnais' creative works and voiced in some of his interviews, it is the writers who present this view, and for this reason it is the writers who take over the role of shaping *Cahiers'* criticism in the 1960s.

The expression of cinematic form in Surrealist terms reveals its hybrid visual-literary nature, because of the character of the Surrealist experience of cinema. The Surrealist engagement with cinema was the creative-critical response by poets to their fascination with a new medium of expression. They described cinema as a dream lived in a state of physical wakefulness and considered cinema to be the source of Surrealist experience in its purest form (see Beaujour 1965: 58). This interest in cinema resulted in a profusion of literary texts: mostly scenarios and poetry. These were considered a new type of cinematographic criticism and referred to as a 'critique synthétique' ('synthetic criticism'). They were singled out because of the creative spontaneity which was associated with their production:

> Rather than analysis, such criticism attempts to find in the disorder, the freshness and the emotions provoked by the work and to give it a kind of poetic equivalence ... This type of criticism is an act of sympathy [with the work]. (Bonnet 1965: 85–6)

A certain affinity exists between the Surrealist project in cinema and that of the MacMahon criticism in the early 1960s, published in the film magazine *Présence du cinéma*. The terms of their criticism and its objects (peplum, westerns, pornographic features, serials) coincided with the interests of the Surrealists (see Mourlet 1987). As was mentioned before the MacMahons continued the critical line of *Cahiers du cinéma* from the 1950s emphasising the critical category of *mise-en-scène*.

Although the critical texts of the Surrealists often took the form of a scenario, they were very rarely made into actual films. Among the rare exceptions are Antonin Artaud's *La Coquille et le Clergyman* (*The Seashell and the Clergyman*, 1927), filmed by Germaine Dulac, and Robert Desnos' poem which provided the basis for Man Ray's *L'Etoile de mer* (*The Star of the Sea*, 1928). The Surrealists' disappointment with cinema came not only from the impossibility of making their scripts into actual films, but also from the divergence they observed between their spectatorial experience of film as a dream, and a very tedious, long and technical process of filmmaking, which did not at all resemble the freedom of a dream. The difficulties with the actual realisation of most of the Surrealist texts in film led to a certain paradox in the Surrealist conception of cinema. Although cinema was supposed to liberate the Surrealists from the constraints of the literary institution, it resulted in the production of a new type of literary text, and ended up perpetuating its growth (see Virmaux 1965: 114). Hence, the framing of cinematic form in Surrealist terms is profoundly marked by literature. In the second half of the twentieth century the character of this literature changed because writing was marked by the experience of cinema.

In his review of *L'Année dernière à Marienbad* Ollier draws a comparison between film narrative and the narrative of the novel *L'Invention de Morel* (1961a: 910). This novel was a fictionalised account of the fascination with cinema experienced by the whole generation which included the Surrealists in the 1920s. Ollier's comparison between *L'Année dernière à Marienbad* and *L'Invention de Morel* focuses on numerous repetitions. Owing to the close relationship between Bioy Casarès and Borges, this comparison brings Ollier's interpretation of cinematic form within the sphere of influence of Borges, already evident in Resnais' position outlined earlier. There also exist close affinities between Borges and Robbe-Grillet. In the preface to *L'Invention de Morel*, Borges argues that cinema in the novel is presented as 'rationalised imagination' and as a 'fantastic premise which is not nonetheless supernatural' (1973: 9, 10). Thus defined, Bioy Casarès' concept of cinema is analysed by Robbe-Grillet in his review of *L'Invention de Morel* in which he also mentions Borges' preface (1953a: 172). We can see here how writers like Robbe-Grillet attempted to incorporate cinema into their reflections on the novel. As we have seen in the discussion of Borges in the context of Resnais' critical activity, such reflections were attempts to redefine the predominant concept of culture and to cast it in new, wider and not just literary terms. Robbe-Grillet's efforts to rethink the nature of culture focus on narrative; from his reflection on narrative in the novel and cinema we can deduce his new vision of culture.

Robbe-Grillet identifies two realities in Bioy Casarès' novel. He shows how the false reality fabricated by the narrator changed its status after it was recorded and became part of the existing film. In the very act of being integrated into the existing recording, it becomes less false. At the same time, this addition manipulates and transforms the original recording and falsifies it to some extent. Describing the reality presented in the novel in terms of 'the imagination and the doubts regarding the exact nature of reality' (1953a: 174), Robbe-Grillet brings to the fore the power of narrative which arranges images in different ways and thus changes their meaning; the existing narrative can thus be transformed by the insertion of new images. The argument of Robbe-Grillet and Borges concerning Bioy Casarès' work relates cinematic and literary narrative; it is not surprising that Borges and Robbe-Grillet connected their views of cinema to the evolution of the novel.

Both critics argued that *L'Invention de Morel* was an important step in the development of the novelistic genre. They remarked on the difference between a modern novel like that of Bioy Casarès and the psychological novel of the nineteenth century. Robbe-Grillet shared Borges' enthusiasm regarding the rigour and discipline of *L'Invention de Morel*, which were the result of formal limitations imposed by the genre of the adventure novel. They also agreed on the fact that the detective novel had replaced the love story of the past. The detective story was considered modern, because it possesses many of the characteristics of the adventure novel which, for the two writers, was the most important modern genre (see Borges 1973: 9; Robbe-Grillet 1951: 1002). Robbe-Grillet's reading of *L'Invention de Morel* demonstrates that changing conceptions of cinema were functions of the prevailing model of the novel. Bioy Casarès' novel shows that the shaping of literary models and their narratives depended on a conception of cinema endorsed by contemporary writers. According to Bioy Casarès, cinema has characteristics of both realist cinema and dream-like cinema. Borges' authorship of the preface of this novel proves that the interaction in the novel between literary narrative and visual elements associated with a fantasy of cinema were transforming not only the novel's narrative but also the whole culture. Literary narrative and literary culture were increasingly saturated by writers' ideas about cinema and Ollier's review was a product of this process.

The changes in *Cahiers'* criticism caused by the emergence of the *nouvelle vague*, and a shift by many critics into filmmaking, brought about changes in the relationship between scriptwriters and filmmakers. It led to the transformation of the nature of authorship, film and literary narratives, and the understanding of culture, which was no longer considered to be strictly literary. These transformations were evident in the more active role played by the literary collaborator of Resnais' second feature, *L'Année dernière à Marienbad*, Robbe-Grillet. The disruption of chronology in cinematic narrative revealed the workings of imagination, thought and dream. Although the Surrealists' interest in cinema was expressed more frequently in the form of written texts than films, these written texts carried strong visual elements. They were written either as a poetic response to films or as film scripts, and the visual element denied these texts' uniquely literary character. The literary production of the Surrealists was hybrid – cine-literary – in nature. Due to this kind of Surrealist engagement with cinema, references to Surrealism provide the most adequate terms to describe the forms of the narratives of Resnais' films and Robbe-Grillet's cine-novel. By the same token, references to the ideas of Borges made by Resnais, Robbe-Grillet and Ollier present literary narrative, whose nature has changed due to the impact of cinema, as reflective of the transformation undergone by the whole literary culture.

LITERARY CRITICS AND *L'ANNÉE DERNIÈRE À MARIENBAD*

The reception of the film and the cine-novel *L'Année dernière à Marienbad* revealed the growing importance of critics associated with literature who were either scriptwriters or other types of writers. The acclaimed lack of difference between the film and the cine-novel and the erasure of the distinctiveness of cinematic and literary narratives had some consequences for the arguments about *L'Année dernière à Marienbad* by literary critics such as Gérard Genette. Firstly, they borrowed some terms from film criticism such as 'caméra-stylo' in order to account for the characteristics of the narrative of the cine-novel. Secondly, they identified the same structural features in literary and cinematic narratives. They also referred to the critical discourse associated with Surrealism and Borges to describe these works. These processes show how new creative developments such as *L'Année dernière à Marienbad* transformed not only film but also literary critical discourses by integrating them through the use of the same critical terminology and references to conceptualise both cinematic and literary narratives. The distinctions between critical discourses of cinema and literature seems to be replaced by their fusion into one. The most striking characteristic of the new discourse shared by cinema and the novel is the adoption by literary critics of terms which originated in film criticism. This is a sign of an important and profound change in the cultural status of cinema which is integrated into literary discourses.

Barthes was one of the earliest critics of Robbe-Grillet's novels, and his reviews reflected an important moment in the literary criticism of the 1950s. In three articles, 'Littérature objective', 'Littérature littérale' and 'Le Point sur Robbe-Grillet' (1954, 1955 and 1962 respectively) Barthes identified cinematic effects in Robbe-Grillet's novels which transformed literary narrative; the visual or cinematic effects in this author's works were directly linked to the disintegration of plot. Barthes presented the opening paragraph of *Les Gommes* (1953b) as an effort by Robbe-Grillet to reconstruct the conditions of film viewing. For him, 'the cubical room is a movie theatre; nudity is the darkness of the movie theatre, necessary for the emergence of the immobile gaze; the window glass, it is the screen, both flat and open to all the dimensions of the movement, even that of the time' (1964b: 37–8). He also argued that the impact of descriptions in Robbe-Grillet's novels on their readers was evocative of the effect that film images have on cinema spectators. In these descriptions 'one recognised the impact of the revolution that the cinema had on vision' (1964b: 37). Barthes suggested that these descriptions oppress the reader and, just like film images, leave the spectator without control and vulnerable to their influence. The new ways of representing space found in Robbe-Grillet's novels were, according to Barthes, also inspired by cinema and modern science. The writer's transformation of traditional ways of representing space 'is not dreamlike or irrational … one should rather think about the mental complexities revealed by science and contemporary art, such as modern physics and cinema' (1964b: 42). Robbe-Grillet's innovations were difficult to account for and classify because the investigation of new novelistic forms had only just begun. It is remarkable that cinema was used so readily by a literary critic to discuss the effects of modern fiction which shows that cinema was an important element of contemporary culture. Barthes' references to cinema also indicate that the concept of cinema was open to interpretation. Its definition loses its flexibility after ten years of *Cahiers*' work, which developed the concepts of *mise-en-scène*.

In identifying the cinematic effects in Robbe-Grillet's writing Barthes thus shaped the concept of cinema in ways most suitable for his argument regarding the *nouveau roman*. In 'Littérature objective' he reduced the experience of cinema in Robbe-Grillet's novels to a succession of flickering images produced by a rotation of the *lanterna magica*, the ancestor of cinema, or to a laborious tracking of the transformation of comic-strip characters, which supposedly imitates movement (1964b: 40). The best way to convey the representation of objects in Robbe-Grillet's novels was that 'time acts as a way of releasing space and constitutes the object as a series of sheets which overlap almost completely with each other; it is in this "almost" relating to space that the temporal dimension of the object is realised' (1964b: 39). As already seen, in the 1950s film criticism was still in its early stages which might explain Barthes' freedom in his treatment of the concept of cinema. Genette's argument in 'Vertige fixé' was very different from that of Barthes'; it was the first time in literary criticism that film terms were used in a literary review to create a platform for the joint evaluation of cinematic and literary works.

Genette's argument was inspired by the cine-novel, *L'Année dernière à Marienbad* – Robbe-Grillet's creative realisation of the concept of narrative developed by literary and film critics in the 1950s. Just like Robbe-Grillet before him, Genette, a literary critic, treated the cine-novel as a film in written form. He employed a number of strategies in his essay in order to make his reading of the cine-novel suitable for both films and literary writing. He absorbed some lessons of the *Cahiers* criticism of the 1950s. He uses terms such as 'camera-pen (caméra-stylo)' in his reading of the cine-novel, and focuses on narrative as a common denominator in the evaluation of Robbe-Grillet's novels and his cine-novel. He also draws on some of the Surrealist and Borgesian elements used in film criticism in the 1960s to define cinematic specificity. These are elements which allowed him to read the cine-novel and literary works from a structuralist perspective, and this structuralist take would be further developed in the second half of the 1960s. Genette's references to the cine-novel are important because they indicate the background to the theoretical developments which will serve as a new common denominator for the joint consideration of cinematic and literary narratives.

Genette's rhetoric in 'Vertige fixé' is exemplary of the ways in which literary criticism absorbed some of the concepts generated by film criticism in the 1950s. Genette 'recycles' Astruc's idea of the 'caméra-stylo' and adopts it for literature; he suggests that Robbe-Grillet uses his pen like a director uses a camera. Genette presented Robbe-Grillet as 'a realist and objective writer who surveyed all the things with an impassive eye similar to the camera-pen' (1966: 69). Robbe-Grillet behaves like a filmmaker who writes novels or literary works, an example of which could be the cine-novel for *L'Année dernière à Marienbad*. The impact of the film criticism of the 1950s on wider literary criticism changed the status of some works from literary to cinematic by altering the language of literary critics. As a result, it became impossible to determine whether Genette's argument about *L'Année dernière à Marienbad* was related to the film or the cine-novel.

The critic's references to the 'caméra-stylo' are among the cultural indicators that show, by the time of *L'Année dernière à Marienbad*, that cinema had achieved the status envisioned for it by Astruc and his fellow critics; *Caméra-stylo* could be used in cinema and literature to create the same type of narrative, and cinema became an art whose form was defined in narrative terms. Genette refers to this aspect of film criticism by pointing out that *L'Année dernière à Marienbad* is as much part of Robbe-Grillet's corpus as his novels *Le Voyeur* or *Dans le labyrinthe*. For Genette, the world of *L'Année dernière à Marienbad* 'is nothing else than the world which Wallas, Captain Laurent, Garinati, Mathias, the husband in *La Jalousie*, the soldier in *Labyrinthe*, the lovers of *L'Année dernière à Marienbad* or *L'Immortelle* perceived, remembered, imagined, sometimes dreamt and often contrived' (1966: 77). He identifies 'points of view, limitations imposed on the frame, ignorance and uncertainty' as the common features of Robbe Grillet's cinematic and literary works (ibid.).

Genette also engages with the cinematic criticism of the early 1960s and uses it in his own argument. He points to Borgesian and Surrealist elements identified in the critical discourse which Resnais, Robbe-Grillet and Ollier developed in response to Resnais' documentaries and feature films. The experience of *L'Année dernière à Marienbad* clearly revealed Robbe-Grillet's affiliation with 'the reversal of the imaginary and subjectivity', which could be understood as a Surrealist effect in his works (1966: 71). Furthermore, Genette claims that the favourite structure of Robbe-Grillet's works is a labyrinth, which is 'this perplexing part of being where we can see coming together in a kind of confusion, the signs of the difference and identity' (1966: 89). He also compares the temporal effect of Robbe-Grillet's work to that found in Borges' writings where 'nothing moves, everything is still, and yet, what vertigo!' (ibid.). The labyrinth as a figure in Robbe-Grillet's literary and film narratives is part of the structure which is achieved through playing with time. Genette argues that these signs of cinematic form are also indicative of a literary one. The conflation of the forms of both arts is achieved at least in part through the merging of their critical discourses. This is most amply demonstrated in Genette's writing on Robbe-Grillet's fictions; it is further supported by the adoption of a structuralist framework by Genette in his argument. The process of the development of literary theory and its filtering into the critical discourse of cinema therefore began.

The debt of French literary structuralist discourse to Borges shows the importance of this writer for debates regarding literary form. It thus points to Borges as a link between the debates about cinematic and literary narrative forms in structuralist terms. According to Dominique Noguez, along with Gaston Bachelard, Georges Bataille, Maurice Blanchot, Maurice Merleau-Ponty, Jean Paulhan, Gaëtan Picon and Leo Spitzer, Borges was a precursor and initiator of the new criticism (*nouvelle critique*) (see Noguez 1967). There are numerous structuralist works which make references to Borges because of this shared 'critical idiom', to borrow the term of Jaime Alazraki (1990). According to this writer, the success of Borges in the French critical context is certainly related to the affinity of ideas between Borges and the Russian Formalists, whose texts, translated into French by Tzvetan Todorov, played an important role in the formulation of the literary theory of narratology in the mid-1960s (see Todorov 1965).

According to Genette, a structuralist reading of narrative offers new terms for describing cinematic and literary form, as it takes to a new level the debates about form understood in narrative terms. He sees narratives as closed structures, whose elements are arranged and rearranged into different combinations of themes which correspond to linguistic paradigms (1966: 84). Genette identifies different ways in which the elements of the structure in the works of Robbe-Grillet are assembled. There are 'analogies naturelles' which means that parts of the novels' and films' landscapes, such as roads, buildings and rooms, are similar. There are also 'reproductions artificielles', which are in fact various *mises-en-abyme* of the works in which they appear: a play in *L'Année dernière à Marienbad* or a cinema poster in *Le Voyeur* (1966: 85–6). At this stage the most important characteristic of Genette's use of structuralist discourse is his identification of the same structural elements in literary and cinematic narratives. Structuralism provides a common critical language for cinema and literature which allows us to envision a new way of describing one narrative form shared by both arts.

The most important element which organises and directs all the variations and transformations in the structure of narrative is chronology. Temporal transformations are also among the most effective ways of illustrating the translation of subjective, unrealistic and dreamy effects in Robbe-Grillet's narratives, usually explained in Surrealist terms, into a structuralist framework. These are 'repetitions and variations of the narrative, which create a subjective universe whose existence in turn justifies all the anachronisms and freedoms the writer takes with the chronology of his own novels' (Genette 1966: 86). Apparently, not only Borgesian but also Surrealist concepts can be effectively translated into structuralist terms. The presentation of cinematic form first in Surrealist and finally in structuralist terms reveals the relationship between film and literary criticism of the 1960s. The importance of chronology for establishing narrative structures and for exploring their functioning also emphasises the critical role of Robbe-Grillet and the impact his critical reflections had on shaping Genette's ideas. This in turn had implications for the development of the concept of authorship. For Genette, the critical ideas of authors are of crucial importance. The difference is that Genette focuses on the critical ideas of scriptwriters, while film critics were preoccupied mostly with the ideas of filmmakers.

For Genette, it was Robbe-Grillet's critical reflections which served as an immediate impulse to evaluate his cinematic and literary works in narrative and then in specifically structuralist terms. He argued that although it might seem that his engagement with cinema 'remains external to the work', the fact is that 'there is a parallel evolution of the theories developed by Robbe-Grillet himself' (1966: 71). One of the most important statements he made in reference to *L'Année dernière à Marienbad* regards the interlocking of story and narrative. The principle of such narration is 'the overlapping of the plot and narration' where the stress is put on the story as it happened in the film. This is an illustrat on of the simultaneous narration described by Genette in *Figures III* as the transparent narration which is a marker of the first novels of Robbe-Grillet described as 'objective literature' and 'the school of the gaze' (1972: 231). Genette's view suggests that Robbe-Grillet's reflection in the introduction to *L'Année dernière à Marienbad* was of fundamental importance for the development of critical ideas regarding cinema and the cine-novel. His ideas facilitated the embrace of structuralism by literary critics such as Genette. The ideas of the scriptwriter inspired the literary critics in the same way that the concepts of filmmakers inspired some aspects of film criticism.

The discourses about film and literature in the early 1960s were a continuation and a development of the critical language of the 1950s. The criticisms of the 1960s expanded the definition of cinematic and literary specificity developed in the 1950s by adding new elements derived from Surrealism and Borges. A Surrealist framework allowed film critics to look beyond realist cinema into the spheres of the unconscious, dreams and memory, whose nature, according to Surrealists, was para-cinematic. Borges' contribution to film criticism regarded the place of the cinematic narrative among predominant cultural forms. For him, Hollywood cinema not only expanded literary culture by adding a new product to it, but, more importantly, it actively transformed this culture into a mixture of audio-visual and verbal elements.

Both stages of criticism, in the 1950s and 1960s, revealed the same dynamics, as critics had to respond to new creative developments. In the 1950s, they focused on American productions of the 1940s, Italian neo-realist works and the films of such artists as Ingmar Bergman and Jean Renoir. In the 1960s, they were faced with the *nouvelle vague* and the revival of a cine-novel; their response was informed by their relationship with literature. In both cases they were trying to develop an understanding of cinema outside of a literary framework but ended up with a concept of cinema which was significantly determined by literature. By dismissing adaptations, the film critics of the 1950s sought to distance their understanding of cinema from the influences of literature. However, they used the literary canon to write the history of cinema, compared filmmakers to writers of novels and revealed a particularly strong interest in narrative. The critics of the 1960s were aware of this literary presence in film criticism and tried to avoid it by developing a critical framework which was not determined by literature. However, just as in the 1950s, they were not successful and essentially lost control of the debate regarding cinema. In the end the shape of the debate in film criticism was determined by literary critics and writers, making literature even more significant for cinema than in the 1950s.

By shifting into filmmaking, the former *Cahiers* critics claimed that they continued their critical reflections in their films. In the case of Alain Resnais, new ways of determining cinematic specificity were established, which drew on ideas from the Surrealists and Jorge Luis Borges. However, these filmmakers were no longer voicing their ideas in the language of criticism. By moving from talking about cinema into making it, they exited the sphere of *parole* (speech) and became, as Resnais had always been, *mute*. They became 'silent' and creatively engaged film critics, as Resnais had always been. This shift proved to be of fundamental importance in the context of French culture, in which writing and speech – the activities associated with language – were the instruments of power in conceptualising culture and its products. They were replaced by writers and literary critics, whose position was strengthened by a number of factors. Their creative works, like the cine-novel of Alain Robbe-Grillet, were a product of the criticism of the 1950s, which had developed a concept of narrative with the same formal character-istics in both media. The critical activity of Robbe-Grillet also inspired that of other new novelists such as Claude Ollier, whose first writings as a critic of cinema, as we have seen, were on *L'Année dernière à Marienbad*. The ideas about cinema expressed by these writers coincided with those of the *nouvelle vague* filmmakers and directors, such as Resnais. This led to the merging of literary and cinematic discourses, facilitated by the Surrealists' and Borges' artistic engagement in both cinema and literature and by the hybrid nature of the cine-novel.

One of the manifestations of the conflation of these discourses was the work of Gérard Genette, in which he used the terms developed by the film critics of the 1950s in his discussion of Robbe-Grillet's *ciné-roman*. Gen-ette's main contribution was based on his conviction that arguments regard-ing cinema could also be employed by literary critics. His position was part of a complex relationship between contemporary literary and cinematic criti-cal discourses which was extended from the early 1950s until the mid-1960s. The dynamics of the process of the conflation of cinematic and literary criti-cal discourses and the different stages in their development can be traced by examining the critical work in cinema and literature of Jean Cayrol, a new novelist and Resnais' collaborator on his next film, *Muriel ou le temps d'un retour*.

III

Fusions: Jean Cayrol

In the story of critical dialogue between the *nouvelle vague* and the *nouveau roman* Jean Cayrol plays a central role. He is a forgotten new novelist, whose work in cinema has been always located on the margins, apart from his two collaborations with Alain Resnais, *Nuit et brouillard* and *Muriel ou le temps d'un retour*. Even though he is largely unknown, it is in Cayrol's critical writings regarding cinema and the novel where we can observe in microcosm the dynamics and the pattern of interactions of the critical discourses of the novel and cinema which led to the emergence of narrative as a common denominator of both arts at the times of the *nouvelle vague* and the *nouveau roman*. Cayrol's emphasis on a narrative voice evoke *Cahiers'* concepts of *écriture cinématographique*. His critical work encompasses both literary and film criticisms, which are organically connected through Cayrol's authorship. He is thus unique among the new novelists and among the film critics associated with the *nouvelle vague* and *Cahiers du cinéma* in that he is *both* a literary and film theorist. However, in spite of the critical and artistic credentials which clearly linked him to both the *nouvelle vague* and to the *nouveau roman*, Cayrol has been sidelined in the historical accounts of both movements. His contribution has been forgotten in a way which parallels the repression of memory of the connections between the literary and cinematic worlds in the French cultural context.

Membership of the *nouveau roman* group was always a problematic matter for literary critics. Questions regarding not only who was and was not a new novelist, but also what criteria to use to define the group, were first addressed in the most comprehensive manner in the special issue of *Esprit* in 1958 (Anon. 1958). Ten writers were singled out: Samuel Beckett, Michel Butor, Jean Cayrol, Marguerite Duras, Jean Lagrolet, Robert Pinget, Alain

Robbe-Grillet, Nathalie Sarraute, Claude Simon and Kateb Yacine.[17] Their
work was grouped together according to the formal characteristics which by
now had become part of the definition of the *nouveau roman* such as rejection of plot, the importance of objects and descriptions and experiments with
pronouns, linked to an unorthodox treatment of characters whose social and
historical origins are secondary. In short, these critics defined the *nouveau
roman* in opposition to the norms of nineteenth-century novels and thus
paved the way for the French post-war modernist novel.

Although the critics attempted to identify shared features in the writings of all ten novelists, the works of some writers received more attention
than others; consequently, the definition of the *nouveau roman* suited some
writers more than others. In the introduction to his 'Panorama d'une nouvelle littérature romanesque', Olivier de Magny explains that Robbe-Grillet
is important not only because of his fiction but also because of his theoretical works (1958: 17). This theoretical writing was the reason why numerous
comparisons were drawn between Robbe-Grillet and Cayrol. The writers
themselves tried to forge some connection among themselves on the basis
of their shared theoretical concerns. It might be the reason why the collective title given by Robbe-Grillet to his theoretical essays, *Pour un nouveau
roman* ('*Towards the New Novel*', published in 1963), echoes Cayrol's own
theoretical study 'Pour un romanesque lazaréen' ('Towards Lazarean fiction') written over a decade earlier (see Cayrol 1964).

Although at the time of the *Esprit* survey theoretical writings were not
studied on their own but only as commentaries on the novels by their authors,
they were subsequently recognised as an aspect of writers' output which determined their membership in the *nouveau roman* group (see Britton 1992).
Thus, for Roland Barthes, Cayrol's critical activity justified his place among
the new novelists (1964g: 245–6). In the 1962 survey conducted by *Tel Quel*
regarding the condition of literature in France Cayrol was interviewed along
with Sarraute, Robbe-Grillet and Butor, which reinforced his position in the
nouveau roman group (see Butor 1962; Sarraute 1962; Cayrol 1963a; Robbe-
Grillet 1963e). By choosing to interview these writers in order to assess the
condition of literature in France, the critics of *Tel Quel* acknowledged the
importance of their theoretical activity as they were all writers and theorists.
It was also evident in the *Tel Quel* decision to publish excerpts of Cayrol's
critical study of cinema, *Le Droit du regard* (Cayrol & Durand 1962).[18]

Cayrol's and Robbe-Grillet's potential as not only writers but also critics
and theorists was increasingly recognised when they became editors at the

publishing houses Seuil and Minuit, respectively. Cayrol, who since 1956 was director of a special collection entitled *Ecrire* with Seuil, was responsible for launching the creative career of Philippe Sollers (see Sollers 1957). Marcel Pleynet and Jean-Pierre Faye also had their literary debut in the collection *Ecrire* along with Claude Durand who later became Cayrol's collaborator on his cinematic projects (see Faye 1957; Pleynet 1957; Durand 1958). Cayrol was also behind the creation of *Tel Quel*, the key journal of literary theory in the 1960s. Among young talents discovered by Robbe-Grillet for Minuit was Claude Ollier, who became not only a novelist but also an important film critic. Ollier's engagement with cinema extended beyond his activity as a film critic. He also acted in Robert Bresson's *Une femme douce* (*A Gentle Woman*, 1968) and in Eduardo de Gregorio's *La Mémoire est courte* (*Short Memory*, 1979). He was a scriptwriter for Hugo Santiago's *Ecoute voire* (*See Here My Love*, 1977). He talks about his experiences in cinema in a book of interviews with Alexis Pelletier (Ollier 1996).

The importance of Sollers and Ollier in shaping the critical response in the field of literature and cinema suggests that they continued to explore the theoretical interests of their 'fathers'. Thus, Cayrol's and Robbe-Grillet's involvement with criticism influenced theoretical developments in France not only in the literary but also in the cinematic field (see Fouché 1998). In spite of Cayrol's importance in shaping the literary scene in the 1950s and 1960s, his profile was rather low in comparison to that of Robbe-Grillet, who was attracting a good deal of attention from the media and even now is clearly identified as the key new novelist. Barthes argues that by 1964 Cayrol's formal research was still in progress and that his findings had not yet been systematised unlike those of Robbe-Grillet or even Sarraute (1964g: 246). Since Cayrol published his main study on the novel in 1950, the question of the systematisation of Cayrol's research regarding the novel is not really convincing. Perhaps what Barthes refers to is Cayrol's work as a poet, scriptwriter and a documentary filmmaker which was accompanied by theoretical writings on cinema. In other words, it was not just Cayrol's creative but also his critical project which was not yet complete. But both Duras and Robbe-Grillet were filmmakers as well and it did not prevent them from being considered canonical new novelists. What Barthes refers to, then, must be Cayrol's theoretical project in cinema, which put him apart from his fellow new novelists.[19] Barthes' assessment of Cayrol's place among the new novelists is therefore a recognition of Cayrol's versatility as an artist and theorist of various arts, which made him difficult to categorise as he did not fit neatly either with the literary or the cinematic worlds; he was an artist of the liminal audio-visual/literary space. Cayrol's pronounced Catholicism was another reason for his exclusion from some of the most important critical writings of the 1960s.

The respect which Barthes had for Cayrol's artistic achievements was not, however, sufficient to justify including even one of his articles on Cayrol in the collection *Essais critiques* (1964a). The reasons for this exclusion are the same as those behind the amnesia haunting cultural memory in regard to Cayrol. Bernard Comment (1993) argues that it was Cayrol's spirituality, related to his experience as a concentration camp survivor, which proved to be most problematic for Barthes in his attempts to forge the concept of 'zero degree' of writing. Where Cayrol saw a survivor of the concentration camps, Lazarus, a new type of hero created in his works, a man who was risen from the dead and thus confronted with a painful and tragic rupture with his past condition, Barthes wanted to find a completely new man without the past and memory, virginal and pure, without any blemish (1953: 60). Cayrol's emphasis on life in the camps as his formative experience as a writer also had some dramatic consequences for the reception of his works; even among his contemporaries he was more readily regarded as an author of testimonial writing than as a new novelist. The possibility of identifying a historical or contemporary basis for his writing also distanced him from a leader of the *nouveau roman*, Robbe-Grillet. Thus, it was the *nouveau roman* defined in terms of the importance of the critical activity, radical formal experimentation and engagement with cinema to which Cayrol belonged most firmly. Yet, by the mid-1960s, his identity as a new novelist was no longer openly acknowledged due to the explicit historical and spiritual inspiration of his works which clashed with the critical trends of that period. Paradoxically, the man who did most to explore the formal aspect of the *nouveau roman* in relation to cinema is hardly mentioned in any studies concerning it; it is for this reason that he deserves as much attention as other new novelists in the context of this study.

Since Cayrol's theoretical writings on the novel, poetry and cinema cover most of the artistic fields explored by the new novelists, they could be seen as a way of foregrounding the importance of the critical element in the artistic activity of the group. His effort to explore ideas not only creatively but also critically makes it possible to argue that for him criticism has a status equal to creative endeavours. Cayrol's works share this discursive feature with Resnais' and also with those *nouvelle vague* films whose directors had undergone their apprenticeship in *Cahiers du cinéma*. The exploration of an intricate pattern of interpersonal and professional relationships which placed Cayrol in the sphere of influence of Surrealists such as Paul Éluard and André Breton, and the critics of the Geneva school – Albert Béguin, in particular – allows us to understand better the creative basis of critical activity in which Cayrol and the *nouvelle vague* filmmakers were involved (see Béguin 1948). This examination also shows how critical activity is a form of artistic expression in its own right. The overlapping of creative and critical work serves as a bridge between the products of filmmaking and literary cultures; it also extends the meaning of the concept of 'cinematic writing' which became a method of expression in both literary and cinematic works. It is only by emphasising the creative dimension of criticism and the critical aspect of works of art that cinematic writing could emerge as a shared idiom of cinema and literature. Cayrol's oeuvre is thus an important step in the direction of creating this new idiom.

Many of Cayrol's ideas regarding literature, especially the central role of dreams, were inspired by the writings of Béguin. In *L'Ame romantique et le rêve* (see 1937a and 1937b), Béguin traces the presence and the role of dreams in Romantic poetry and argues that, with Surrealism, poetry inspired by dreams managed to establish a profound connection between readers and poets (1937b: 440–1). A reader or a critic can respond almost 'automatically' to Surrealist poetry; Béguin was trying to recreate this reader/poet synergy in his own work, which was largely focused on literary criticism. Sarah Lawall suggests that Béguin-the-critic thought of his critical work as a creative act akin to Surrealist automatic writing (1968: 67). Furthermore, the effect of his critical writing on readers was not dissimilar to that of Surrealist poetry evoking Béguin's and his readers' 'shared cultural mind' (see also Béguin 1955a: 169; 1955b: 450). In the post-war period, Béguin found echoes of his critical ideas in the works of young critics such as Roland Barthes, Jean Poulet, Jean-Pierre Richard and Maurice Blanchot. They were particularly taken by their stress on the work as referring to its own formal structures rather than to some historical, social or psychological reality. What is fascinating about Béguin is that the act of creation and the reader's response were both hypnotic and dream-like. His idea also implies that the artist and the reader must be in a very similar state of mind or may even be the same person. All these elements along with Béguin's treatment of critical works on a par with creative ones are found in Cayrol's own reflection on art known as 'Lazarean fiction' first presented in *Lazare parmi nous* (Cayrol 1950c).

Cayrol himself was a concentration camp survivor deeply traumatised by the experience, and full of compassion and empathy towards the plight of his fellow prisoners. Lazarean dreams described in *Lazare parmi nous* were fantasies of life out of the camp, which allowed prisoners to survive their experience. Tragically, when freed from the camps the prisoners remained in a dream-like state, numb and unable to find their way to normality. What was their salvation in captivity turned into a curse when they left the camps. In a brilliant *tour de force* Cayrol establishes the prisoners', and by extension his own, dream-world as the source of his art which must be destroyed for this art to be created. His art is nurtured by the dreams the prisoners had in the camps; the same dreams which helped them overcome the hypnotic numbness of their post-camp life. Like Béguin's reader, Cayrol's reader and creator can share their state of mind and communicate in the 'automatic' way because they are literally one; Cayrol, as a former camp prisoner, engages in the Lazarean artistic project in order to find a way out of the double-bind of salvation and curse offered by dreams.

Camp prisoners' dreams which help them resist death are echoes of the ontological theory of cinema developed by André Bazin. Cinema was not just a total illusion of reality but also a continuous repetition and triumph of life after a film ended, which was underlined by the possibility of screening the same film over and over again. The 'Lazarean' conception of Bazin's cinema, the film's life-likeness and its multiple resurrections through repeated screenings, were appealing for Cayrol who knew Bazin's writings from the pages of *Esprit*, especially his articles on Italian neo-realism (Bazin 1949; 1997c). Cinema first presented itself as a potent metaphor for Cayrol's Lazarean fiction emphasising the importance of the visual element in his critical reflection on art. In time it was the hypnotic nature of the cinematic image which led Cayrol to attempt to translate the concept of Lazarean fiction from literature into film. In spite of Cayrol's extreme versatility and flexibility as an artist and critic, he has always emphasised his identity as a poet (see Cayrol 1988: 118). His creative and critical roots were always in literature and for this reason the verbal linked to his literary interests would always dominate the treatment of the visual in his writing and filmmaking resulting in a tension between the verbal and the visual. The cinematic image, just like the prisoner's dream, is the source of the verbal, of the writing and expression, which has to be destroyed for the verbal to exist. Paradoxically, by destroying the image the language destroys its origins and risks its own existence. A balance full of tension thus has to be maintained between the visual and the verbal; this tension between the two elements will prove to be a constant feature of his literary and film criticism and can be found in 'Pour un romanesque lazaréen', *Le Droit du regard* and in the script of *Muriel ou le temps d'un retour* (see Cayrol 1963b; Cayrol & Durand 1963). It constitutes the very core of the Lazarean *ciné-écriture*.

At this stage it is also worthwhile to mention briefly the figure of Chris Marker who in the early 1950s, just like Cayrol, was bridging the literary and cinematic worlds and was seen by Cayrol as one of the most prolific and innovative documentary filmmakers (see Cayrol 1982). Marker was mentioned in the credits of *Nuit et brouillard* and, according to Resnais, he played the key role in adjusting Cayrol's commentary to the images shot by Resnais (Resnais 1987: 49, 53–4). Marker's first identity, before he became a filmmaker, was that of a literary and film critic for *Esprit* and *Cahiers du cinéma*, a novelist and an editor at Seuil (see Marker 1950a; 1950b; 1952; 1953a; 1953b). Cayrol and Béguin played an important role in initiating Marker on his literary path by writing very positive reviews of his novel, *Le Coeur net* (1950) and of a critical study of Jean Giraudoux, respectively (see Cayrol 1950b; Béguin 1952).

Marker's literary and critical works, just like those of Cayrol's, express a profound engagement with the visual. His study of Giraudoux is a collage of photographs from the production of Giraudoux's plays and excerpts from his literary works. A special collection of Seuil, which he edited, *Petite Planète* (1954–81), consisted of travelogues which were an intricate and intriguing *montage* of photographs, cartoons, drawings, reproductions of works of art and text. Both their form and content foreshadow Marker's documentaries resulting from his travels all over the world.[20] The title of his first documentary, *Lettre de Sibérie*, stresses the literary dimension of his work and echoes the critical essays, *Lettre de Hollywood* and *Lettre de Mexico*, he published in *Cahiers* (1953a; 1953b). But it was Marker's decision to publish the scripts of all his documentaries, including those which had never been made into films, which relates Marker most closely to Cayrol. Imaginary films, which only possess a textual identity, evoke Cayrol's Lazarean dreams. The scripts of unmade films, just like cine-novels, are very strange creatures, which both mobilise and destroy the visual; they absolutely need the visual to exist, but it is only by constantly deferring the visual, repressing it and making it secondary, that their existence can be justified. After all, why would we need the script if we already have the film? Marker's scripts and cine-novels written by the new novelists are expressions of the fine balancing act between existence and destruction of the visual found at the centre of Cayrol's Lazarean fiction.

Cayrol's conception of art is inextricably linked to and determined by his experiences in the Mauthausen concentration camp during World War Two. The haunting memory of terror, pain and ever-present death, and the impossibility of resuming a normal life after liberation, inspired the former poet to search for artistic means to express the condition of the survivor. In 'Pour un romanesque lazaréen', he compares the concentration camp survivor to Lazarus who was miraculously raised from the dead and given a second chance to live (1964: 214). Those who returned from the camps felt disconnected from the reality which surrounded them and lived in their own world. They were alienated and solitary, incapable of communicating their emotions and forming loving and affectionate relationships with others. Starved for affection but unable to reciprocate it they experienced all human contact, even the most distant and disembodied, as touch (1964: 217). Their communication with others was not coded as language; indeed it was instinctive and mediated through the senses. Lazarean fiction was about making the senses reveal themselves in a narrative voice and creating an idiom to express the Lazarean experience.

Cayrol's immediate inspiration for his artistic project comes from the realisation that survivors' alienation from post-war reality and the impossibility of communicating their experiences made their lives after the Liberation not so different from their life in the camps. For Cayrol the reality of post-war France and that of the concentration camps were in some way parallel. To his surprise, and perhaps horror, Cayrol realised that even those who knew the camps only by hearsay started behaving as though they lived through them (1964: 201). He experienced post-war French society as numb or mechanical in the same way the former camp prisoners were, and thus post-war French culture and society itself had echoes of a prison camp. One could speculate as to what made Cayrol see the France of his times as such a problematic and hopeless place. The rise of popular culture, consumerism, censorship and the uncomfortable memory of the war-time Vichy regime might have had something to do with his views. The malaise of modernity is found at the origins of Cayrol's own attitudes. Perhaps more important than the reasons for drawing a comparison between the reality of the concentration camps and that of post-war France are the consequences of this comparison. The artistic project Cayrol was proposing turned out to be not just an example of testimonial literature but a much wider and ambitious endeavour which was to capture the condition of those living in post-war France.

Camp survivors are in some sense prisoners of their memories in the same way that they were mesmerised by their dreams when they were in the camps. Not only memories of the camps but also the dreams fantasised in the camps were generated in comparable emotional circumstances, such as an alienation from reality which Cayrol describes as 'doubling' and 'disembodiment'. The goal of Cayrol's artistic project was to give expression through his Lazarean art to the experience of the prisoner caught between these two worlds (1964: 203). Cayrol outlined his conception of the art of the novel in two texts, 'Rêves lazaréens' and 'Pour un romanesque lazaréen', which were published in 1950 under the title *Lazare parmi nous*.

The first text describes the development and transformation of the dreams which the prisoners experienced in the concentration camps. According to Cayrol, these dreams helped prisoners survive the reality of the camps (1950c: 10). In the more theoretical part of *Lazare parmi nous*, 'Pour un romanesque lazaréen', Cayrol outlines the characteristics of the new art which give expression to the condition of the survivor whose memories of the camps are as alienated from reality as his dreams were in the camps. The writing belonging to this 'Lazarean fiction' does not engage in any social and psychological portrayal of the characters. Its narrative is not driven by plot but is marked by numerous descriptions and a special importance is given to objects, which convey the emotional burden of the novel (1964: 219, 226–7). In other words, Lazarean fiction breaks with the formal norms of the nineteenth-century novel and presents a new idiom which Cayrol believes can be applicable not only to literature but also to other arts (1964: 203). In this sense Lazarean fiction shares all of the aims and objectives of the *nouveau roman*.

Dreams and memories form an integral part of the experience of the camps and consequently are also central to the concept of the Lazarean fiction. The prisoners are like spectators of their own dreams – they view them, identify with them and, when asked, give an account of them. The dreams resemble internal films screened in prisoners' consciousness. The prisoners are captivated by their dreams in a way that the spectators of cinema are gripped by film images. The fact that cinema appears to be central to Cayrol's conception of the Lazarean fiction finds support in his conception of the creative imagination which can be called 'a cinematic state of mind'

(1963a: 55), which leads him to compare his work as a writer to that of a film editor. This cinematic metaphor evokes Béguin's 'shared mind' of a writer and a reader. Cayrol expects his readers to be also spectators, so that they could enter a communion with the writer, who is also a kind of film director. Bridging of the cinematic minds of the reader/spectator and the writer/director also recalls psychic automatism, which Béguin associated mostly with Surrealist poetry, that could have in fact found its complete realisation in cinema which thus comes to symbolise both the origins and attainment of a better world. Cinema as a signifier of utopia to be realised once the old order collapses had already been expressed in Surrealist writings; a short poetic piece by Bernard Roger (2000), a Surrealist, imagines an impressive cinema created on the bottom of a lake once the old world is wiped out.

The new literary idiom created by Lazarean fiction has at its origins an involvement with dreams which is a metaphor for the spectatorial experience of cinema. Lazarean fiction is a search for the formal literary means of describing the alienation and distance from external reality of somebody who is absorbed by the internal cinema of his/her dreams, and Cayrol's description of the arrangement and functioning of the camps evokes conditions normally associated with cinematic spectatorship. The first memory he has of the concentration camps treats it as a stage illuminated by the spotlights emerging out of a sea of darkness (1950a: 21). Once in the camp, the prisoners enter a state of hypnosis because the camp is such an unusual, almost unreal, place. Cayrol stresses that this hypnotic stage was immediately accompanied by the experience of dreams. The reality of dreams contrasted with the reality of the camp which was a kind of hallucination, a detachment created by frightening, alienating and absurd camp ceremonies of disinfection, hours of waiting on the camp square, and death (1950a: 22). Cayrol's descriptions of long spotlights piercing the darkness, the detachment from reality and the focus on dreams evoke the experience of film-viewing centred on the images created by the projector's beam. Just as the material conditions of the camps bring to mind movie theatres, so the feelings experienced by camp prisoners evoke those of cinema spectators. They are lonely and silent in the way that a cinematic spectator might feel once the movie theatre darkens (1964: 212). Cayrolian characters, just like spectators, can listen and look but they are not allowed to speak. It is by the means of two senses only, sight and hearing, that Lazarean characters perceive reality (1964: 213).

It is only in cinema that an almost perfect illusion of reality can be forged by engaging these two senses. This illusion has a certain peculiar characteristic, namely it empties spoken language of physicality which it normally possesses due to the actual presence of the speaker. The prisoner 'is no longer used to the marvellous movement of the lips, to the warmth of speech, to the embodied verb' (1964: 223). The experience of language which lacks the physical dimension is associated with movie-viewing. At the same time spectatorship depends on evoking a sense of pleasure by establishing a specific relationship between the spectator and the screen. For this reason Lazarean fiction emphasises the element of pleasure by attempting to convey an 'aura' whose constituent elements are sound, 'une résonance', and sight, 'un lustre', which are also the basic ingredients of cinema (ibid.). It is in these conditions of the camps which evoke cinema-viewing that dreams are generated. Similarly, the dreams also display some cinematic characteristics especially associated with silent cinema.

The overall effect of prisoners' dreams is thus undeniably filmic. It is the existence of the temporal dimension which relates dreams most closely to cinema. In *Lazare parmi nous*, Cayrol stresses the imbalance experienced by the prisoners between real, chronological time and the achronology of dreams based on memories of the past. The time of their horrifying daily life in the camps contrasted with the 'atemporal' time, which was 'preserved, petrified in their dreams' (1950a: 18). The different stages through which the prisoner goes before he comes 'to live simultaneously between the two universes without rejoining either of them completely' (1950a: 26–7) in fact mark a shift between the ways in which he experiences time – from the chronological to the achronological. The process begins with the difficulties the prisoner faced in keeping track of time despite the efforts to do so; marking the calendar on the wall of the cell did not stop the dates from getting mixed up (1950a: 27). The prisoner's grasp of chronology was further weakened by his increasing lack of interest in the life of the camp; he was living his memories or dreams more intensely than reality itself (1950a: 23).

The existence of this fourth dimension, time, is signalled through the problems which his fictional characters had in capturing an image; they perceive others as being in a state of continuous flux. It is transformation through time which can be held responsible for the inability to take a 'snapshot' of what the character is looking at. Instead, 'the face is multiplied infinitively ... he [the prisoner] is not able to choose a moment of the face; the transformation [of the face] is constant and illogical' (Cayrol 1964: 221). These overlapping and fractured images bring to mind the avant-garde experiments of the cubist Férnand Léger in *Ballet mécanique* (1924) and the films of Man Ray. It is this avant-garde cinema of the 1920s which comes to mind as the main source of inspiration for Cayrol's cinematic metaphor.

The changing perception of time was closely linked to the disembodiment or 'désincarnation' which Cayrol identified as characteristic of the prisoner's condition. This suggests that Cayrol associates the body with chronological time while the mind, the source of the prisoner's internal spectacle, is linked with achronological time. Cayrol's literary project envisages doing away with disembodiment, which means overcoming the dichotomy of body and mind and ultimately connecting the two notions of time.

Cayrol also compares dreams to a spectacle by evoking the memory of a dream about a painting whose elements began to move. The painting Cayrol dreamed was one by Breughel which he entitled 'Les Dessous d'une table' whose elements were slowly coming to life and became animated as the dream unravelled (1950a: 41–2). By making dreams the basis of a new Lazarean art, Cayrol thus also engages with the history of the visual arts, especially its accounts given by Bazin and Malraux. They argued for the existence of a direct relation between the emergence of cinema and the struggle present in the history of Western visual art to represent movement. Cayrol also evokes the importance of musical composition and colours for the creation of dreams, whose memory contributed to the emergence of the intangible and throbbing dreamy world; he gives examples of some prisoners for whom the memory of certain colours, associated with the feelings experienced prior to imprisonment, helped them live through the emotionally monochrome life of the camps (1950a: 40, 49–51). Evocative of painting, music and colour, the dreams described by Cayrol emerge as a thrilling visual symphony comparable only to cinema, which was considered from the earliest days of film criticism to be a synthesis of all arts (see Abel 1993).

In his description of dreams, Cayrol emphasises the fact that prisoners' excessive belief in their dreams had a lethal effect on them. The most dangerous being dreams which involved the fantasy of a return home; these were also the most realistic (1950a: 59). The lethal effects of some dreams and of the prison circumstances in which this internal cinema unfolds inevitably bring to mind Adolfo Bioy Casarès' story of Morel's invention (1973). In this novel, the main character is a prisoner who escapes to an island where he is imprisoned anew by the images projected with an apparatus invented by Morel. The protagonist desires to become part of the recorded world to such a degree that he is ready to give up his life for it. He dies once he becomes part of projected reality – the dream of a woman who captivates his mind and heart. Both Cayrol and Bioy Casarès use cinema as a metaphor for a fantasy which is dangerous and threatening if it is wholly 'believed'.

BARTHES' AND CAYROL'S FICTION

The Lazarean fiction project is presented as Cayrol's challenge to spectatorial passivity, which is in some way parallel to the state of the French nation in the post-war period. In his novels Cayrol experiments with literary forms and invents artistic solutions to the problems discussed in *Lazare parmi nous*. Barthes' reviews of Cayrol's fiction suggest that he was very familiar with the writer's conception of the art of novel presented in 'Pour un romanesque lazaréen'. This is apparent in Barthes' emphasis on the past concentration camp experience with which Cayrol's characters attempt to come to terms. The critic calls this experience 'a cataclysm without a name' (1952: 484). Barthes presents Cayrol's fiction as an attempt to move beyond the experience of the camps by challenging the passive spectatorial position of the fictional characters. In his review he also makes references to cinema.

The arguments presented in Barthes' reviews of Cayrol's novels herald many of the ideas regarding the theory of the novel which Barthes developed fully on the pages of *Le Degré zéro de l'écriture* (1953). In these reviews it is the formal or self-referential aspect of Cayrol's novels which seems to be of the greatest importance to Barthes. He refers to his writing as 'pure novel' or 'true novel' and argues that it is necessary 'to consider his work as a work which is in the course of being made' (1952: 482). In *Le Degré zéro de l'écriture* Barthes continues this argument when he mentions Cayrol among the writers of 'neutral writing' for whom the investigation of form is a central concern (1953: 9–10, 30). From the perspective of Barthes' reviews of Cayrol's work, the literary idiom of Lazarean fiction based on breaking away from a certain condition akin to spectatorship is a characteristic of the theoretical investigation into novelistic specificity conducted by Barthes in *Le Degré zéro de l'écriture*.

Barthes' theory of the novel describes the characteristics of the process in which Lazarus manages to give some expression to the memories which haunt him and to establish a connection with the external world. It could be compared to the process of leaving a darkened cinema auditorium after the screening of a film and attempting to make sense of the surrounding reality. It is not by coincidence that Barthes identifies small hotel rooms and cinemas as places where the entrance of *l'homme cayrolien* into the world originates

(1952: 484). The key element in this shift is first-person narration which Barthes refers to simply as the 'voice' which is 'a word extended between the image and the rejection of the novel' (1954: 151). The effort to articulate which the existence of the voice implies is an expression of the will to move on – the crucial moment in the life of the camp survivors. For Barthes this voice rising slowly from the debris of the experience of the camps, from the silence of dreams, is the first step in expressing the condition of the survivor. The voice narrates the experience of breaking out of the hypnotic spectacle of memories or dreams unfolding in Lazarus's mind. The importance of the first-person narration here lies in its ability to generate new literary forms. Cayrol's narratives relegate chronology to a secondary position and lack plot. The result is a loose narrative in which descriptions of objects abound (1952: 483). This narrative signifies the appearance of a new novelistic idiom which, according to Barthes, redefines the novel's specificity and differentiates modern novels from nineteenth-century writing (1952: 495).

Barthes contrasts Cayrol's novels with the kind of writing he refers to as 'classical literature' which is characterised by a certain degree of realism. It is a representation of the social position of characters linked to their family past, financial status and the historical circumstances in which their personal story develops. Cayrol's novels focus on the process of arriving at this stage when the work can be labelled 'Literature'. Barthes says that it is 'the prehistoric and pre-novelistic sphere which Cayrol made into the object of his novel' (1952: 488). This evolution is exemplified through the passage from first- to third-person narration and the characters' ability to establish and maintain their relationship with the world.

There is an optical element, associated with traditional literature, to which the characters are exposed but whose experience is marked by passivity and stillness. Barthes contrasts the immobility of the character subjected to the spectacle with the importance of walking and active exploration of the world for *l'homme cayrolien* (1952: 492). The condition of the character in traditional literature resembles, to a large degree, the position in which prisoners found themselves in the camps. They were numb and exposed to a spectacle that dominated their minds but over which they had no power. It is precisely this situation of being 'imprisoned' in cinema which was described in Cayrol's rendering of the camp dreams. For it is necessary to emphasise the paradoxical and double-nature of the dreams; dreams helped some to survive the camps by establishing a kind of internal exile. For Cayrol, breaking out of this 'spectacular' prison also meant developing new formal means of artistic expression; his novels are a reaction against traditional literature and a search to assuage the symptoms of Lazarus's withdrawal from the world. This happens when Lazarus establishes a new relationship with objects.

L'homme cayrolien looks at objects and people and then enters into a physical contact with them which is key to Cayrolian aesthetics (1952: 489). Barthes rightly points out that it is literature that triumphs in the last volume of Cayrol's trilogy he reviews; they are novels about appropriation of people and objects through affection. The movement in Cayrol's novels is from *looking* to *embracing*. It can be compared to a difference between fascination with close-ups of objects or people on screen and the possibility of an actual physical contact with them in reality (1952: 495). This is the reason Barthes can call Cayrol's novel 'an act of human kindness' (1952: 499). It is by developing this tender and affectionate relationship with people and objets that *l'homme cayrolien* manages to break out of the internal cinema of his thoughts.

LE DROIT DU REGARD

Cayrol envisioned Lazarean fiction as a revolution taking place in various arts. Picasso's paintings were among his key examples (1964: 203). For Cayrol himself, it was his work in cinema which was a continuation of his artistic quest initiated in literature. His engagement with cinema began with the commentary to Alain Resnais' groundbreaking film *Nuit et brouillard*. It was followed by the script to Resnais' *Muriel ou le temps d'un retour* and culminated in Cayrol's directing his own films.[21] Some of the results of Cayrol's work in cinema were included in the form of film-scripts in his collection of essays on cinema, *Le Droit du regard*, which he co-authored, just like his films, with Claude Durand, a translator of Spanish literature, a film editor and a future novelist.[22]

The essays in *Le Droit du regard* are Cayrol's and Durand's attempt to describe the characteristics of the language which was created through a 'translation' of the literary project of Lazarean fiction into the language of cinema. In doing so they made claims for this new cinematic language that considerably broadened the terms in which it had previously been considered. Lazarean fiction also claimed cinema's right to research and self-discovery and to possess its own cultural memory (Cayrol & Durand 1963: 13). Paradoxically, perhaps, the terms of this translation process were inspired by literary research into its own specificity. If Cayrol and Durand were able to establish such a close relationship between cinema and literature this was because they stressed the importance of the verbal element over the visual one in both idioms of Lazarean fiction, the literary and the cinematic.

Cayrol and Durand draw parallels between the two arts in order to create a common ground which will facilitate the investigation of cinematic language in the context of Lazarean fiction. They begin by comparing the work of a filmmaker to that of a poet. Thanks to technological advances cinema had become capable of creating new means of expression that allowed a filmmaker to realise some of the creative dreams of poets and writers (1963: 33–4). This comparison between the work of a filmmaker and that of a poet suggests that the latter had already envisioned or dreamt of cinema even before it was invented. Thus understood, cinema is less of a new art than an art that had already existed in anticipation. Such a view allowed Cayrol and Durand to advance an idea that the language of the novel presented in 'Pour un romanesque lazaréen' is just a way of entering the poetic imaginary.

Initially, while speaking of cinema, Cayrol argues that it is by bringing the elements of both arts together that a new language of cinema, which is neither purely cinematic nor purely literary, can be created (1963: 13). In *Le Droit du regard*, he describes the characteristics of this new language which he compares to metaphor. He stresses that text and image are interdependent and it is by a merging of the visual and the verbal that new formal structures can be created. He is talking about 'the metamorphosis of both languages, their alloying into one, which can be grasped at once' (1963: 91). This is how the representation of the world in cinema gains the coherence of a poem and becomes a way of entering the poetic imaginary shared equally by cinema and literature (1963: 24). The fact that Cayrol chooses to call this new language metaphoric is significant because it establishes a degree of equivalence between visual and verbal elements. It also suggests the possibility of interchange or 'metamorphosis' between these elements and, as Barthes' reviews showed, between cinematic and literary idioms.

The formal languages of cinema and literature are made indistinguishable by Cayrol to the extent that Barthes, in his review of Cayrol's novel *Les Corps étrangers*, compares the effect of *Muriel ou le temps d'un retour* to those encountered in his novels. The name of the director, Alain Resnais, is never mentioned. As a result the impression is created that the novelist, Jean Cayrol, is the author of the film. For instance, Barthes identifies time as one of the central themes of Cayrol's fiction, which can also be found in *Muriel ou le temps d'un retour* (1964g: 241). An ambiguity regarding the nature of the work, namely whether Barthes is referring directly to the film or to the script, hovers over the review, but is never properly addressed or solved. This is best reflected in Barthes' ideas about the use of *montage* in Cayrol's novels and then in the film. According to Barthes, the assembling of Cayrol's literary narratives brings to mind cinematic *montage*. And the editing of the film supposedly reflects the nature of Cayrol's narratives (1964g: 242). Although as a scriptwriter Cayrol had nothing to do with the actual editing of *Muriel ou le temps d'un retour*, it is not important for Barthes, because for him too the formal language of cinema and literature are interchangeable due to their shared characteristics. This enables each to be talked about in terms of the other.

Cayrol's desire for the verbal and the visual to play an equal role in this new cinematic language, however, is challenged by the importance he gives throughout the book to commentary and dialogues in relation to images. According to Cayrol, although images possess a unique quality of capturing the past, they are not capable of preserving its meaning and conveying it fully as time goes on; only language is capable of conveying time. The role of a commentary is to actualise an image by bringing out the signification it had for the participants of the recorded events (Cayrol & Durand 1963: 20). In fact, Cayrol subscribes to the belief that images are meaningless in themselves. Their full impact is achieved only with or through a commentary (1963: 93). The verbal and visual elements do not complement each other and are not equivalent; rather, the text is indispensable for images to signify. It is this understanding of the relationship between the composite elements of cinematic images as unequal which brings the cinematic language described in *Le Droit du regard* even closer to Cayrol's vision of literary language presented in 'Pour un romanesque lazaréen'.

The circumstances of Cayrol's artistic career which led him to the critical evaluation of the formal language of cinema in *Le Droit du regard* evoke to some degree those which inspired his critical examination of the formal language of literature. The critical element present in the literary idiom of Lazarean fiction was a result of Cayrol's conceptual move from the visual fiction of the dreams to the critical discourse in which he outlined the characteristics of the Lazarean artistic project. In the same way, the creation of a cinematic idiom was the result of Cayrol's work in cinema as a scriptwriter for *Nuit et brouillard* and the maker of a number of films. It is the visual element which is made problematic and treated critically in the literary and cinematic idiom. However, this domination of the verbal over the visual in the cinematic idiom is not made apparent from the start of Cayrol's argument in *Le Droit du regard*.

Cayrol's interest in foregrounding the importance of the text in cinema is longstanding and can be traced back not only to his arguments in 'Pour un romanesque lazaréen' but also to his later concerns regarding the representation of the concentration camp experience. In his article 'Témoignage et littérature', written in 1953, he points to the dangers of what can be called the 'mediatisation' of the concentration camp experience which led to the representation of the concentration camps becoming increasingly commercialised. As a result, its authenticity is compromised if not irrevocably lost. Everything becomes an image and the historical events such as the existence of the concentration camps is turned into 'fiction or a fable', or a handful of clichés at best (1953: 575). It is through language that this seamless representation might be broken, made problematic and uncomfortable. Cayrol's work with Resnais on *Nuit et brouillard* was a deliberate counter-representation of the camps through the exploration of the images of the past with the new artistic means offered by cinema. The collaboration of Cayrol and Resnais on *Nuit et brouillard* is an exploration of this new language shared by cinema and literature which was later theorised in *Le Droit du regard*. The status of the images and the text, and the interaction between the two, best reflects the power relationship between the visual and the verbal in the cinematic idiom established by Cayrol.

It is important to note that formal concerns were central for both artists working on the film. Resnais revealed that their interest in exploring the formal language of cinema while working on *Nuit et brouillard* became a source of certain moral qualms owing to the nature of the subject treated:

> The idea that stimulated us in our work was, 'Do we have the right to do formalist research with such a subject?' But maybe with this element, it would have more of an audience. For me formalism is the only way to communicate. (1989: 213)

Resnais' request to work on *Nuit et brouillard* with an actual concentration camp survivor was one of the ways of safeguarding the authenticity of the testimony presented in the film. According to Georges Perec, who wrote on the testimonial literature of Robert Antelme, the identity of the author is essential in reaching the truth not only about life but also about literature, or more widely art. Antelme fulfilled this requirement and for this reason his own testimonial writing, such as *L'Espèce humaine* (1957), was expressing the truth about literature and about the world (see Perec 1992: 114). Authors of testimonial writing such as Cayrol or Antelme argued that formal experimentation is necessary for conveying the experience of the camps. Giving a sense of this experience to the readers called for new forms of expression in all arts (Cayrol 1953: 576). *Nuit et brouillard* is one of the most powerful examples of such a formal project.

The film explores not only the nature of the text/image relation, but also that of different types of images; those of the past (in black and white) and of the present (in colour) are juxtaposed. Hence, Cayrol's commentary not only actualises those relating to the past but also explores the tension between the two kinds of image. Annette Insdorf describes the combined effect of the commentary and the images in *Nuit et brouillard* in the following way:

> The vacant images of the ovens are brutally defined by black-and-white photos, and *montage* activates the silent railroad tracks covered with green grass into sputtering newsreels of transports. The 'picture postcard' becomes a stark nightmare, as *Nuit et brouillard* assumes the function of an X-ray: through the spine of documentary footage and Cayrol's calmly vigilant meditation, we are forced to see the deformities hidden from the unaided eye (and camera), and to struggle against the imperturbability of surfaces. (1989: 40)

Insdorf points to the quality of the colour images in *Nuit et brouillard* which correspond to Resnais' experience and understanding of the concentration camps. She refers to him as an artist trying to make sense out of survival (see 1989). Cayrol's commentary is that of a survivor of the concentration camps, and it is this commentary that makes the images of bygone worlds intelligible and the existence of these past worlds irrefutable (see Cayrol & Durand 1963: 94). It is not only in literature but also in cinema that the verbal element is dominant. The only way in which the formal language of cinema and literature can become comparable is by granting the verbal primacy over the visual.

MURIEL OU LE TEMPS D'UN RETOUR: FILM AS LITERATURE

The script of *Muriel ou le temps d'un retour* constituted a new departure for Cayrol in his approach to cinema. This is evident in the different treatment that the script received compared to that of *Nuit et brouillard*. Although the latter film also resulted from a collaboration between Resnais and Cayrol, the script was not published until the mid-1990s. Hence, the decision to publish the script of *Muriel ou le temps d'un retour* soon after the release of the film was a significant gesture on the part of Cayrol in that it emphasised the importance of the literary aspect of the film. The publication of the script should be also seen in the context of a wider trend which was becoming more pronounced in 1960s France – a rebirth of the cine-novel as a genre. Alain Robbe-Grillet, Marguerite Duras and Chris Marker all published the scripts of their own films or films on which they collaborated. The publication of the script after the release of the film and the presence of the stills from the film made by Resnais allow us to see the script as a critical evaluation of the visual, that is the film itself. As already seen, a critical approach to the visual was a shared characteristic of literary and cinematic idioms.

There exist at least two ways through which the arguments about cinematic idiom in *Le Droit du regard* and also those of 'Pour un romanesque lazaréen' about literary idiom both found their way into the script of *Muriel ou le temps d'un retour*. Firstly, in the pattern which can be discerned throughout Cayrol's artistic career, the script of this film occupied a place comparable to the one which his novels had. This is why the script is seen as a realisation of the formal problems discussed in *Le Droit du regard* in the same way that Cayrol's novels addressed the formal questions raised in *Lazare parmi nous*. Secondly, 'Pour un romanesque lazaréen' was reprinted in the 1964 edition of *Les Corps étrangers*. Hence, *Muriel ou le temps d'un retour* could be read from the perspective of Cayrol's arguments regarding the form of both novel and cinema. The narrative not only serves as a *mise-en-abyme* of the central aspects of Lazarean fiction – its literary and cinematic idiom – but also explores a new feature of Cayrol's formal representation – the dramatic storyline which is necessary for establishing the dominant position of verbal over visual elements.

Muriel ou le temps d'un retour focuses on the characters' effort to come to terms with their memories. In the case of Bernard they concern his experiences during the Algerian War where he participated in the torture of local people including a young woman, Muriel. For Hélène the past is locked up in the memory of a passionate love story in her youth which took place during World War Two. These past events are preserved and presented in the film in two different ways. Bernard has an amateur documentary which shows scenes of torture committed in Algeria; cinema is thus represented as a recording of violence and the locus of the unspeakable. Hélène's love story dominates her mind and is her most powerful memory. Bernard and Hélène are like modern Lazaruses attempting to live their lives after a total disaster that took place in the past and completely determines the subsequent course of their lives. It is essential for them to deal with the past in order to be fully integrated into the present flux of life. Cayrol explained that he wanted 'to understand the mechanism of returning; of how one comes back from a tragedy, from a passion, in what state [of mind] and for what reason' (1982: 110). Bernard accompanies the screening of the film footage with his own commentary regarding the torture episode; Hélène confronts her former lover, Alphonse, about their past affair and manages to deal with some of the memories in this active act of remembrance. This is the way in which the story of *Muriel ou le temps d'un retour* thematises the key tenets of Lazarean fiction. According to Philip Dine, this is also linked to a formal investigation present in the film:

> The revelation of the nature of Bernard's Algerian crimes – which he committed, to pick up his own expression, 'comme tout le monde' – will thus be inextricably bound up with a characteristically modernist reflection on the generation of fictional meaning itself. (1994: 225)

The way in which Hélène and Bernard come to terms with their memories becomes a *mise-en-abyme* of the central problem of Cayrolian fiction – the characters' attempts to deal with their memories. Barthes further highlighted this quality of the film when he said that '*Lazare [parmi nous]* is the best commentary for *Muriel*' (1964e: 245). It is important to remark that *Muriel ou le temps d'un retour* conducts a parallel investigation into the formal language of cinema and literature from the perspective of Lazarean fiction. Bernard's association with film makes it possible to see his coming to terms with his memories as a thematisation of the formal language of cinema:

> His memory found refuge in his camera and in his tape-recorder, in his guns, and in his films; he needed an intermediary to capture the others, to become close to them, and [at the same time] he could only approach them by surprise. (Cayrol 1963b: 21)

Hélène's past is only expressed through her memories. Her situation resembles that of the prisoners who returned home traumatised by their experiences in the camps. As we saw earlier, this problem was central to the formal investigation in *Lazare parmi nous*. Consequently, Hélène's condition can be associated with the formal language of literature. The fact that Hélène invites Alphonse to pay her a visit is like re-entering the sphere of the most painful and upsetting events of her life. Hélène's state of mind is comparable to the reaction Cayrol had on his return to the concentration camps to work on *Nuit et brouillard*. Occasionally, he felt completely overwhelmed by the memories of the camps and on the verge of madness (1982: 108–9). He relived his memories through the film and the commentary he provided to illustrate the images. In the case of Hélène the visual element, which is expressed in the form of a fantasy about the past, must be verbalised through dialogue.

According to Cayrol, the only way in which the characters can deal with their haunting memories is through drama; this is a new element in his literary and cinematic idiom. Drama was a kind of shock or catharsis which could initiate the process of acclimatisation into normal life, of putting down roots and enjoying the healing effect of memory where past experiences could be contained (Cayrol 1963b: 15). On the formal level, this drama must create a situation in which the verbal element can emerge and express the visual one. In the case of Hélène, dining with her friends and family is a pretext to set up some of the most dramatic events of the narrative. Eating together is a community-building encounter which takes the characters out of their solitary experience. The dinner and lunch at Hélène's place are the moments of confrontation between various characters who remember the events of the past.

The dramatic tension surrounding Bernard's memories is associated with the threat of destruction to which the footage is exposed on a number of occasions. At one point Françoise, who pretends to be Alphonse's niece, touches by accident the record button on Bernard's tape-recorder containing the tape of Muriel's voice and nearly erases it. Bernard becomes angry and hits her; she is punished for threatening the preservation of memories. This incident becomes more significant when Françoise's ambitions to act are taken into account. She is associated with commercial cinema and has already done some acting in historical films on television. The film shows her looking at cinema posters in Boulogne and going to the cinema in her spare time. The threat which she poses to the recording of Muriel's voice is a confrontation between two visions of cinema – documentaries presenting true events and commercial cinema generating a marketable version of history. The former, not the latter, is supposed to serve as the basis for Lazarean fiction. Françoise is a lesser threat than Robert – a young man from Boulogne who accompanied Bernard in Algeria and participated in the torture incident. Robert realises that Bernard wants to share his memories hoping for a sympathetic response from the French public. In his view, Bernard's desire is impossible to realise:

> Do you want to tell the story of Muriel? This story cannot be told ... Every Frenchman feels lonely and dies of fear. He erects a barbwire fence around himself. He does not want to hear any stories. (Cayrol 1963b: 110, 115)

Bernard kills Robert in one of the final sequences of the film; his voice must be silenced in order for Bernard's to be heard. In the end, the narrative will 'resort to an ingenious combination of properly literary and documentary strategies to convey its vision of the Algerian conflict' (Dine 1994: 225). The dramatic events allow for the story of *Muriel ou le temps d'un retour* to be told while the archival footage is being screened.

In his review of the film, Claude Ollier emphasises the verbal at the expense of the visual and the role of Cayrol in the making of the film. The visual is relegated to a secondary position in relation to the verbal, which manifests itself mostly in dialogue. The importance of the verbal is shown in that the past in the film is constituted by memories, which are not revealed through flashbacks but through speech. The emphasis placed on the role of the scriptwriter and on the primacy of the verbal as far as the overall effect of the film is concerned suggests that Ollier saw it as a manifestation of the most important aspects of Lazarean fiction. In light of the importance Ollier gives to the verbal, his review compromises the film, which exists as an independent entity, by stressing the importance of the script. In other words, he seems to be reviewing a written text rather than a film.

The story of Hélène and Alphonse and the consequences of Alphonse's visit to Boulogne play a central role in Ollier's reading of the film. Alphonse's return constitutes the dramatic tension of the film and triggers a process in which the past is unlocked from the safe-box of memory (1981: 142). It is this aspect of the film which thematises the workings of Lazarean fiction. The memories which are unleashed by the appearance of Alphonse take the form of verbal exchanges (ibid.). As a result it is the verbal which gives expression to the visual. As mentioned before, the tension between the visual and the verbal creates a drama or a plot-driven narrative. This dramatic tension is one of the characteristics of Lazarean fiction and it is not surprising that Ollier identifies it in *Muriel ou le temps d'un retour* when he says that 'Cayrol and Resnais decided to tell a story which can be very easily followed thanks to its chronology' (1981: 141–2). It is the story which brings out the memories.

The importance of the verbal is also stressed by the comparison which Ollier draws between the aims of this film and the *nouveau roman* more generally; it is the simplicity and mediocrity of the characters which connects all the feature films of Resnais and relates them to the characters of the *nouveau roman*. Ollier identifies as a shared goal of Resnais and the new novelists the research into the flattening type of representation of the fictional characters, which functions as a 'pretext to uncover new structures of logic' (1963: 21). It is as though characters have to be deflated in the psychological sense in order for the modernist novel and cinema to become ways of developing a new area of critical reflection on human nature and culture. In spite of its groundbreaking character this investigation can only happen in the realm of language.

Resnais supports the emphasis Ollier places on the verbal and suggests that the character of Bernard and his role in the film reflects to some degree the director's understanding of the whole project. The film grows out of the discomfort that both Resnais and Cayrol felt at the idea that the most atrocious forms of violence can grow banal and mundane, and become integrated into the fabric of everyday life (see Resnais & Cayrol 1963). The film relates Bernard's impassioned recording of war crimes to the banal images of modern Boulogne. There are some ghosts and horrors in this apparently peaceful French provincial town filmed in 1963 (see Beylie 1964: 65). It is for this reason that Resnais stresses the importance of Bernard's monologue in making the images of war signify. Resnais would agree with Ollier that the verbal seen as an expression of memories is so important in the film that it is manifested in the architecture shown in the film:

The images of the past are inscribed into the film, not like in *Hiroshima, mon amour* where they take forms of mental phenomena, but rather through dialogued motives, linked to the actual perceptions, which recall the pre-war period. This is particularly true of [these parts of the city] where elements of old urban décor are still present (railway stations, gates, city walls, monuments). (1981: 150)

The mention of dialogue is of key importance here. It suggests that the verbal is not just inscribed but almost incarnated in the architecture of Boulogne and by extension also in the visual elements of the film. The emphasis put on language in the context of Boulogne's architecture show language as the architectural, or structural, principle of the whole film. Resnais also points to the equivalence between the aspects of the *mise-en-scène* provided by the director and Cayrol's commentary. The director talks about 'a profound relationship between the confessional [element of the film] and images' (Resnais & Cayrol 1963: n.p.); the drama of the confession arises from the calmness of the images which is oppressive. For Resnais, it is Cayrol's script which to a large extent evokes the signifying power of images. The vision of an almost organic bond between image and text refers to the metaphoric relationship which Cayrol wanted to establish in a new formal language of cinema. Resnais admits the vital importance of the verbal aspect for the film. For him, '*Muriel* appeared in the midst of ink stains' (ibid.).

The fact that Ollier gives so much importance to the verbal is connected to his professional identity as a critic of *Cahiers du cinéma* and a new novelist involved in the artistic project related to that of Cayrol. By the same token we could argue that Resnais' endorsement of the literary aspect of the film is related to a concept upheld also by *Cahiers* according to which cinema was trying to become an artform equal to literature. It is partly because of this aspiration of cinema critics that it has been possible to identify the elements of Lazarean fiction in their critical methods. The support given to Lazarean fiction by Ollier and Resnais is an expression of an extreme position because of the degree to which cinema was becoming a part of the formal project of literature.

Jean Cayrol's work as a film theorist, scriptwriter and filmmaker foreshadowed new trends which appeared in film criticism in the period between 1963 and 1967 with the advent of theory and in response to the growth of avant-garde cinema, exemplified in the films of Alain Robbe-Grillet. Cayrol's adaptation of Lazarean fiction for the needs of cinema, which he described in *Le Droit du regard*, showed the importance of literary criticism and literary ideas for shaping critical discourse about film. This was linked to the dominance of the literary element in film criticism. In the period between 1963 and 1967, we will see how ideas associated with semiotics and the structural analysis of narrative were absorbed into film criticism. An almost exclusive focus on narrative is a manifestation of a predominance of the literary element in film critical discourse. Cayrol's ideas regarding cinema were developed in the course of his work as a writer, scriptwriter and filmmaker in his own right. The same elements can be identified in the career of Robbe-Grillet who, in the early 1960s, became not only a scriptwriter but also a filmmaker. Such comprehensive artistic engagement called for a theoretical framework which could explain the works and formulate some understanding of them. For Cayrol, this framework was Lazarean fiction, developed as a literary theory which could also be translated into the filmic terms. In the case of Robbe-Grillet, it was literary theory which was adopted for the needs of cinema. Cayrol's work as a film critic is largely forgotten, because even in its own times it was treated as marginal due to its avant-garde and literary elements. Cayrol had to fight his way into film criticism and struggle for recognition; a similar fate awaited the works of Robbe-Grillet. The entrance of theory into film criticism was associated with negotiating the status of avant-garde production in relation to commercial works.

IV

Theory: 1963–67

By 1963 the *nouvelle vague* experienced its first commercial failures which resulted in a mounting criticism directed at it. Faced with attacks from different directions the former *Cahiers* critics – Jacques Rivette, François Truffaut, Jean-Luc Godard, Jacques Doniol-Valcroze and Pierre Kast – decided to return to criticism, while continuing to make films, in order to defend the creative cause of the *nouvelle vague* and the new kind of cinema it was representing. When back at the *Cahiers* offices they demanded a sharp change in the direction of the magazine headed by Eric Rohmer. At the turn of the 1950s and 1960s the most radical voices of *Cahiers* promoting the notion of modern cinema – André S. Labarthe, Michel Delahaye and François Weyergans – were operating on the margins of the magazine's *cinéphilic* centre headed by Rohmer, who continued to argue for the concept of classical cinema embedded mostly in the exploration of American film. The *nouvelle vague* group of critics returning to *Cahiers* claimed that the magazine needed to embrace modernity in the area of film criticism in the same way that the *nouvelle vague* filmmakers embraced it creatively. Film criticism should not be an exercise in film history, a guided tour across the museum of cinema, but an instrument in the fight for new kinds of cinema, a call to arms, a passionate engagement on the side of new directors and films which can push the boundaries of the medium in a radically new direction. This engagement happened by incorporating into critical reflections on cinema the analysis of the developments in contemporary arts and human sciences. Jacques Rivette, who took over the editorial control of the magazine from Rohmer in 1963, was very interested in new philosophical ideas associated with semiotics, structuralism and psychoanalysis. He treated developments in the serial music of Pierre Boulez, Anton Webern, Alban Berg and Karl-Heinz Stockhausen and the painting of Mark Rothko, Max Ernst and Jackson Pollock as a bridge between the modern cinema he was defending and the new set of theoretical postulates which were shaping the era (see de Baecque 2003: 316–7).

The new model of film criticism was a departure from the *cinéphilic*, romantic and existentialist treatment of the cinematic object and an embrace of a scientific and theoretical take on cinema. The relationship between the spectator and cinema was to be that of comprehension and not fascination (see de Baecque 2003: 323). This theoretical engagement with cinema was based on a radically different set of values and informed by different objectives than criticism was. While criticism was seen as empirical and subjective (and in the 1960s also as preoccupied with the cinema of the past), theory was objective and deductive, and very importantly, progressive and focused on the contemporary cinema and cinema of the future. This new approach meant that sometimes ideas about cinema, the models of thinking about it, were becoming as important if not more so than the films themselves. This was a change from the 1950s when cinema was at the centre of the activity of the *cinéphilic*-minded critics. That *cinéphilic* culture was forged in opposition to the university culture; many of the *Cahiers* critics were university drop-outs. The belief in theory led them to embrace academic debates because this is where the momentous intellectual shift of the period was taking place. In the *Cahiers* of the 1960s one could find interviews with not just filmmakers but also literary critics and theorists, such as Roland Barthes and Christian Metz. The theoretical turn occurring in the magazine was fuelled by the energy of young critics who joined its staff: Jean-Louis Comolli, Jean Narboni, Jean-André Fieschi, Paul Vecchiali and Serge Daney.

The influx of ideas associated with structuralism and semiotics into *Cahiers*, and their focus on questions of narrative in modern cinema, became a vehicle for literary critics such as Jean Ricardou and Claude Ollier, and new novelists, Alain Robbe-Grillet in particular, to put their stamp on *Cahiers*. In this period the new novelists, Robbe-Grillet, Marguerite Duras and Jean Cayrol, began making their own films which were seen as examples of modern cinema in *Cahiers*.[23] Although these various literary figures were crossing over to film, their interest in promoting and supporting cinema was underpinned by their concern with literature; they incorporated cinema into their literary debates by extending the definition of literature to include cinema as well. This became particularly evident in the critical writings of

Ricardou and had already been signalled by Gérard Genette's article about *L'Année dernière à Marienbad* in 1966.

Ricardou's essay 'Plume et caméra' ('Pen and Camera') (1967a) was composed of answers to a survey directed in 1961 to a number of contemporary writers in a special issue of *Premier Plan* devoted to Alain Resnais and edited by the literary critic Bernard Pingaud. Michel Butor, Claude Ollier, Jean Ricardou, Claude Simon, Phillipe Sollers and Jean Thibaudeau were asked whether Resnais' collaboration with the new novelists created a real rapprochement between literature and cinema. Although the focus of this issue of *Premier Plan* is Resnais, the survey was addressed to writers and focused on their own work rather than on Resnais' films alone. Ricardou's answer was crafted to address the problems he encountered in his work as a writer. For this reason the definition of the art of cinema which he proposes remained completely dependent on the literary nature of his own work and of the inquiry organised by Pingaud. In the same way, Ollier's literary background also determined the shape of arguments regarding the questions of cinematic and literary narratives presented in the 1966 special issue of *Cahiers du cinéma*, '*Film et roman, problèmes du récit*'. Even though Ollier claimed that cinematic and literary narratives were distinct, there is a strong sense that the urge for posing the question in narrative terms, rather than using a more cinematic framework of *mise-en-scène* or *montage*, came from the world of literature. The publications in *Premier Plan* and in *Cahiers du cinéma* emphasised the importance of other than audio-visual elements for the definition of the art of cinema. In the 1950s a literary impulse was provided by the culture dominated by the written word in which debates about the potential of cinema as art were growing. In the 1960s cinematic culture thrived alongside the novelistic, poetic and essayistic one and it was the contribution of literary critics working in all areas of cultural activity which gave the strong literary, and increasingly linguistic, flavour to any new ideas about cinema.

In the 1960s, film criticism became subject to new influences and arguments regarding cinematic art and cinematic *écriture* derived from semiotics, structural linguistics and Russian Formalism. These theoretical developments created a new platform for relating cinema and literature. Ricardou's argument in 'Plume et caméra' brings in the science of signs which transforms the context in which the presentation of his argument takes place. In the same way Ollier's argument centres on the problem of narrative, which becomes the focus of his investigation of cinematic and literary specificity. It is theory, rather than literary criticism, which now offers the framework for understanding cinema, as theory provides conceptual tools to establish new terms for the interactions between cinema and literature. It is not only that film critics are interested in theory, but also that the theorists display their interest in cinema. Their reaching out to cinema is evident in the research of the magazine *Communications*.

Communications was a publication by Centre d'Etudes des Communications de Masse, which was part of L'Ecole Pratique des Hautes Etudes. In the introduction to the first issue we read that the aim of the Centre was to provide a sociological analysis of phenomena of mass communication: press, radio, television, cinema and advertising (Anon. 1961a: 1). Their intention was to establish a forum for the development of a method or theory for the study of these mass phenomena. Cinema was the centre of their attention, especially in 1961, when the cinema of the new generation, the *nouvelle vague*, had not yet lost its momentum. It is not by chance that in the first issue they present 'Enquêtes et analyses: les films de la *Nouvelle Vague*' (see Morin 1961; Bremond *et al.* 1961). At that time, this kind of sociological analysis was absent from *Cahiers du cinéma*, which still focused on aesthetics and formal analysis. The development of the sociological approach in the study of culture and society conducted on the pages of *Communications* took place in two stages which, in turn, had an impact on film criticism. The first stage was the publication of a series of articles about semiology, and the second was the development of the structuralist analysis of narrative. Both researches into semiology and narrative took cinema into account. In *Communications* 4 (1964) devoted to 'Recherches sémiologiques', we find a text on photography, Barthes' 'Rhétorique de l'image' and Metz's essay on cinema, 'Le Cinéma: langue ou langage'. In *Communications* 8 (1966) also devoted to 'Recherches sémiologiques. L'analyse structurale du récit', we can find Metz's 'La Grande syntagmatique du film narratif'. In other words, cinema was one of the primary testing grounds for these new methods of semiotic analysis.

In the introduction to 'Recherches sémiologiques', Barthes argues that semiology is a science which makes it possible to study any sign system: images, gestures, rites or spectacles (1964f: 1). It drew on linguistics, information theory, formal logic and structural anthropology to develop its analytical tools. By demonstrating that both cinema and literature are systems of signs, semiology created an opportunity for the joint and comparative analysis of cinema and literature by establishing parity between the two forms as objects of study. It became the basis for the arguments of such literary critics as Jean Ricardou who claimed that cinematic and literary signs are comparable because they are both systems of signs, and different because the cinematic and literary systems are distinct from each other.

A new method of studying narrative presented in 'Recherches sémiologiques. L'analyse structurale du récit' was another platform on which cinema and literature were brought together using different terms. Barthes argues that there is an infinite number of narratives in the world, but that there must exist some underlying structure or set of rules which is shared by all these narratives; he calls 'theory' the study of these rules underpinning narrative (1966: 2). One could begin by identifying language with literature and by comparing the sentence with narrative. In other words, at the basis of the study of narrative, one can find structural linguistics. The aim of the theory is to describe narrative structure, while disregarding its chronological and psychological aspects. It seems that Barthes associates chronology with plots in narratives; it is only by dismantling the chronological element that it becomes possible to analyse the structure of narrative (1966: 12). The study of literary narrative in France led to the development of a new discipline, 'narratology', whose main figures were Gérard Genette and Tzvetan Todorov.

The special issue of *Cahiers*, '*Film et roman: problèmes du récit*' was thus an attempt to introduce this interest in narrative into the study of cinema. For *Cahiers* critics this issue of the magazine was an attempt to engage with contemporary theoretical debates especially those ongoing in *Communications* (see Bontemps 1966: 8). Narratological analysis had clearly introduced a new dynamic into the cinema-literature relationship which is why critics writing in this issue of *Cahiers* were interested in both literary and cinematic narratives. Narrative came to be regarded as a system of rules which could be shared by both without compromising the specificity of either. As with semiology, there was a sense that cinema and literature could approach each other as partners engaged in a shared enterprise which put narrative at the centre of analysis for film and literary critics. The study of cinema centred on the structural analysis of narrative introduced narrative as a new category for examining cinema, to replace *mise-en-scène* and *montage*. Just like *mise-en-scène* and *montage* the critical category of narrative could be used to discuss a great variety of films including avant-garde, popular, art and documentaries.

Barthes points to the works of the Russian Formalists as one of the sources of inspiration for his study of narrative. A selection of their writings appeared for the first time in France in 1965, translated by Todorov who emphasised the coincidence between the formal research of the Russian Formalists and that of literary critics in France. He gives the example of the study of point of view which had been addressed by Jean Pouillon, Claude-Edmonde Magny and Georges Blin before the analytical tools of the Russian Formalists for tackling questions of narrative structure became available (see Todorov 1971: 39). This continuity between studies undertaken in the French context and those of the Russian Formalists is important from the perspective of the study of cinematic narrative as well because traditionally in France the study of cinematic narrative had been framed by developments in literary criticism. Such continuity is also present between the study of cinematic narrative and the analysis of the Russian Formalists. Todorov points out that the theoretical concepts developed by the Russian Formalists were accompanied by avant-garde artistic production; he identifies a similar coincidence in France in the 1960s and says that there is 'a direct link between formalism and contemporary art' (1965: 15). The analysis of the Russian Formalists is particularly well-suited to avant-garde works such as Robbe-Grillet's films. In other words, a new kind of artistic production calls for an innovative type of critical analysis. This is reflected in the critical reception of Robbe-Grillet's works which were embraced by theorists such as Christian Metz and Noël Burch and rejected by other *Cahiers* writers such as Jean Narboni. While Robbe-Grillet's work certainly does not account for all the avant-garde production in that period, the reception of his films is nevertheless exemplary of the process of transformation undergone by the critical discourse of cinema at that time.

One of the reasons why the theoretical type of analysis was particularly well-suited to describe avant-garde cinematic production and to transform the dynamics of the cinema/literature relationship is connected to its stress on artistic practice. Todorov points out that the French artists whose reflection on literature coincided most strongly with that of the Russian Formalists were both writers and critics of literature: Stéphane Mallarmé, André Gide, Marcel Proust and Paul Valéry (1965: 21). Artists such as Robbe-Grillet and Cayrol continued the same tradition while expanding their literary creative practice into the realm of cinema as well. The theoretical type of analysis was most suited to address their practical involvement in cinema. Theory offered ways of describing the hybrid cine-literary character of the *nouveau roman* scripts and films. It did this by focusing on the structural analysis of narrative which had the same characteristics in cinematic and literary works.

Theory was a way of casting in new terms and expanding the *Cahiers* view of the 1950s according to which narrative had the same characteristics irrespective of its medium. Theory was also welcomed because the earlier *Cahiers* criticism of narrative did not account for such hybrid works as those produced by the new novelists or that of Resnais. The emergence of theory had two important consequences. Firstly, it emphasised to a much greater degree than previous analyses the importance of the literary element in the analysis of cinematic narrative. Secondly, this emphasis made it possible to see not only scripts (cine-novels) but also novels as cinematic works.

The emergence of theory as a new critical paradigm in writing about cinema can be traced on the basis of the critical response to Robbe-Grillet's films, *L'Immortelle* and *Trans-Europ Express*. The period between these two films, 1962–67, witnessed the emergence of semiotics and the structuralist analysis of narrative which were used in the process of building a new understanding of cinematic narrative. Robbe-Grillet's engagement with filmmaking, like that of Cayrol, was largely motivated, if not encouraged, by the rhetoric of *Cahiers du cinéma* criticism of the 1950s which emphasised the equivalence between literary and cinematic works. It perpetuated the myth of cinematic writing which made films equivalent to novels. Robbe-Grillet's practical experience of cinema caused him great disappointment in this respect, revealing gross differences between the creative processes of filmmaking and fiction writing. This resulted in his conviction that, by the virtue of their creative processes, the arts of cinema and literature are completely different. Ricardou supported Robbe-Grillet's position and examined it using a purely semiotic type of analysis. However, he failed to establish convincingly a difference between cinematic and literary signs. The weakness of Ricardou's argument lies in the fact that he treated the script of *L'Année dernière à Marienbad* as though it was a film in written form. Ricardou's line of argument regarding the difference between cinematic and literary signs and the specificity of cinematic and literary narratives collapsed because he did not foresee the consequences of his own assumption regarding the equivalence of films and their scripts. The semiotic type of analysis chosen by Ricardou supports the existence of hybrid cine-literary works and emphasised parallels between cinematic and literary narratives instead of undermining them.

With the advent of Russian Formalism, structural narrative analysis allowed critics to address the hybrid nature of cinematic and literary narratives produced by the new novelists as well as Resnais. This analysis emerged as a platform for the joint consideration of cinematic and literary works. The introduction of structural analysis occurred in three stages. Firstly, it was necessary to establish that all cinema and not just commercial cinema was narrative in nature. This is why Metz's analysis could be seen as a direct response to the view of Barthes, who refused to use narrative analysis to deal with the avant-garde works of the *nouveau roman*. Metz put forward a thesis about the ways in which avant-garde cinema expanded and developed the definition of narrative. Secondly, film critics analysed the hybrid cine-literary nature of the narratives in avant-garde films. Their theoretical analysis emphasised the literary element present in cinematic narrative. It was found there either because of the contribution of a scriptwriter or because of the structural elements present in both cinematic and literary narrative. Thirdly, film and literary critics jointly established that literary narrative was also cinematic in nature. Noël Burch showed that both the literary and cinematic works of the new novelists were hybrid. The consequences of the existence of cinematic characteristics in literary narrative were then further analysed by Robbe-Grillet.

L'IMMORTELLE – THE IMPOSSIBILITY OF LITERARY CINEMA

The years 1961 and 1962 were eventful for Alain Robbe-Grillet. He was a scriptwriter for Resnais' *L'Année dernière à Marienbad* and became a director of his first full-length feature, *L'Immortelle*. It was his work as a film director which made him change his mind regarding cinema and its relationship with literature. He argued that cinematic narrative was different from literary narrative and that it was impossible to 'translate' a literary narrative into a cinematic one. The medium, whether cinematic or literary, had the power to determine the shape of the narrative. This view was a departure from the ideas of the 1950s literary and cinematic criticisms.

Why was it the practice of cinema rather than that of scriptwriting which led Robbe-Grillet to question the critical concepts of the 1950s? Robbe-Grillet found Resnais' realisation of the script of *L'Année dernière à Marienbad* very successful and convincing, and regarded the film as equivalent to the script and vice versa. Resnais' skill and mastery as a director could explain why Robbe-Grillet, an inexperienced filmmaker, found the cinematic adaptation of *L'Immortelle* diverging so much from the script. It might have been easier to claim that Resnais' film was just as Robbe-Grillet imagined it in his script, because the writer did not film it and thus was not exposed to all the difficulties and challenges which are integral to the practice of cinema. Hence, Robbe-Grillet's lack of experience with the concrete practices of the cinematic medium was among possible explanations for his idea that cinematic and literary narratives are different. The difficulties Robbe-Grillet experienced filming *L'Immortelle* were also indicative of something more important than the writer's lack of skills as a filmmaker; namely, the problematic nature of the idea that cinematic and literary narratives are somehow equivalent.

L'Immortelle is a story of a French professor's search for a beautiful stranger, set in the unsettling atmosphere of the secret and labyrinthine city of Istanbul. The professor meets Leila upon his arrival in Istanbul. She becomes both his guide through the city and his lover. One day she disappears and the professor tries to find her in places they had been together. He runs into her but she seems to be very troubled. She is followed by a man in sunglasses. Shortly after her encounter with the professor, she dies in a car accident. The same fate seems to await the professor; we see his car crashing. However, the final scene of the film shows the stranger alive and laughing. This scene changes our understanding of the film. What we took for real events turns out to be a dream or fantasy sequence repeated in different combinations and with only slight changes of content throughout the film.

Robbe-Grillet's methods of filming, his ways of conceptualising his role as a director and the parallels between writing and filmmaking show how closely allied cinema and literature were in the wake of the *nouvelle vague*. The novelist's shift to filmmaking is the legacy of *Cahiers du cinéma* criticism of the 1950s which promoted the concept of filmmaker as *auteur* and suggested that filmmaking had its origins in writing. All these elements are reflected in the views held by Robbe-Grillet when he embarked on his career as a filmmaker in 1961. The practice of cinema led him to question the assumptions on which he based his original views as a filmmaker.

In the 1950s while searching for ways to strike the final blow to novelistic realism and replace it with radically new forms of writing Robbe-Grillet often evoked cinema in the same way that *Cahiers*' critics referred to literature in their critical discourse, and many of his ideas regarding narrative and its elements overlapped with the findings of *Cahiers*' critics in this area. Robbe-Grillet's aim in his essay 'Temps et description dans le récit d'aujourd'hui' (1963e) was to discuss the specificity of narrative in his writings, where descriptions played a new and important role. The *nouveau roman* changes the function of literary description from that of the nineteenth-century novel.

Descriptions were no longer there 'to recreate the reality which already exists'; rather descriptions were about fathoming their own 'creative potential' (1963e: 127). They do not focus on conveying some external *verisimilitude* but on the workings of the mind. Literary descriptions, like cinematic images in modern cinema, highlight the tension between the subjective and the objective. This is evident in *L'Année dernière à Marienbad* and in *L'Immortelle* where it is very difficult to discern which images are fantasised by the characters and which sequences are realist representation. Like modern cinema, Robbe-Grillet's fictional writing explores 'the domain of the subjective and imaginary' (1963e: 128). For this reason, the object of literary description is 'at the same time solid and unstable, existing and dreamt, alien to the man while it is all the time being reinvented in the man's spirit' (1963e: 127). Robbe-Grillet's references to cinema in the presentation of his literary project suggests that the new novelist clearly saw cinema and literature as comparable. *L'Immortelle* put to the test this idea of the interchangeability of cinematic and literary narratives based on the parallels between descriptions in the *nouveau roman* and the nature of images in modern cinema.

Before embarking on *L'Immortelle*, Robbe-Grillet was convinced that the traffic between literature and cinema is both possible and desirable, and in a sense unproblematic given the apparently shared objectives of the two media. He appears to have taken quite literally the *Cahiers* idea of the camera as a pen and the filmmaker as an author which had been realised through the ascetic filmmaking style of Robert Bresson, one of *Cahiers'* canonic filmmakers. Robbe-Grillet shared Bresson's desire for the absence of any facial expression on the part of the actors and neutrality of their verbal expressions which at first made the characters seem to lack any psychological depth. Just like Bresson, Robbe-Grillet became infamous for having numerous takes of the same scenes, and for discouraging improvisation, which reveals a desire for a kind of automatism and a view of the actors and their performance as a material of the film and a constitutive element of its formal structure. Robbe-Grillet and Bresson also both focus on the nature of the image and envision a film as a closed formal system, which explains their adherence to some specific methods of filmmaking (see Bresson 1957; Smith 1992: 29). Jean-Louis Trintignant, an actor in *Trans-Europ Express*, said about Robbe-Grillet that it was he who guided the actor, 'no creative act was initiated by the actor' because with Robbe-Grillet 'an actor can only be free if s/he succumbs to the demands of his style' (1972: 177–8). Despite some striking parallels between Robbe-Grillet's and Bresson's cinematographic project, these two filmmakers differ as far as their relationship with the text is concerned. André Bazin argues that Bresson wants to overcome and surpass the text which is the origin of his film. His aim 'is not to create a film which is "comparable" or "worthy" of the novel, but a new aesthetic entity which is the novel multiplied by cinema' (1997d: 124). This is in contrast to the position of Robbe-Grillet, who wants to achieve the most faithful recreation of the text on screen. This discrepancy, however, does not change the fact that Robbe-Grillet's project in *L'Immortelle* reflected Bresson's conviction that through audiovisual means it is possible to achieve a novelistic effect in cinema (see Bresson 1975). Marie-France Pisier, who acted in *Trans-Europ Express*, noted that through filming *L'Immortelle* Robbe-Grillet tried 'to find again some of the precision of novelistic writing' (1972: 169). This idea of a parity between filming and writing was inscribed into the narrative of the film and revealed in one of the descriptions of N – the narrator:

> Why is his name N? For sure to indicate his very special position in the narrative, which is a little bit like that of a narrator in a contemporary novel. He is the narrator who does not tell any story, but whose eyes see everything, his ears hear everything, and whose mind imagines everything [in the narrative]. (1963f: 9)

N is a character who can be found in both Robbe-Grillet's films and his novels. For him, filmic and literary narration means filtering through the character's imagination the signals transmitted through his ears and eyes, which act like a human microphone and camera. Gérard Genette argues that such a form of narration is 'internal focalisation', illustrated in Robbe-Grillet's *La Jalousie* (1957). Genette describes an example of an interior dialogue in which 'the main character is reduced – and derived – from his own focal position' (1972: 209–10). Since both writing and filming depend on this human apparatus, the implication is that a man of literature should be perfectly capable of making a film.

The ideas about cinema which informed Robbe-Grillet's work on his first film proved to be a source of great disappointment for him when put into practice. The direction of the film was marked by numerous disagreements with crew members who were not able to execute what the writer regarded as very precise directions for the film. Françoise Brion, who acted in *L'Immortelle*, remembers how strict Robbe-Grillet was about following the script, which he called his 'Talmud' (1972: 166). Robbe-Grillet's description of the behaviour of the main character, N, in relation to cinema, written after filming was completed, was a reflection of the writer's experiences with the visual medium. N's clumsiness and his lack of character are nothing like that of cinematic heroes we are accustomed to see in cinema. His awkward manner corresponds somehow to the technical errors evident in the framing of the image or in editing (Robbe-Grillet 1963f: 9). The behaviour of N seems to show how ill at ease Robbe-Grillet felt in his attempts to adjust the literary project to the material conditions of cinema. It was this discrepancy between the theory and practice of filmmaking which led Robbe-Grillet to conclude that cinema and literature are too different. This view is presented in the introduction to the *ciné-roman*, *L'Immortelle*, when he argues for the primacy of the film over the written text and compares the *ciné-roman* to an operatic libretto or a musical score (1963f: 7–8). The predominance of the visual over the verbal marks Robbe-Grillet's distance not only from the *Cahiers* criticism of the 1950s but also from Cayrol's reflections on cinema.

CINEMATIC SIGN – AN EXAMPLE OF CINE-LITERARY HYBRID

In order to argue for the difference between cinema and literature, which became evident through such works as Robbe-Grillet's *L'Immortelle*, Jean Ricardou, one of the most important critics of the *nouveau roman*, focuses on the points of divergence between literary descriptions and film images. This shows how closely he engages with the theoretical writings of Robbe-Grillet. Ricardou discusses the differences between them on the basis of the cine-novel of *L'Année dernière à Marienbad*, which he treats, as did Robbe-Grillet, as the equivalent to Resnais' film. It is his focus on the cine-novel which is the main weakness of Ricardou's argument. He attempts to challenge the equivalence between cinematic and literary signs by drawing on the theory which postulated the existence of this equivalence in the first place. Ricardou's definition of the cinematic image based on the cine-novel reveals characteristics which they share with literary description. As a result, Ricardou fails to define clearly the difference between literary descriptions and cinematic images.

Ricardou became a fiction writer and a literary critic at a moment when literary criticism was being transformed by structuralism and semiotics; in 1967, Dominique Noguez identified Ricardou among those critic-writers who were marked by these contemporary ideologies (1967: 494–5). Ricardou's fate was inextricably linked to *Tel Quel*, headed by Philippe Sollers, and to the *nouveau roman*. In the 1960s and 1970s he published a number of critical studies of the *nouveau roman*. The membership of this group and the *problématique* was changing dramatically in Ricardou's accounts. These shifts and contradictions were his response to the changing intellectual climate in which he worked (1971: 125). They also mirror the trends of the era in which they were conceived, presenting the *nouveau roman* as an eclectic, varied and multifaceted literary and cultural phenomenon. For Ricardou, the *nouveau roman* group includes such artists as Alain Robbe-Grillet, Claude Simon, Michel Butor, Claude Ollier, Philippe Sollers, Edgar Allen Poe, André Breton, Marcel Proust, Jean Paulhan and Raymond Roussel. The membership of this group is determined by those structural elements of their writing which Ricardou considers to be related to 'the real questions of the novelistic research' (1971: 11) In *Pour un théorie du nouveau roman* he extends his definition of the *nouveau roman* to include Paul Valéry, Gustave Flaubert, Jean-Louis Baudry and Jorge Luis Borges. But it is not until *Le Nouveau roman* (1973) that Ricardou limits his definition of the group to contemporary authors and outlines the process of the emergence of the *nouveau roman*. He determines membership on the basis of their participation in the Colloque de Cerisy entitled 'Nouveau Roman: hier, aujourd'hui' in July 1971. He claims that it was a principle of self-determination which brought together Michel Butor, Claude Ollier, Robert Pinget, Jean Ricardou, Alain Robbe-Grillet, Nathalie Sarraute and Claude Simon. He also traces the formation of the phenomenon of the *nouveau roman* from a cultural, ideological and sociological perspective (1971: 17). In *Le Nouveau roman* Ricardou attempts to outline some of the common preoccupations of the new novelists; he singles out their experiments with narrative as a common feature of their writings and identifies various types of narrative in the texts of the new novelists (1973: 24). It is telling that in his last assessment of the *nouveau roman*, he refers to narrative as the common denominator of their works.

Ricardou's interest in the *nouveau roman* was initiated by his critique of Robbe-Grillet's fiction, published in the pages of *Tel Quel* in such articles as 'Réalités variables' (1963), 'La Querelle de la métaphore' (1964b) and 'Expression et fonctionnement' (1966). He identifies contradiction as the main feature of Robbe-Grillet's theoretical and fictional writing (1963: 31); however, Ricardou also remarks that some of the contradictions which are present in the writer's theoretical essays are resolved in his fiction. For example, although Robbe-Grillet rejects the use of metaphor because he sees it as a tool of subjective expression, he employs it as a structuring device in his fictional writing (1964b: 60). Ricardou concludes that Robbe-Grillet's fiction is thus exemplary of the process in which 'expression and imposing a structure are in a way two conflicting vectors and it is the tension between them which determines the contemporary creative [literary] space' (1964b: 62). In other words, he seems to identify a creative tension resulting from the clash of two critical frameworks: one acknowledging the agency of the author and the other a structuralist one.

Ricardou's description of the divergence between Robbe-Grillet's theoretical and fictional writing determines the way in which he positions his theoretical project concerning Robbe-Grillet. He contests Robbe-Grillet's theoretical writings by referring to his fictional texts and frames them in the terms of structural discourse (see Noguez 1967: 495). There is one aspect of theoretical analysis where Ricardou seems to be caught up in the same set of contradictions as Robbe-Grillet. This concerns the relationship between description and image, be it photographic or cinematic. 'Plume et caméra' presents his argument, which at first seems to address the issues raised by *L'Immortelle*, of the irreconcilable differences between cinematic and literary signs.

In this essay, Ricardou sets out to outline the difference between film images and literary images created by means of description. His arguments contest the view that literary descriptions and film images developed on the basis of the new novelists' engagement with cinema are equivalent; he does not consider the formal aspects of Robbe-Grillet's novels to be cinematic. At the same time, his argument implies that the cine-novel is representative of both cinematic and literary signs. He uses the example of the cine-novel *L'Année dernière à Marienbad*, which is a written text and not a film, to argue for the existence of formal differences between cinematic and literary signs.

According to Ricardou, the main difference between cinematic and literary signs lies in their reception. The cinematic medium allows for immediate synthesis and global perception of the film object. In literature, the reader becomes acquainted sequentially with different elements of the object, which eventually create its composite image (1967a: 70). Ricardou illustrates this point with descriptions present in *L'Année dernière à Marienbad*. He argues that in the cine-novel Robbe-Grillet juxtaposes literary descriptions, which are detailed and analytical, with film images, which are wide-ranging and not as exact (1967a: 71). This analysis leads to a paradoxical situation in which the specificity of cinema is established on the basis of written texts such as the cine-novel. It is for this reason that one could argue that Ricardou's view does not describe a difference between film and literary images, but rather a difference between the two types of description – both of them literary.

Ricardou argues that the cine-novel of *L'Année dernière à Marienbad* was a step forward in the evolution of cinematic art. Robbe-Grillet's script for the film was so successful in reflecting the non-temporal nature of cinematic images that it managed to liberate them from the burden of storytelling (1967a: 77). By including some of the film's technical prescriptions in the cine-novel Resnais was relieved of the obligation to tell a story in film. Ricardou's argument makes Resnais' film largely redundant, for cinema is already produced in the form of the cine-novel. However, to say that Ricardou disregards the actual film production is not fair. Rather he has a very particular vision of the filmmaker's role, which is made evident in his argument about the differences in the production of cinematic and literary signs.

The number of objects present in the cinematic image is unlimited, whereas that found in literary descriptions is finite. This difference has implications for the creative activity of writers and filmmakers: writers have to control the representation and the number of objects; filmmakers may want to be – but are not able to be – as controlling (1967a: 70). Such an understanding of cinema is derived from the ontological myth of cinema. This is evident in Ricardou's belief that the camera just films objects, providing a seamless representation of the world. Whether the filmmaker chooses to intervene or not in this process, a cinematic sign will be produced. There is a strong idea of automatism, which underlies such an understanding of cinema, implying that the filmmaker's role is ultimately dispensable.

The characteristics of the cinematic sign described by Ricardou have two important implications for cinema: they curtail its efforts to produce a narrative and limit the role of the filmmaker to a minimum. The stress on the contingency of objects in the production of cinematic signs minimises the importance of close-ups, framing or studio sets. They not only direct the spectators' attention to particular objects or to particular elements of the image but are also crucial for the construction of narrative by providing cues. Weaving objects into the narrative fabric abolishes the individuality of film objects emphasised by Ricardou. Although he admits that a filmmaker can regulate the automatism of film production, he completely disregards the importance of editing in the process of filmmaking. This omission is significant because editing is fundamental to cinematic storytelling, as the example of Resnais so amply demonstrated.

Ricardou's reading of cinematic signs as non-narrative and automatic puts into crisis the institution of filmmaking and of narrative cinema. It also goes some way to explain why it was so easy for him to equate film with the cine-novel in the case of *L'Année dernière à Marienbad*. Hence, Ricardou's argument shows that no difference can be established between literary and cinematic signs if the impact of actual film practice, formal aspects of cinema and film narrative are not taken into account. It becomes necessary to find ways of conceptualising cinematic practice and of establishing a difference between cinema and literature. This new framework would replace the paradigm which can be found at the origins of Robbe-Grillet's engagement with cinema – the ontology of cinema and the belief, which dates back to Astruc, that a film can take the form of a novel.

The need for this new framework is also evident in the reaction of the critics of *Cahiers du cinéma* to *L'Immortelle*. The film elicited little interest from the magazine, which was reflected in critics' reluctance to review it. It is certainly possible to argue that the cool reception of *L'Immortelle* had to do with the fact that it was competing not just with a wave but a flood of very good films. *L'Immortelle* was not particularly successful, but given the identity of its director and the theoretical response it solicited in literary circles, *Cahiers'* silence is curious. It might be that the conceptual tools of the critics were not adequate to deal with this film. In rejecting *L'Immortelle*, they began to question the critical tradition which allowed for the emergence of the *nouvelle vague*. In the end Jacques Doniol-Valcroze was the only *Cahiers* critic willing to write a review (1963). He had an especially close and intimate relationship with the film, having acted in the role of the film's protagonist, and his reading of *L'Immortelle* brings to the fore the question of cinematic form in terms which provide a basis for determining the difference between cinema and literature.

Doniol-Valcroze argues that *L'Immortelle* is an example of modern cinema which explores its formal aspects at the expense of telling a story; by abandoning plot, cinema – like music, painting and literature – can focus on its structural elements (1963: 55). It is important to note that neither Doniol-Valcroze nor Ricardou differentiate between plot and narrative. They only contrast plot/narrative with the formal structures of films. They imply that films without tight storylines and plots are not narrative, which is not necessarily true. In fact, both critics remark that films such as *L'Immortelle* or *L'Année dernière à Marienbad* eliminate a dominating plot which is then replaced by a variety of interpretive possibilities offered by the film. Doniol-

Valcroze begins his review of *L'Immortelle* by giving a short summary of the film and concludes that it is just 'one of the ways of presenting the film but certainly not the only one' (ibid.). Hence, when Ricardou and Doniol-Valcroze say that modern cinema explores film's formal structure they in fact acknowledge the existence of narrative but lack the vocabulary to distinguish between plot and narrative. An important film critic and theorist and contemporary of Ricardou and Doniol-Valcroze, Noël Burch, might have been right when he said that 'the filmmaker's (or film critic's) vocabulary is a reflection of the way of thinking about cinema' (1986a: 11). In the case of Doniol-Valcroze and Ricardou it was necessary to await Todorov's translation of the writings of the Russian Formalists which offered theoretical tools to distinguish between narrative and plot by drawing a distinction between *fabula* and *sujet*. Doniol-Valcroze's argument suggests that, by focusing on its structural elements, cinema can discover its differences from other arts, including literature. This implies that the presence of the plot homogenised cinema and literature, while their narratives can be specifically cinematic or literary. As we will see, this problem will be addressed by Ricardou a few years later in his essay 'Page, film, récit' (1967b).

In 'Plume et caméra' Ricardou focuses on another homogenising element of cinema and literature – the doctrine of realism. Traditionally, this doctrine was at the origin of the association of cinema with literature. According to Ricardou, it is by removing this false common denominator that the specificity of literary and cinematic signs can be established; he suggests that cinema must become a linguistic system in order to establish itself as an art with its own specificity (1967a: 78). As a result, it becomes possible to develop non-mimetic systems of cinematic and literary signs. Ricardou's vision poses a serious problem for cinema because it implies that only non-representational cinema can be made up of signs. Doniol-Valcroze's argument is equally problematic in its conviction that the focus on structure will make it possible to differentiate art cinema and cinema of entertainment (1963: 57).

Ricardou's argument was a response to the changing creative and critical landscape of French arts in the 1960s. In the avant-garde cinematic production of this time, the bulk of non-mimetic cinema was made by artists with a literary background, or writers such as Robbe-Grillet, Duras, Philippe Sollers and Georges Perec.[24] Hence, at its core, thus defined and produced, the cinematic sign will remain literary. By inscribing non-mimetic cinema into a semiological framework Ricardou essentially ends up extending the field of literature again.

SEMIOTIC ANALYSIS OF NARRATIVE IN POPULAR CINEMA

When *Cahiers* critics invited Roland Barthes for an interview in 1963, they regarded him less as a literary critic than as a leading semiologist and theorist of culture (Delahaye & Rivette 1963). By that time, his most frequently referred to works were no longer *Le Degré zéro de l'écriture*, but *Mythologies* and the essays which appeared in *Revue Internationale de Filmologie* (Barthes 1957; 1960a; 1960b). His first piece of cinematic criticism was a review of Bresson's *Les Anges du péché* (*The Angels of Sin*, 1943) (Barthes 1997). The champion of 'the zero degree of writing' was writing about the champion of the most rigorous form of film *écriture*. In *Mythologies*, which aimed to identify various 'mystifications which transform middle-class culture into the universal one', Barthes devoted a substantial number of essays to cinema (1957: 7). His semiological analysis of cinema emphasises its sociological and ideological elements, an approach which was already present in his articles on cinema written for the *Revue Internationale de Filmologie*. Edward Lowry (1985) argues that with these articles Barthes established the link between filmology and structuralism which was later developed by Christian Metz. All this suggests not only that cinema was important for Barthes' semiological analysis, but also that his impact on film criticism was quite substantial.

His proven interest in cinema puts into question Jonathan Rosenbaum's claim that 'far from being a film specialist, Barthes could be even considered somewhat *cinephobic* (to coin a term), at least for a Frenchman' (1995: 45). Rather than calling him cinephobic it would be more appropriate to emphasise his antagonism towards the established institution of cinema. Barthes experienced a certain discomfort when faced with the pressure to follow cultural and critical prescriptions about cinema. He said that 'the films which one is *supposed* to see conflict with the idea of unpredictability, and complete availability that cinema represents for me' (in Delahaye & Rivette 1963: 21). Although Barthes accepts and acknowledges cinema's development into art, he is nostalgic for a different type of cinema which is closely related to the Surrealist ideal; he longs for the cinema of the early years of the twentieth century when it was considered a lower form of entertainment, uncodified by aesthetic norms, and constituted an example of popular culture *par excellence*.

Barthes' essay on Robbe-Grillet's and Cayrol's writing suggests that the critic recognised and shared the writers' fascination with dark movie theatres conveyed in more or less overt ways in their novels and critical writings. By allying his vision of cinema with the one professed by Surrealism, Barthes launches 'a critique of the institution of cinema as art' (ibid.). Both Resnais and Robbe-Grillet attempted to conceptualise in Surrealist terms the effects created in narratives where less emphasis was put on chronology and causal relationships between events. Given Barthes' understanding of cinema inspired by Surrealism it is surprising that it is precisely avant-garde cinema which is excluded from his analysis. In his view, only realist and narrative cinema can be treated in semiological terms. He also argues that only this type of analysis can be related to literary narrative.

Barthes believed that Robbe-Grillet failed to create the narrative of film and did not realise the objective of cinematic art, which was to develop a cinema of narrative signs. This suggests that Robbe-Grillet's cinematic experiment lay outside the ways of conceptualising cinema proposed by Barthes. It also leaves unanswered the question of the relationship between Robbe-Grillet's experience in cinema and *Cahiers'* criticism of the 1950s from which Barthes' analysis grew. The only way in which continuity can be established between the analysis of avant-garde cinema proposed by Resnais and Robbe-Grillet in Surrealist terms and that of Barthes, who envisioned realist cinema in semiological terms, is by finding means to consider the avant-garde cinema of Robbe-Grillet's narrative forms from a semiological perspective. Such an argument would also highlight the relationship between cinematic and narrative structures and show the links between the earlier *Cahiers* criticism and the developments in theory in the second half of the 1960s.

In his analysis of film narrative, Barthes uses terms from contemporary linguistic discourse: 'metaphor' and 'metonymy' and analyses cinema's potential to develop narrative by referring to the opposition between metaphor and metonymy. He begins with a claim that in order to see cinema in linguistic terms, it is necessary to find those elements of cinema which are continuous and analogous or metonymic. Barthes' reflection on the analogical nature of film images was initiated in his article 'Le Problème de la signification au cinéma', where he remarks that in cinema 'to signify crying, it is necessary to cry' (1960a: 89). In other words, all symbolism and metaphor must be avoided. Narrative is an element of cinema, which seems for Barthes to imitate the metonymic nature of cinematic signs (see Delahaye & Rivette 1963: 24). Film narrative is tightly linked to the metonymic nature of cinema, which is based on the linking up of signs whose significance arises as a result of such linking. It is because of the importance of *montage* that cinema can be established as a metonymic art rather than a metaphoric one assuming that, thus created, narrative is chronological, causal and plot-oriented. The novels and films of the *nouveau roman* were excluded from Barthes' linguistic analysis of film narrative. According to Barthes, from the linguistic perspective, the *nouveau roman* fictions and films are not metonymic but metaphoric and for this reason not narrative.

In 'Le Problème de la signification au cinéma', an example of the signifiers Barthes gives is décor, which is usually a very stable element in film. Gestures and facial expressions are also signifiers, whose character is fleeting, changing and more circumstantial. By showing what the signifiers refer to, Barthes makes speculations about the nature of the signifieds. The signified is an idea which goes beyond the immediate signification of the film; it exists outside the film but needs the film to be realised (1960a: 87). To illustrate this point, Barthes gives an example of some events or circumstances which are important to the plot of the film but which are not shown on the screen. Spectators must grasp their meaning and importance as though in spite of the developments of the film. The more elliptical and demanding the film is in this respect, the closer it seems to come to the 'problematic literature' or 'literature of suspended meaning' that Barthes mentions in a *Cahiers* interview (Delahaye & Rivette 1963: 28). Only the definition of cinema based on the unique analogous nature of its signs could produce a narrative which matches a literary one. This conclusion leaves avant-garde prose and films outside the scope of linguistic analysis, and for this reason makes Barthes' position problematic and limits the range of work he covers.

But even cinema which matches 'problematic literature' is not easy to develop. As an example, Barthes discusses Luis Buñuel's *El Angel Exterminador* (*The Exterminating Angel*, 1962) where the filmmaker manages to establish and maintain a fragile balance between the arrangement of signs, which give a sense of urgency and necessity, and a feeling that this arrangement does not build into a resolution which is unified and final; we are presented with a metonymic narrative whose meaning is not determined but suspended. This is an example of a film 'which provokes responses but does not give any' (ibid.). The increasing but unresolved tension which Barthes admires in Buñuel's film can be explained in the context of the critic's attempts to codify cinematic style. In 'Problèmes de la signification au cinéma' he divides cinematic signs into two categories: the nexus and the periphery. The nexus is easily identifiable by spectators because of their previous knowledge of cinema. The periphery exclusively concerns those signs which convey the personal style of the filmmaker; they are the zone where the art and originality of the filmmaker are situated (1960a: 84). According to Barthes, the source of the originality of the filmmaker is the distance which the filmmaker is able to establish between signifier and signified without breaking the link between the two. It is in the context of *El Angel Exterminador* and this theory of the filmmaker's style that Barthes launches a critique of Robbe-Grillet's venture into cinema.

He contrasts *L'Immortelle* with *El Angel Exterminador* and argues that Robbe-Grillet does not manage to suspend meaning in the way Buñuel does; rather he blurs it by making his cinema metaphoric (in Delahaye & Rivette 1963: 30). Barthes argues that repetition, which is a central feature of *L'Immortelle*, constantly refers us to the same signifieds and that this is metaphor rather than metonymy. In other words, there is no progression or development as we get in *El Angel Exterminador*; there is no story 'with the beginning, the end and suspense', which are the elements Barthes most admires in cinema (ibid.).

Jean Ricardou and Roland Barthes attempt to inscribe cinema into a semiological framework. The films they focus on and their reasons for engaging in these projects are different. Ricardou's project is motivated by the new novelists' shift to filmmaking and their involvement with film production. The difference between literature and cinema was becoming fluid and Ricardou was trying to find ways of establishing the difference. The focus of his analysis was the avant-garde cinema of the new novelists and their fiction writing. He claimed that only non-mimetic and non-narrative cinema that focused on formal structure can be made out of those cinematic signs which were different from literary signs. His analysis excluded narrative and realist cinema. The analysis of Ricardou's position here demonstrates that there was no difference between the literary and cinematic narratives of avant-garde prose and films.

Individually Barthes and Ricardou proposed two conceptual frameworks based on semiotics which between the two of them covered avant-garde and commercial cinema and mapped their relationship with literature. However, there was no one framework which would make it possible to read all cinema in semiotic terms. Hence, this common denominator still remained to be found. Their analyses amply demonstrated that such a shared framework would be related to or even derived from literature. After all, literature, be it avant-garde or more traditional, could be found at the centre of the analyses conducted by both critics. It is Christian Metz who can be credited with the emergence of such a common framework for the consideration of all cinema. As we will see, he highlights the importance of the literary elements in his argument, which demonstrates that avant-garde cinema is also narrative. As a result, Metz manages to 'translate' the *Cahiers* criticism of the 1950s into semiotic and structural terms.

NARRATIVISING AVANT-GARDE CINEMA

The only way in which avant-garde cinema could be included in a linguistic analysis was by finding the way in which metaphoric cinema could be presented as narrative. This problem was essentially a call for a different definition of narrative. It was Christian Metz, a great promoter of structuralism and semiotics in cinema, who presented the argument which defined narrative in such a way that it became a common ground for both commercial and avant-garde cinema. While his argument challenged some of the key elements of the *politique des auteurs*, it also made explicit the parallels between the structures of cinematic and literary narratives. Metz's emphasis on cinematic narrative and its links with literary narratives, present in his structural analysis of cinema, were expanding and casting in new terms the definition of cinema proposed by the *Cahiers* critics of the 1950s.

Metz was never a film critic but a researcher and scholar who in the early 1960s decided to combine his research in linguistics and semiology with the study of cinema. He was trained in linguistics, German and classics; in other words he was 'an academic of the best kind' (Gauthier 1991: 148). He was a young member of the inner circles of Parisian intellectual life who developed and cultivated his interest in cinema not by associating with *Cahiers du cinéma* critics, but with the filmology movement which was introduced into the university context in the 1940s and 1950s (see Cohen-Séat 1946). This was an approach to cinema which was historically parallel but very different from that of André Bazin and *Cahiers du cinéma* (see Lowry 1985: 5); rather, it drew on various sciences in order to develop a comprehensive approach to cinema and to come up with a general theory of film. It attracted the attention of such academics and intellectuals as Georges Sadoul, Edgar Morin, Etienne Souriau and Roland Barthes who jointly taught a course dealing with social, anthropological and historical considerations of cinema at the Sorbonne. They conducted research at the Filmological Institute, founded by the Association for Filmological Research, and their findings were published in the *Revue Internationale de Filmologie*.

Edward Lowry demonstrates the ways in which Metz's *Language and Cinema* (1971) was directly inspired by the research of such filmologists as Anne Souriau (1985: 93–4; Souriau 1953a; 1953b). As a result, Metz's approach to cinema remained scientific and rigorous, although it always displayed traces of an authentic film culture and a passion for cinema. He acknowledges his debt to the filmological tradition in numerous references in his early essays to the writings of Etienne Souriau and Gilbert Cohen-Séat (see, for example, Metz 1968c). In the early 1960s, he began to publish articles about cinema in *Communications* where he continued to draw on some of the filmological discoveries of the 1950s. Metz found himself in the avant garde of structural research at the time. His semiological analyses were fuelled by exposure to the works of the Russian Formalists and the structuralist analysis of narrative which their writings inspired. As a result, this new conception of narrative appeared as an innovative way of framing the debates of the cinematic and literary critics.

Metz's first article appeared in *Cahiers du cinéma* in 1965 and was followed by 'Le Cinéma moderne et la narrativité' (1968a; 1968b). A historian of *Cahiers du cinéma*, Antoine de Baecque, claims that when Metz published in *Cahiers*, the magazine critics knew him only as a German translator of a book on jazz – Joachim Berendt's *The New Jazz Book* (1991b: 153; Berendt 1963). This book was one of the first extended publications about jazz in France (see Tournès 1999). Berendt suggested that jazz was changing so quickly that jazz criticism could not keep up with it properly; he argued that 'the aliveness of jazz is such that standards are constantly overthrown – even where old models and entities remain connective' (1964: 248). It is possible that, in some way, this influenced Metz to adopt an unorthodox position towards the prevailing dogma of cinema criticism. Another view is that put forward by Francesco Casetti who suggests that the success of Metz may have come partly from the fact that he was a product of his times – a new type of research called for a new type of researcher, and the result was that Metz performed a replacement of ontological theories by methodological ones (1999: 104–5).

In his essay 'Le Cinéma moderne et la narrativité' Metz challenged the prevailing conviction of film criticism according to which the most important characteristic of some examples of modern cinema – that of Resnais, Robbe-Grillet, Godard and Antonioni – was the absence of narrative (1968b: 186). This form of criticism was developed by the critics of *Cahiers du cinéma* such as Bazin, Leenhardt, Astruc and Truffaut. As we have seen, it was also endorsed – albeit as a negative characteristic – by Roland Barthes. Their criticism implies that modern cinema underwent some dramatic change:

> Everybody agrees that new cinema is defined by the fact that it surpassed, rejected or clarified something; but the identity of this *something* – [understood as] spectacle, narrative, theatre, 'syntax', single meaning, 'strings' attached by the scriptwriters etc, is different to different critics. (Metz 1968b: 187–8)

Metz concludes that, rather than eliminating narrative, these modern films succeeded in extending the limits of narrative (1968b: 221). He begins by contrasting his type of analysis with *Cahiers'* film criticism, whose objective is not only to analyse films but also to support the cinema critics love. Metz proposes a less *cinéphilic* and more rational, theoretical approach. He sets out to undertake 'theoretical analysis of the cinema we all love', which will allow him to counter the anti-narrative myth professed by traditional film criticism (1968b: 187). Hence, Metz's is the first attempt to openly use the structuralist method to engage with cinema.

This theoretical mode of analysis allows Metz to provide an alternative to the *Cahiers* tradition established by Bazin. He emphasises a number of literary elements in the new cinema, including the importance of the scriptwriter and the common characteristics of literary and cinematic narratives. Hence, his argument emphasises cinema's association with literature; modern cinema can be considered narrative if its link with literature is made explicit. Metz challenges the view of the *Cahiers* critics that modern cinema is essentially realist. By emphasising the non-realist aspect of cinema, Metz shows his support for Ricardou's position expressed in 'Plume et caméra'. Metz also claims that Bazin is responsible for the constant presence of the idea of realism in film criticism (1968b: 193). In his opinion, it was Robbe-Grillet's film *L'Immortelle* and his reflections on questions of subjectivity and objectivity in cinema which allowed him to challenge the ideas of Bazin (1968b: 193–4). Metz refers to *L'Immortelle*, made by a new novelist who, as we know, was not much loved by *Cahiers'* critics, in order to contest some of these critics' ideas about cinematic realism. He suggests that Robbe-Grillet, along with Resnais, Varda, Marker and Henri Colpi, belong to an avant-garde of modern cinema and even seem to detach themselves from the rest of modern cinema because of their rejection of realism. This suggests that in that period even more mainstream cinema could be considered modern cinema and experimental. For it is important to remember that the backdrop to these avant-garde film productions was the *nouvelle vague*, with its impressive volume of films and varying degrees of formal experimentation. Hence, in light of this competition from formally innovative and often commercial cinema, it became important to defend the merit of films whose shared characteristic was commitment to radical experimentation and commercial failure (1968b: 187). Metz found it necessary to emphasise cinema's parallels with fiction writing, that of Robbe-Grillet and Butor in particular, in order to defend the avant-garde cinema and its commitment to narrative. That constituted an open challenge to the fundamental tenets of *Cahiers* criticism.

The *Cahiers* critics defined modern cinema on the basis of the *politique des auteurs* according to which directors are in total control of their films. Metz points out the importance of scriptwriters in the cinema he defends. As an example he uses Resnais' collaboration with various writers and describes them as 'the films of scriptwriters' (1968b: 199). He argues that this avant-garde cinema was an attack on one of the most important taboos of the *politique des auteurs* by emphasising the importance of a filmmaker's co-operation with the scriptwriter. This implies that it is the scriptwriters who are responsible for the elaboration of the film narrative before the film is made. Metz identifies some of the characteristics of narrative in this avant-garde cinema using the example of Godard's *Pierrot le fou* (1965). The narrative of this film shares these characteristics with narrative techniques used by Robbe-Grillet in his novels, especially repetition of the same events with only slight variations (1968b: 213). In the same way the use of 'voix off' in *Pierrot le fou* and *L'Année dernière à Marienbad* is seen as 'the embodiment of narrativity rather than of the author' (1968b: 215). This suggests that the designation of avant-garde cinema as narrative cinema not only reveals its shared characteristics with novels but also establishes the centrality of the narrative at the expense of the author or filmmaker whose position becomes secondary in relation to narrative structures. This is yet another way of contesting the premises of the *politique des auteurs* which was brought by the advent of structuralism.

Metz uses theoretical analysis in order to argue that avant-garde cinema is narrative. He establishes narrative as a common denominator of all cinema, both avant-garde and more traditional, plot-driven productions. His argument bridges the analysis of Ricardou and Barthes, and his theoretical method poses a challenge to the premises of the *politique des auteurs* and *Cahiers du cinéma* criticism with its emphasis on realism in cinema and cinema's links with literature. At first, it may seem surprising that such an open challenge to *Cahiers'* tradition occurs in the pages of the magazine. Metz's essay is part of the special issue of *Cahiers* entitled '*Film et roman: problèmes du récit*' which, as we will see, features other articles which question the critical line of *Cahiers*. The presence of these articles suggests that *Cahiers* is changing under pressure from structuralism and semiotics. Furthermore, it shows that there has always been room in this magazine for the defence of avant-garde cinema and for a radical change of the critical line. This interest in cinema had been gaining prominence since the success of Resnais' *Hiroshima, mon amour*. As previously mentioned, one of the features of this film was the importance of the scriptwriter for the development of the film. Hence, this *Cahiers* line was more significant for the exploration of the forms taken by the cinema/literature relationship in the context of French cinema. It is logical, then, that one of the central characteristics of Metz's analysis is the explicit link between literary and film narrative structures.

This effort to redefine all cinema in narrative terms and the impact this had on some fundamental elements of *Cahiers'* criticism of the 1950s brings to mind the similar results of Jean Cayrol's attempts to adopt 'Lazarean fiction' for the needs of cinema in *Le Droit du regard*. Metz, like Cayrol, demonstrates parallels between cinematic and literary narrative. Cayrol's analysis encompasses both commercial and avant-garde cinema; it also presents a challenge to the basic tenets of the *politique des auteurs* and *mise-en-scène*. This shows that Cayrol's critical work in cinema foreshadowed the advent of theory and structuralism. It also demonstrates an important link or even an overlap between the work of avant-garde writers and filmmakers and that of film theorists. In his analysis, Metz identifies the elements of literary narrative in film narrative. However, he does not explain the ways in which narrative could be specific to literature or cinema because of the differences in the media. This question is addressed by Jean Ricardou.

STRUCTURALIST NARRATIVE

The difference between the medium of cinema and that of literature raises an important question regarding the degree to which it could make cinematic and literary narratives medium-specific. Ricardou discusses this issue in his article 'Page, film, récit'. His thesis about the difference between cinematic and literary narratives grows out of his argument in 'Plume et caméra', where he presented ways in which cinematic and literary signs diverged. But as in that earlier discussion, so in 'Page, film, récit' Ricardou fails to present evidence sufficient to allow him to establish the specificity of the forms of cinematic and literary narrative. For this reason, in spite of Ricardou's efforts, Metz's view regarding the structural similarities between the narratives of both arts is not challenged.

The participation of writers in French cinematic culture and the strong presence of some literary critics, such as Claude Ollier or Jean Ricardou, among film critics brought the debate about the specificity of cinema and literature to a new level. Literary/film critics, who, like Ollier, were actually involved in filmmaking, gained more insight into the cinematic medium. In 'Page, film, récit', Ricardou refers to *L'Année dernière à Marienbad* as a film, rather than as a cine-novel as in his previous article 'Plume et récit'. For the first time, literary critics were making clear distinctions between the cine-novel and actual films. Making Ollier responsible for a special issue of *Cahiers du cinéma* was a sign of the editors' recognition of writers' contribution to cinematic production in the 1960s. Following Metz's view, Ollier argued that narrative is a shared feature of all films although 'until now this common denominator of almost all filmic products has been largely ignored' (1966: 12). Narrative also emerged as a new variable in assessing the difference between cinema and literature and was discussed by Ricardou in 'Page, film, récit'.

Ricardou's interest in the question of narrative predates the publication of Todorov's *Théorie de la littérature* (1965) and can be traced back to his avid interest in the works of Jorge Luis Borges in the early 1960s. Ricardou contributed to the special issue of *Cahiers de l'Herne* on Borges and wrote a review of Bioy Casarès' *L'Invention de Morel*, which was prefaced by Borges (1964a; 1965). As mentioned above, Borges' 'Narratif et l'art magique' was important for bringing narrative to the attention of the *Tel Quel* critics. In 'Page, film, récit' Ricardou emerges as a careful student of the Russian Formalists. His article is a response to Claude Bremond's analysis of narrative, 'Le message narratif' (1964), based on Vladimir Propp's *Morphology of the Folktale* (1968).

Bremond argues that the same plot can be represented in different media and remain unaltered. The plot can curtail or change medium because of the limitations imposed by the chronology, which is an integral element of the plot. The plot can limit the medium, but no medium alters the plot (Bremond in Ricardou 1967b: 80–1). Ricardou points out that the only situation in which the medium can display its full potential is when the domination of chronology disappears and the plot is no longer the driving force of the narrative. He already suggested this in 'Plume et caméra' where he argued that the disappearance of plot reveals the film's formal structure. *La Jalousie* serves as an example of such a new type of fiction where chronology and plot are challenged and replaced by a different type of logic, which is based on textuality. He calls *La Jalousie* 'the novel of pagination' because the feeling of jealousy, which is the main subject of the novel, 'has nothing to do with the chronological progress of the events, but rather refers to the combinations of the events and descriptions of the characters happening from one page to another' (1967b: 82). In such types of fiction, cinematic and literary signs become 'narrative signs', which are responsible for forming cinematic and literary narratives respectively (1967b: 83).

Ricardou agrees with Bremond that plot-driven narratives are comparable because plot and chronology can constrain literary or cinematic signs in such a way that they lose their specificity. At the same time, Ricardou emphasises the fact that cinematic and literary narratives are different if they are not determined by plot and chronology but by the specificity of their signs. It is for this reason that his analyses of the differences between cinematic and literary signs in 'Page, film, récit' are essential for establishing the specificity of the respective narratives of film and literature. However, the examination of the differences between cinematic and literary signs shows that there are numerous similarities between them. As a result the assemblies of cinematic and literary signs, described and analysed by Ricardou, are not capable of generating media-specific narratives.

Ricardou identifies four categories which allow him to juxtapose literary and cinematic signs and argue for their specificity. Firstly, he suggests that literary signs are linear while cinematic ones are spatial with various audiovisual layers superimposed one onto the other: image, dialogue, music, sound, and so on (1967b: 83). In his analysis Ricardou focuses primarily on avant-garde cinema and attempts to establish a difference between literature and avant-garde cinema, which in turn suggests that more popular forms of cinema which rely on the principles of continuity editing and cause/effect plots might be in fact related to literature. As we have seen, Barthes argued that cinematic signs associated with commercial cinema were metonymic, hence closer to what Ricardou considers to be a characteristic of literary signs; avant-garde cinema was seen by Barthes as metaphoric, which according to Ricardou's taxonomy appears to be a feature of cinematic signs. Secondly, Ricardou repeats his argument outlined in 'Plume et caméra', according to which the number of objects appearing in literary description is necessarily limited, while that appearing in cinematic signs is unlimited and as though automatic (1967b: 84). Thirdly, he emphasises that cinematic signs are analogous and realistic while literary ones are 'unmotivated' (1967b: 83). Fourthly, he suggests that cinematic and literary signs are different, because the workings of the camera cannot be imitated in writing (1967b: 85–7).

The second and third sets of oppositions define cinematic signs in such a way that they simply are not capable of generating narrative. Although in 'Page, film, récit' Ricardou believes that such cinematic signs can produce cinematic narrative, he does not explain how this could actually happen. At the same time, it is important to remark that literary and cinematic signs reveal more similarities when they are taken out of their respective categories. As Barthes points out in the *Cahiers* interview, the linearity of literary signs is comparable to the analogous and continuous nature of cinematic signs, even if their arrangement is not determined by plot and chronology. The spatiality of cinematic signs requires the association of various signifiers such as sound and image and the identification of a message which results from bringing all this information together. This process of synthesis is abstract in nature and therefore could make the cinematic sign thus defined comparable to abstract literary signs.

In the fourth category of signs Ricardou contrasts the nature of camera movements with that of literary descriptions. Camera movements are characterised by two extremes: the camera can move around a fixed object or it can frame a rapidly moving object (1967b: 87). A literary description is not capable of capturing the movement of an object because it is difficult to convey the transformation of the object. For this reason, writers prefer to describe objects which are not mobile – photographs or paintings (1967b: 85). However, Ricardou's distinction between cinematic and literary signs is not quite convincing. It is equally difficult for the camera to frame a moving object as it is for a writer to describe it. The camera is more capable than a description of immobilising an object through framing.

In his argument, Ricardou attempts to demonstrate the difference between cinematic and literary signs: he wants to establish their specificity in order to show that narratives differ depending on the medium in which they are conveyed. He thus advances the hypothesis that avant-garde cinema is narrative and made up of signs. As we have seen, Ricardou's position is different from that of Barthes, who believed that only commercial cinema was narrative, yet Ricardou did not manage to establish the specificities of literary and cinematic signs. The weakness of Ricardou's argument supports Metz's view that all types of cinema are narrative and related to literary narrative.

Ricardou bases his argument on examples of the avant-garde cinema of Robbe-Grillet. However, the differences described by Ricardou can be easily contested from the perspective of Barthes' argument about commercial cinema. This is particularly revealing in two cases. Firstly, Ricardou proposes that literary signs are metonymic, which for Barthes is a characteristic of the cinematic sign in commercial cinema. Secondly, Ricardou argues that literary signs are abstract in nature, while cinematic ones are realist and analogous. However, Barthes demonstrated earlier that the interaction of sounds and images in cinema makes cinematic signs abstract in nature. It is narrative which can emphasise the linear aspect of literary signs.

Contextualising Ricardou's view from the perspective of Barthes' and Metz's arguments and, as a result, identifying the shortcomings of Ricardou's position reveals an important development in the critical discourse of cinema. Perhaps the greatest innovation and eventually the crucial weakness of Ricardou's position stems from this attempt to establish the specificity of cinematic and literary narratives without taking into account the arguments of either Barthes or Metz. Historically, their arguments developed from the views of the cinematic and film critics of the 1950s who, like Ricardou, attempted to establish the specificity of their respective arts. Yet analysis of these earlier arguments shows that, despite the critics' efforts to maintain the specificity of their arts, narrative emerged as their shared feature. Ricardou was simply trying to cast these arguments in semiotic terms. Critical analysis of Ricardou's argument also allows us to establish that both cinema and the novel share the same type of narrative.

In *Praxis du cinéma* (1986), the critic and theorist Noël Burch discusses common features of literary and cinematic narratives. An 'American in Paris' is one way to describe Burch, who decided to live in France as a young adult in the early 1950s with the intention of becoming a filmmaker. Annette Michelson calls him a 'brilliant outsider', operating on the margins 'of the purlieu of French academic life and the traditional philosophical culture of the Parisian *agrégé*' (1973: xiii). One cannot help but draw a parallel with another *étranger* on the Parisian cultural scene – the very talented engineer Alain Robbe-Grillet, whose work inspired the majority of Burch's insights in *Praxis du cinéma*. Burch graduated from L'Institut des Hautes Etudes Cinématographiques (IDHEC) but found it difficult to begin his career as a filmmaker. Originally, the essays from *Praxis du cinéma* were published as a series of articles in *Cahiers du cinéma*. Hence, Burch had a dual identity as a practitioner and a theoretician of cinema.[25] In 1973, Burch wrote that for him 'filmmaking, teaching and writing were indissoluble parts of the same epistemological search' (1973b: xvii). Hence, his excursion into theory, which began with *Praxis du cinéma*, was not just an expression of a temporary intellectual passion but an essential part of a life-long endeavour. It was also a way of inscribing himself into the French tradition where artists often combined their artistic activity with criticism.

Michelson rightly points out that *Praxis du cinéma* was both the result of and a contestation of the concept of the avant-garde developed by André Bazin, which offered 'an endorsement of the conventions of our narrative cinema that was to produce the orthodoxy of the 1960s and its attendant strategy, *la politique des auteurs*'; for her, Bazin 'laid the foundation for that revision of the canon that was to animate the critical orthodoxy of the post-war period and continue well into the 1960s' (1973: v). She continues that 'it is within and against the context of this orthodoxy that one must read and understand *Theory of Film Practice*' (1973: vi). This indicates that Burch's work marks an end to the reign of Bazin's school of thinking but it is also indebted to it. Burch can be seen as a champion of the avant-garde represented by Robbe-Grillet, Godard and Marcel Hanoun. At the same time, his interest in narrative structures and in the ways in which 'film's narrative can be generated out of technical parameters' seems to be an attempt to rewrite in structuralist terms *Cahiers'* vision of cinema centred on *mise-en-scène* (Bordwell 1985: 279). Burch's reflections regarding the evolution of narrative in modern cinema continue in his article 'Propositions', where he sets up a taxonomy of narrative and develops a theory of 'textual production' (in Burch & Dana 1974: 42). Burch's conception of structure continued to be informed by an effort to establish parallels with 'serial music, non-figurative painting, non-narrative dance and conceptual structure' (ibid.). More generally, his ideas could also be seen as a development of Ricardou's arguments emphasising formal aspects of cinema as generators of cinematic narrative.

Michelson points out that *Praxis du cinéma* theorises the great discoveries made by the generation of intellectuals to which both Burch and Michelson belonged (1973: xiv–v).[26] These involved, on the one hand, a search for an avant-garde which developed against the constraints of the film industry and the possibility of seeing the films discussed in *Praxis du cinéma* as examples of this avant-garde production (1973: xii). On the other, the discoveries outlined in *Praxis du cinéma* signified an effort to introduce contemporary anthropological and linguistic discourse into film criticism. Burch was constantly involved with the contemporary avant-garde and looked back to the avant-garde of the 1920s. In the series *Cinéastes de notre temps*, he made a programme about Marcel L'Herbier and the avant-garde of the 1920s. Later, he wrote a study of L'Herbier's cinema (1973a).[27] He was also the author of a two-part programme in the *Cinéastes de notre temps* series about Robbe-Grillet's career as a filmmaker.[28] As though in response to contemporary intellectual tendencies, *Praxis du cinéma* incorporated the tools of formal structural analysis into the study of film. In this way, structuralist theory became a new mode of film criticism also practised by Christian Metz.

The earlier discussion of Metz's 'Le cinéma et la narrativité' showed how structuralist theory allowed him to present avant-garde cinema in narrative terms. In *Praxis du cinéma* Burch demonstrates how theory dramatically changed the nature of the cinema/literature relationship. Using the example of Robbe-Grillet's literary and cinematic works, Burch widened the definition of cinema to include Robbe-Grillet's novelistic writing as well. He also identified common structural elements in literary and cinematic narratives. The concepts of *découpage* and 'parameters' were central in the process of defining this new extended cinema. While *découpage* emphasises the literary dimension of the final stage of the film script, 'parameters' refers to film techniques which can also be found in literary texts. According to Burch, *découpage* was unique to French film and to French language. It is neither a script nor a transcription of the finished film but rather a presentation of the film before it is made which takes into account the work which will be accomplished during the editing of the film. *Découpage* emphasises the fact that film could be understood as an assembly of 'slices of time and slices of space' (1986a: 11); it was a way of rendering the narrative in the forms of scenes and sequences before the actual shooting took place, an imaginary film *par excellence*. Along with cine-novels, *découpage* was regarded as another species of film/literature hybrids which, in the context of French film and literary criticism, were gaining a status equal to that of film proper. It is enough to mention the ambiguous status of Robbe-Grillet's *découpage* of *L'Année dernière à Marienbad* in relation to Resnais' film. In *Praxis du cinéma*, Burch uses *découpage* to trace the development and transformation of cinematic style. In this type of analysis, *découpage* and film are both expressions of a filmmaker's style. *Découpage* thus emphasises the textual dimension that filmmaking has in Burch's view.

Burch calls the classical Hollywood style which renders changes of shot unnoticeable, 'the zero degree of cinematographic writing' (1986b: 22). Such designation of the cinematic style recalls Barthes' term and shows how its meaning changed in Burch's writing by comparison with its original meaning. Contemporary cinema distances itself from the cinematic techniques which had been responsible for establishing 'the zero degree of cinematographic writing'. In this, it severs its link with novelistic structures and supposedly replaces them with new ones, which are inspired by serial music.[29] Burch refers to them as 'parameters' and announces the advent of a creative effort which arranges them into new structures (1986b: 28–9).[30] Such an effort is particularly evident in the works of such artists as Robbe-Grillet whose work, both in cinema and literature, is structuralist because it reworks the structures which are travel itineraries (1986b: 100). This suggests that Robbe-Grillet's works such as *Trans-Europ Express* could be analysed by using the mode of travel itinerary as a conceptual tool. The film starts when a train departs from Paris and ends when it arrives in Anvers. During this journey all the elements of the film, like characters and events, are introduced and their narrative potential explored, developed and exhausted. Burch's main point about 'itinerary-like structures' is that they present the abstract nature of narrative structure in a less abstract manner if they are constructed around such easily recognised and understood organising principles as travel (1986b: 101). Flashback is another structural element which Burch examines. Like voice-over, it was first used in writing and later adopted in cinema. The identical nature of flashback and flashforward in cinema was exposed and examined by Robbe-Grillet in the *découpage* of *L'Année dernière à Marienbad* (Burch 1986a: 18). It is striking that a written text was capable of presenting the various tenses used to capture the nature of film, which lacks tense. The implementation of the flashback in the *découpage* of *L'Année dernière à Marienbad* shows the struggle of a written text to approach film by limiting its temporal dimension to the present tense. This also makes evident how the ambiguous nature of *découpage* allows Burch to conduct a comparative analysis of Robbe-Grillet's cinema and his literary works.

Burch argues that the choice of the subject of films is essential for formal development in cinema, because 'a subject creates forms, and for this reason the choice of a subject is necessarily an aesthetic choice' (1986b: 240). Aesthetics grow out of thematics. He shares this view with the critics of *Cahiers du cinéma*, who addressed formal questions about film by analysing its subject (1986b: 199). Burch argues that his approach is particularly close to that of the *Cahiers* critics who became filmmakers:

Our goal is on the one hand to make cinema, and on the other to watch it, but to watch *as though we were making it*, which means [to see it] as a perceptible reality. (1986b: 242)

Hence, Burch's perspective implies a connection between criticism and creative work. In other words, the critical approach proposed by Burch, which he describes as 'theoretical', is a way of conceptualising cinema by those who make film rather than by those who merely consume or analyse the final product. In this respect, Burch's analytical framework is different from the tradition of *Cahiers*. Theory also presents a step forward from the *politique des auteurs* and Burch claims that for him 'it is only the *works* which matter' (1986b: 245). Making the work central brings to the fore the questions of *mise-en-scène* and style which are reframed in theoretical terms derived from structuralism and serial music.

According to Burch, Robbe-Grillet's work is a major step towards developing 'the functional subject', in which formal developments are managed and driven by the subject. Burch counts both Robbe-Grillet's cinematographic and literary works as contributing to this process. For him, Robbe-Grillet's novels are examples of 'written cinema' (1986b: 206). He constructs this claim on the basis of a rather clichéd understanding of the cinematic element in Robbe-Grillet's fictional work. In search of new novelistic forms, this new novelist created 'the pseudo-cinematographic writings' such as superimpositions, dolly tracks and panoramic shots while his long descriptions constituted 'an attempt to recreate the objectivity which characterises the cinematic image' (1986b: 207). His belief in the presence of cinematic forms in Robbe-Grillet's novels led to Burch's claim that cinema was a real extension of Robbe-Grillet's literary works (ibid.). Cinema appears as the most natural and obvious creative engagement to be pursued by this writer. It is the stress he places on the formal elements of Robbe-Grillet's oeuvre which allows Burch to consider Robbe-Grillet's literary works as part of cinema and to rationalise and naturalise Robbe-Grillet's shift into filmmaking. Hence, theoretical analysis succeeds in connecting cinema and literature in a new way.

The 'multiplying narration' present in *Le Voyeur* (1955) was one such formal element which literature shared with cinema. This type of narration was used and improved in *L'Année dernière à Marienbad*. The key characteristic of this narration was its tight and circular formal structure, mirrored in different elements of the narration, which functioned as a kind of *mise-en-abyme* (1986b: 208), and analysis of the 'multiplying narration' in *L'Année dernière à Marienbad* explains how its formal structures function and become evident. The spectator's memory is central to discerning the characteristics of this type of narration:

> Each sequence, each event refers us (through repletion, 'deviation' or contradiction) to one but generally numerous other moments of the film; so, it is by relying on the spectator's memory, by testing his recollections of the film which is unfolding before the eyes of the spectator, that the authors achieve an effect whereby at every moment the mechanism of the film reflects, in microcosm, the very subject of the film. (1986b: 209)

The structure of such films depends on the spectator's ability to link and relate its different elements. Hence, at a given moment, what is unseen seems to be even more crucial than what is seen. Burch says that 'the subject is the summary of the action, even if this action is purely mental' (1986b: 213). This emphasises the abstract nature of theoretical analysis.

It was Burch's critique of Resnais' failure to capture the essence of Robbe-Grillet's narrative experiment in *L'Année dernière à Marienbad* which led to his praise of *L'Immortelle* as an example of a most perfect realisation of 'multiplying narration' (1986b: 210). Burch characterised *L'Immortelle* as breaking down realist conventions in cinema in a very controlled manner. The objective of *L'Immortelle* 'is a gradual "deterioration" of the *vraisemblable* [something that is true or plausible] through a combination of a maze of coincidences which are increasingly artificial in nature' (1986b: 211). It is possible that the challenge to the *vraisemblable* could imply the reintroduction of some of the chance elements into film narration present in early cinema, but eventually codified and harnessed by the rules of classical Hollywood filmmaking (1986b: 157–8). Among others, it was this element of 'le hasard'/chance, present in cinematic narration, which made cinema so attractive to the Surrealists. Burch is referring to these Surrealist preferences when he compares the type of narration used in *L'Immortelle* to that found in the works of H. P. Lovecraft and in other fantastic novels (1986b: 211). With its focus on the formal structure of literary and cinematic works, theoretical analysis offered conceptual tools to explain Surrealist experiments with literary and cinematic narration as well. This link between Burch's analysis and Surrealism also shows how Burch developed new terms to express those elements of narrative which were previously described through references to dreams and the unconscious. Theory made it possible for critical discourse to enter a new conceptual phase.

PURITAN NARRATIVES

Burch's *Praxis du cinéma* demonstrated that cinematic and literary narrative shared a number of structural elements. This allowed him to argue that literary narratives, especially those created by avant-garde artists like Robbe-Grillet, who was experienced in both arts, could be treated as part of cinema. Robbe-Grillet's reflections following his work on his second film, *Trans-Europ Express*, explore Burch's vision further, revealing that the nature of narrative structures is determined by literature, which brings to mind Jean Cayrol's arguments regarding Lazarean fiction. Cayrol and Robbe-Grillet both endorsed the idea that narrative expresses the visual or cinematic and thus dominates it. It is the domination of the visual by the verbal which seems to be responsible for a successful adaptation of narrative created in these terms for the needs of the novel.

Trans-Europ Express is the story of two parallel journeys from Paris to Amsterdam, one of them real and the other imagined. Robbe-Grillet himself in the role of a scriptwriter, Jérôme Lindon, the founder of the Editions de Minuit, as a film-producer, and Catherine Robbe-Grillet acting as a continuity girl spend their travel time on the Trans-Europ Express writing a script for a new film about smuggling drugs from Paris to Antwerp. The scriptwriter imagines the main character, Elias, who travels on the Trans-Europ Express on his first assignment. In Antwerp he has a casual encounter with a prostitute Eva, whom he strangles once he discovers that she has betrayed him: the first in a series of betrayals which lead to Elias's arrest by the police. In the course of the film, the scriptwriter grows sceptical about the authenticity of the facts, while Elias becomes more and more confused as to the loyalty of his partners.

Trans-Europ Express was an attempt on the part of Robbe-Grillet to incorporate the lessons he learned while working on *L'Année dernière à Marienbad* and *L'Immortelle* into his new cinematic project. After the experience of *L'Immortelle*, Robbe-Grillet did not write a detailed script before the film was made but instead decided to be more spontaneous during the shooting. This decision perhaps reflects his increased confidence as a film-maker and his greater familiarity with the film medium. The narrative struc-ture of the film is more complex and self-reflexive than that of *L'Immortelle*. It is also much more explicit in terms of pornographic images, which result-ed in a trial against Robbe-Grillet and the film in Italy (see Van Wert 1977: 4).[31] In the context of Robbe-Grillet's oeuvre *Trans-Europ Express* is unique, because for the first time he delayed the publication of the cine-novel until after the film was finished; the cine-novels of *L'Année dernière à Marienbad* and *L'Immortelle* were completed before the films were made. The published versions were altered but not substantially. The case of *Trans-Europ Express* was made more difficult because there was no final script of the film; the preparations for the writing of the cine-novel of *Trans-Europ Express* initi-ated a new phase in the conception of the cinema/literature relationship.

In spite of Robbe-Grillet's promises, the cine-novel of *Trans-Europ Ex-press* was never published, but the writer's experience making this film found its way into his fiction, for example in *Projet pour une révolution à New York* (1970). For the first time in Robbe-Grillet's career, the cinema's impact on literature had become evident. The new role of cinema was reflected in the function and treatment of the erotic element in *Trans-Europ Express* and in Robbe-Grillet's theoretical reflections inspired by his work on this film. But this new role for cinema was only possible because cinema was dominated by literature, as narrative became a way of encompassing and expressing the cinematic.

Robbe-Grillet identifies cinema with erotic images of women and for this reason his treatment of the pornographic images of women in *Trans-Europ Express* reflects his understanding of cinema. The example of the script-writer in the film suggests that the creation of narrative structures which are not plot-driven is central in this process. The scriptwriter is so preoc-cupied with maintaining the coherence and logic of his plot that he misses out completely on the very prominent erotic element of the film (in Capdenac 1967: 18). *Trans-Europ Express*, which was scripted and directed by Robbe-Grillet, portrays him as just this sort of artist. He argues that the nature of pornographic images is altered if they are arranged into new formal struc-tures (in Smith 1992: 32–3). The lawyers' defence of *Trans-Europ Express* in the Italian court was built around this idea. The film was not pornographic because Robbe-Grillet undercut 'the erotic element with obvious insertion of lies, performance/ritual and shifting point of view' which acted as 'dis-tancing devices between the viewer and the film viewed' (Van Wert 1977:

30). Narrative structures can alter the nature of pornographic images, and by extension that of cinema, by making them into a literary device. Even though the investigation of narrative form is shared by cinema and literature, the origins of narrative are in literature. This is evident in the adjustments cinema must make to develop a narrative structure. This point was already demonstrated by Jean Cayrol whose Lazarean fiction was an artistic concept initially developed for the needs of the novel. It privileged the verbal element associated with narration over the visual one.

Robbe-Grillet argues that novel writing possesses two defining characteristics: it is both subjective and abstract (1967: 132). The subjectivity of writing is linked to the character of the medium – language where 'the sentence does not represent anything else than itself, that is the mind that created it' (1967: 135). Cinema can be comparable to literature only if it possesses some of these characteristics. This is difficult because cinema, unlike literature, is objective and sensuous. Hence, it is only by breaking or denying in some way its objective and sensuous nature that cinema approaches literature. This happens through the operation of *découpage* and *montage* (1967: 134). *Découpage* could be understood as a process of making a literary text cinematic prior to filming, while *montage* is a way of reworking the filmed material. Through *découpage* and *montage* cinematic narrative comes to resemble literary narrative.

The origins of Robbe-Grillet's association of cinema with eroticism, pornography and sexual crime could be traced to the way he treats images of women in his writing. It is his preface to Jean Berg's *L'Image* (1956) which is very revealing in this respect. Robbe-Grillet argues that Berg describes there an image of a woman who 'regards herself with an anxious gaze while at the same time she remains an object which is looked at, raped, sacrificed and always reborn, whose pleasure consists of contemplating her own image through a subtle interplay of mirrors' (2001: 52). The female body and image are similar in that they are malleable and changeable at the will of a master or a filmmaker. Robbe-Grillet transfers this view onto cinema, which he defines as 'doing pretty things to pretty women' (1992: 145). *Trans-Europ Express* made it evident that narrative tools are indispensable in this process of manipulating and assembling images. At the same time, cinema began to emerge as 'a favoured tool used to confront, empower or surpass this real against which Robbe-Grillet struggles' (Robbe-Grillet 1987: 179). This instigated a change in the cinema/literature relationship when Robbe-Grillet returned to literature with *Projet pour une révolution à New York*. This change was not brought about by his first film projects, *L'Année dernière à Marienbad* and *L'Immortelle*, which were followed by *Instantanés* (*Snapshots*, 1962) and *La Maison de rendez-vous* (*The House of Assignation*, 1965), respectively. One of the reasons might be that the cine-novels rather than the novels were the forum for experimenting with narrative which naturally reflected their cinematic origins. For this reason, the absence of a cine-novel of *Trans-Europ Express* opened the way for experiments in the novel.

In *Projet pour une révolution à New York*, the literary narrative reveals some cinematic characteristics. The narrative techniques and the imaginary of this work show how the tools developed in cinema can also be used in literature. For instance, the narrative of the novel is created through an interaction between changing images from a book cover and sounds recorded on tape. Hence, in this novel Robbe-Grillet seems to be trying to recreate some of the sensuous nature of cinema through direct address to the spectator (1962: 8). The relationship between the reader and the text will come to resemble that between spectator and film by becoming erotically charged. Eroticism is a vehicle for achieving in literature the visceral and sensuous impact associated with cinema which is not just restricted to images but seems to define the very experience of cinematic spectatorship (1962: 41). Robbe-Grillet also uses cinematic vocabulary, such as 'cut', in the body of the text, which makes the novel resemble a *découpage* in its form. This creative project is strongly influenced by cinema. The theory of cinema and literature, when it is cinematicised (or eroticised) loses its abstract character and becomes more intuitive and emotionally charged. As a result, it is more accessible.

CAHIERS' DISTRUST TOWARDS THEORY

Robbe-Grillet's films received a less than enthusiastic reception in *Cahiers du cinéma*. Rather than seeing this purely as a personal attack on the new novelist, it is worth considering wider critical tendencies that this rejection by *Cahiers* demonstrated. It was a reaction to the advent in film criticism of structuralist analysis which privileged narrative, associated with literature, at the expense of the visual, and placed scriptwriters and writers-turned-filmmakers in the critical spotlight. For these reasons, it is not surprising that *Cahiers'* reaction to Robbe-Grillet's films was to a large degree foreshadowed by their reception of Cayrol's work as a film theorist and a filmmaker. The fact that Robbe-Grillet constructs his defence using the terms derived from *Cahiers'* criticism of the 1950s nevertheless demonstrates the strength of this original criticism and the difficulty of challenging it. Jean Narboni, who contests Robbe-Grillet's project in *Cahiers*, contrasts it with the films of Godard, whom he considers one of *Cahiers' auteurs*.

The energy and forcefulness with which Narboni defends Godard and attacks Robbe-Grillet should not be read solely as a value judgement passed by the critic on these filmmakers. Instead, Narboni's position is a reflection of some strong tendencies present in *Cahiers'* criticism. It shows that the arguments of the critics of the 1950s were so deeply rooted that they became a basis for the majority of the statements found in *Cahiers* in the late 1960s. The difference between the reception of Robbe-Grillet and that of Godard points to certain continuities present in *Cahiers'* criticism in the late 1960s regarding the *politique des auteurs* and the understanding of cinema in terms of *mise-en-scène*.

In his review of *Trans-Europ Express*, 'La maldonne des sleepings' (1967), Narboni juxtaposes Robbe-Grillet's attempts at filmmaking with Godard's achievements. Robbe-Grillet in *Trans-Europ Express* and Godard in *Pierrot le fou* both engage in artistic projects which are concerned with narrative, but according to Narboni, Godard is much more successful because of his superior understanding of the cinematic medium. Narboni's criticism of Robbe-Grillet is best understood in the context of the transformation that *Cahiers* was undergoing at the time. The *nouvelle vague* was considered finished, although it had had a huge impact on formal developments in national cinemas all over the world (see de Baecque 1991b: 99–149). At the same time, French cinema was in crisis with commercial production dominating the scene. In January 1965, a special issue of *Cahiers du cinéma* was published under the title '*Crise du cinéma français*' ('Crises of French cinema'). The release of *Pierrot le fou* in 1965 and Bresson's *Au hasard Balthasar* in 1966 began to restore the *Cahiers* critics' confidence in the aesthetic achievement of French cinema. Narboni's critique reflects some of the enthusiasm of *Cahiers* for Godard's films, but it does not yet use the new critical language that *Cahiers* was in the process of developing. Although *Cahiers du cinéma* had already seen the publication of a special issue on narrative in film and cinema, the first articles by Christian Metz and Noël Burch and an interview with Roland Barthes, Narboni's article does not mention these new trends and tendencies coming from structuralism and semiotics. Years later, Robbe-Grillet was still very bitter about the reception his films got in *Cahiers* and claimed that they never managed to break out of their Bazinian way of conceptualising cinema (1987: 175).

Robbe-Grillet was dismissive of the critical efforts of the *Cahiers* critics. Unfortunately, it was they who had the decisive voice in the reception of his films, not only immediately after their release, but also in the years to come. Robbe-Grillet's antipathy towards *Cahiers* reflects the filmmaker's insistence that his films needed a different critical language from that traditionally associated with *Cahiers*. Robbe-Grillet's or Cayrol's films were artistic experiments which could be conceptualised most successfully in the terms derived from literary theory, adopted for the purposes of film criticism. This explains their emphasis on narrative and associations with formal structures of their novelistic works.

The fact that Narboni in some way by-passes the contemporary research undertaken in *Cahiers* is evident in his preoccupation in his discussion of narrative not with narrative structures, but with the creative act and the role of the artist. In this Narboni qualifies Doniol-Valcroze's definition of a modern work presented in his review of *L'Immortelle*. Doniol-Valcroze argued that the lack of plot was the modern work's key characteristic. Traditional films had a closed structure which masked the presence of the author, while modern works are unfinished and open. For his part Narboni focused on the unsettling impact the critical intervention of a filmmaker had on the work itself because this intervention 'takes a form of doubt rather than the proud affirmation of his powers' (1967: 65). This loss of control over the work was something Narboni found very unsettling.

Cahiers' focus on narrative and on the role of the filmmaker was an expression of the *politique des auteurs*. Along with the cinema's relationship to other arts and the question of realism, these are the terms of traditional *Cahiers* criticism and they provide the basis for Narboni's argument. Robbe-Grillet's interviews and critical writing allow him to reconstruct his defence around the same issues. Hence, the critical paradigm adopted by Robbe-Grillet was derived from and built on that of *Cahiers du cinéma*. Robbe-Grillet's response and Narboni's criticism also show how the two critical tendencies appear to coexist on the pages of *Cahiers* in the latter part of the 1960s, despite the advances made by theory into film criticism.

Narboni based his understanding of Godard's cinematic achievement on the ontological concept of cinema, which dates back to Bazin's essentialist idea of cinema and to the *politique des auteurs* which paired the characteristics of cinema with those of other arts. According to Narboni, Godard truly succeeded in transforming cinematic narrative because he made his films not into artificial constructions, but rather into films, which were 'increasingly intimate in their texture', created through 'erasure, scribbling and ink stains' (1967: 65). Godard's success was therefore based on his intimate engagement with the medium, as he managed to transform the very texture of the film which could be made subject to the same processes as paper, or more widely, the text-based medium of literature.

Narboni suggests that Godard's images are as close to painting as they are to writing. He argues that the filmmaker disintegrates the image into colours and sounds and makes it more abstract (ibid.). Godard revealed the close affiliation of his images with painting and music when he said that cinema's only means of expression are 'music and painting, which as you know, live without ever uttering a word' (1989d: 259). He also related his project in cinema to that of Michel Butor in fiction (in Comolli *et al.* 1989). Clearly Godard wanted to be like a writer in cinema: the level of abstraction which he tries to attain and his interest in the projects of modern writers suggest that his engagement with the medium is an expression of the idea of the camerapen or, rather, the camera-brush.

Both Narboni and Godard subscribed to an old *Cahiers* idea, debated in detail in the 1950s by Eric Rohmer, about cinema as being comparable to different arts. Godard based his work in cinema on this idea. It led him to the conclusion that

The history of cinema is that of errors: an error of wanting to represent ideas better than music, to illustrate actions better than a novel and to describe feelings better than painting. In short, one could say that *errare cinématographicum est...* (1989a: 212)

Narboni may have found in Godard a filmmaker who took the ideas of critics very seriously, mainly because he never ceased to consider himself a critic and tested these ideas creatively. Before he made *Pierrot le fou*, Godard had remained within the critical paradigm of André Bazin. Each of his films was an engagement with Bazin's theory, its commentary and critique. *À Bout de souffle* (1959), *Une femme est une femme* (*A Woman is a Woman*, 1961), *Vivre sa vie* (*It's My Life*, 1962), *Les Carabiniers* (*The Carabineers*, 1963), *Le Mépris* (*Contempt*, 1963) and *Bande à part* (*The Outsiders*, 1964) all broke the code established for their respective genre, whether it be thriller, musical or war film. In Godard's films one has the impression of 'a sequence which was not an image, an idea, or a reflection of the world, but something amputated from the world, a living flesh ripped out of the infinite body'

(Narboni 1967: 65); Godard carves shots and sequences of his films out of the 'flesh' of reality. This is connected to Godard's idea that a creative act in cinema is like an act or sign of life. In spite of his critical attitude towards Bazin's ideas, Godard was essentially supporting them.

Narboni was very critical of Robbe-Grillet's work in cinema and contrasted it with that of Godard. Robbe-Grillet, he claims, did not manage to transform narrative, but only to put it in doubt by peppering it with 'perhaps' and 'it seems that' (ibid.). Robbe-Grillet merely qualified segments of his narrative. Narrative, Narboni contended, was at the centre of Robbe-Grillet's interest and created the basis for his engagement with cinema; it also provided a focus for his theoretical investigation. Hence, Narboni's criticism of Robbe-Grillet is that of a different critical paradigm.

Narboni also argued that Robbe-Grillet's cinema is full of clichés which he only repeats and with which he does not engage creatively. He holds that the erotic in his films is a manifestation of the 'pure stereotypes' which 'can hardly be qualified as erotic at all' (ibid.). This position conflicts with that of Robbe-Grillet; for him, clichés, myths, stereotypes and dreams, expressed in contemporary advertisements and fashion present in the streets and in window displays constitute our collective imaginary and result in 'the civilisation of the image' (in Capdenac 1967: 18). It is the erotic clichés which are among the most potent elements of culture used by Robbe-Grillet as material for his works (see Gardies 1983: 116). At the same time, Robbe-Grillet believes that clichés manage to preserve some of the dual nature of cinema because they are a constant interplay between dream and reality, the subjective and the objective. He can thus say that 'dream figures are those of reality' (in Gardies 1983: 115). His films explore cinema and reality in a very complex way which is different from that of Godard. The real difference between Godard and Robbe-Grillet is that the latter manages to establish a stricter separation between the level of the *vraisemblable* and that of fantasy, reality and fiction, in his *Trans-Europ Express*. The only moment when fantasy is brought uncomfortably close to reality is when Elias is also identified as Jean-Louis Trintignant, the actor. Godard mixes reality and fiction in a way which makes them truly indistinguishable. Robbe-Grillet's investigation of cinematic forms is more controlled than that of Godard which could be associated with the writer's explicitly theoretical preoccupations linked to structuralism.

Narboni also reproaches Robbe-Grillet for being a writer working in cinema. He criticises his use of clichés because Robbe-Grillet's method is literary and does not reveal any grasp of the cinematic medium (1967: 66). Narboni's negative evaluation of Robbe-Grillet's film project shows that the opinion of *Cahiers* regarding this artist had not changed since his first film. In fact, Narboni points out that in *Trans-Europ Express*, 'Robbe-Grillet continued down the road already indicated in *L'Immortelle* where he tells a vague detective story made of elements which are improbable, doubtful and perhaps completely imagined' (1967: 65).

Yet Robbe-Grillet saw his work in cinema as completely different from his work in literature (see Robbe-Grillet 1967: 134). The raw material of cinema is in stark contrast with the abstraction of language, which is the material of writing. In other words, Robbe-Grillet argues that his experiment in cinema is that of a filmmaker not a writer. For him, this film institutes a breach between his understanding of cinema and that proposed by the *Cahiers* critics of the 1950s. Later this rupture led to the development of that theoretical discourse which also encompassed Robbe-Grillet's films. This development restored cinema's breach with literature on a different level – that of theoretical discourse.

Narboni appears to be both one of the fiercest critics of Robbe-Grillet's films and one of the most ardent defenders of the *politique des auteurs*. Godard is presented as *Cahiers'* filmmaker *par excellence* who accepts and questions the ontological myth of cinema, sees his films as affiliated with other arts, and compares himself to a writer in cinema. Unlike Godard, Robbe-Grillet's engagement with film narrative is superficial. This evokes Barthes' criticism of Robbe-Grillet's films, the infamous 'confusion of meaning' instead of suspending meaning. For both critics, Robbe-Grillet's identity as a writer precludes him from understanding the medium of cinema in the way filmmakers like Godard do. Narboni reproaches Robbe-Grillet for stressing too strongly the independence of narrative in cinematic production and for making the literary element too prominent in his films.

Narboni's criticism reveals the co-existence of two tendencies in film criticism in the 1960s. There are the remnants of earlier *Cahiers* criticism which proposed the *politique des auteurs* and privileged film directors over all other contributors to films. This tradition was still very strong and had the power to explain and interpret new phenomena in cinema, such as Godard's films. It was also fiercely opposed to new critical trends and tendencies, especially those which in any way privileged the literary element in film criticism. For this reason, *Cahiers* critics rejected Robbe-Grillet's and Cayrol's ventures into filmmaking, and were reluctant to accept the arguments of

semioticians and structuralists who had become prominent among film critics. Nevertheless, the critical tendencies associated with theory and the shift
of writers into filmmaking is very important in the history of film criticism.

Narboni's argument shows that new developments associated with the advent of theory were related in two ways to the *politique des auteurs* of the
1950s. On the one hand, theory was a logical step in the development of film
criticism which resulted in the search for a new critical language. The search
for this language accounts for the shift of the new novelists into filmmaking.
On the other, Narboni's argument also demonstrated the importance and
strength of the arguments associated with the *politique des auteurs* in the
late 1960s. What made the critical discourse of cinema in that period so rich,
diverse and exciting was the coexistence of and tensions between different
critical tendencies.

The developments in semiotics, structuralism and the formal analysis of
narrative in the 1960s were crucial for the growth of theory into a new critical language of cinema. They reflected a shift in cinema's relationship with
literature, resulting from the new novelists' engagement with cinema as film
directors in their own right. The importance of theory can be only understood in light of the critical discourse which preceded it – the *Cahiers* criticism of the 1950s – which established narrative as the common denominator of cinematic and literary works. For these *Cahiers* critics, narrative had
the same characteristics whether it was part of the cinematic or the literary
medium. Paradoxically, thus defined, narrative was also supposed to convey
the specificity of each art. Moreover, in the 1950s, literary and cinematic
production was considered distinct. This critical assumption waited to be
tested until the shift of the new novelists into filmmaking. They believed
that cinematic and literary narratives were the same in nature. It was the
creative process of filmmaking which convinced artists like Robbe-Grillet
that cinema and literature were in fact distinct and different. This moment
of crisis did not overshadow the fact that, with their films, the new novelists succeeded in bridging cinematic and literary production in the work of
the 1960s avant-garde. Theoretical discourse focused on defining the terms
with which this new phenomenon could be described, and these terms were
derived from a structuralist analysis of narrative. Critics such as Noël Burch
identified the same structural characteristics in literary and cinematic narrative, and theory was introduced into the critical discourse of cinema gradually, in stages. This reflected the chronology of the development of semiotics and the structural analysis of narrative which took place in the 1960s.

Firstly, there was an attempt to conceptualise cinema and literature in terms of signs, exemplified in the works of Jean Ricardou and Roland Barthes. Secondly, Christian Metz identified common structural elements in literary and cinematic narrative. Thirdly, Noël Burch argued that, thus defined, narrative included literary works. Theory thus not only offered an alternative but also extended the definition of narrative common to literary and cinematic works proposed by the *Cahiers* criticism of the 1950s. This was a development which concluded two decades of thinking and writing about cinema, which began in the early 1950s with the work of young *Cahiers* critics, directed and inspired by André Bazin, and ended in 1968, when Jacques Rivette, one of the *Cahiers* critics and *nouvelle vague* filmmakers, stopped being the chief editor of *Cahiers du cinéma*. Thus, an important and exciting period in the history of the critical discourse of cinema ended.

Conclusion

The events of May 1968 introduced politics into French culture in a way that was unprecedented in the post-war period. Cinema was affected by this 'political storm' because, as Alain Resnais said in an interview with Jacques Belmans, by then 'cinema joined other arts' (1968: 188). Resnais' statement signalled the end of a period which had lasted nearly two decades and was marked by an astonishing richness and variety of creative works and critical reflections. Through the prism of the cinema/literature relationship developed on the creative level by the new novelists and the *nouvelle vague* filmmakers, and mirrored in the critical discourses of cinema and literature, we have observed the processes through which the art of the novel and the art of cinema were described. Their definitions were cast in terms of narrative, which was believed to have the same features irrespective of the medium. Jean Cayrol's critical work in cinema and literature has been central in shaping the ideas presented in this study. Cayrol's theoretical writings presented the principles of an interaction of cinematic and literary elements in the cine-literary narrative of cinematic and literary works. These cine-literary narratives revealed themselves as highly dynamic structures in which cinematic or visual elements are found at the basis of narratives in cinema and in literature, and expressed by the verbal element. Cayrol showed that such cine-literary narrative was not just the expression of the arts of the novel and cinema, but also a model for the interaction between the critical discourses of the *nouveau roman* and the *nouvelle vague* during the years 1951–67. The cinematic scene was invigorated and changed by a former new novelist, Marguerite Duras, who became a filmmaker in her own right. It was also marked by the radical experiments of Jean-Luc Godard and Jacques Rivette, and by the ongoing work in cinema by Alain Resnais, Alain Robbe-Grillet and Jean Cayrol. In the late 1960s and early 1970s, when the *nouveau roman* and the *nouvelle vague* were slowly disappearing, the aesthetic and historical concerns of the past did not perish but were transformed.

Cayrol's attitude changed the least in the second half of the 1960s, after he finished his collaboration with Resnais on *Muriel ou le temps d'un retour*. In 1965, in co-operation with Claude Durand, he made *Le Coup de grâce*, and in 1969 he directed his last film, *Do Not Disturb = Prière de ne pas déranger*. Cayrol's films continued to be a realisation of the concept of cinema presented in *Le Droit du regard*, whose roots are found in *Pour un romanesque lazaréen*. The continuity between his projects was evident in the form of the script for *Le Coup de grâce*. The introduction was divided into sections entitled: 'décors', 'les faits', 'les personnages', 'rapport et tensions entre les personnages', and thus resembled that found in *Muriel ou le temps d'un retour*. It would not be an overstatement to say that Cayrol incarnated the spirit of the period in which he was making films. For this reason it might be surprising that in 1969 he decided to end his career in cinema so definitively. Some critics blamed Cayrol's problems with the distribution of his features for it. For his part, Cayrol explained that, for him, filmmaking was a way of finding himself at a time of his greatest desperation. He gave up filmmaking when he felt 'saved after the dark years when [he] had lost all hope' (1982: 111). The real reasons for Cayrol abandoning cinema are found in the transformation of the critical debates of both cinema and literature in the late 1960s. Yet Cayrol's heritage remained very prominent in subsequent debates concerning literature's relationship with cinema and the connections between aesthetics, politics and commercialisation.

Alain Resnais was a filmmaker whose work showed a remarkable coherence of ideas and interests across time. In the films which followed *Muriel ou le temps d'un retour*, he continued his collaboration with writers: Jorge Semprun on *La Guerre est finie* (*The War is Over*, 1966) and Jacques Sternberg on *Je t'aime, je t'aime* (1968). Although they were not associated with the *nouveau roman*, the character of and motivation for Resnais' collaboration with these writers seemed to be the same as his collaborations at the time of the *nouveau roman*. It is enough to read Sternberg's account of his work with Resnais to realise the degree to which it resembled that of Robbe-Grillet and Resnais on *L'Année dernière à Marienbad* (1968: 192–9). Literary collaborations in the late 1960s allowed Resnais to engage and to experiment with the problems which had been his concerns in the earlier stages of his career. The question of memory remained at the centre of his attention and was explored in historical and scientific ways.

In terms of both its subject matter and its aesthetics, *La Guerre est finie* was indebted to Cayrol's critical and creative work. The themes of the Spanish Civil War and the resistance movement made this film a continuation of both *Nuit et brouillard* and *Muriel ou le temps d'un retour*, as well as the expression of growing concern with subversive politics among French filmmakers. The second-person narration employed in the commentary of the film was an exploration in cinematic terms of a narrative technique found in Michel Butor's *La Modification* (*A Change of Heart*, 1957). This commentary could be seen as 'an acknowledgement by the filmmaker [Resnais] of the similarity of his medium to that of narrative fiction and to the art of storytelling' (Sweet 1981: 97). As before, formal experimentation on the level of narration in cinema was continued by filmmakers such as Resnais.

Resnais' next film, *Je t'aime, je t'aime* developed the themes of memory already expressed in *Toute la mémoire du monde*. As a science-fiction film, *Je t'aime, je t'aime* is related to Godard's *Alphaville* (1965) and Truffaut's *Fahrenheit 451* (1966), which explored the future of a French culture dominated by books and literature. The film's critics drew a comparison between *Je t'aime, je t'aime* and *La Jetée* (1963) by Chris Marker, who was Cayrol's close friend and companion during his career as a filmmaker and film critic (see Benayoun 1980: 130; Sweet 1981: 101). *La Jetée*, subtitled 'a photo-roman', was made out of a series of still pictures. The film's radical form provided a powerful means to express its main theme – scientific experiment with time and memory. The script of the film was also published, which allows us to see Marker as a practitioner of the cine-literary narrative, a form which was also inspired by Resnais. In *Toute la mémoire du monde* a library is a brain containing all written knowledge and culture, and in *Je t'aime, je t'aime* the brain of a writer is probed and examined. In both cases, cinema provides the possibility of exploring the collective and individual literary mind. In *Toute la mémoire du monde*, Resnais argued that cinema and literature make equal contributions to literary culture. In *Je t'aime, je t'aime* he uses cinema to explore the workings of the literary mind dominated by dreams, memories and fantasies.

After 1967, Robbe-Grillet and Resnais continued to make films, while engaging in contemporary debates, exploring new areas of artistic experimentation, and building upon their previous experiences in filmmaking. Robbe-Grillet did not publish scripts or cine-novels for his two films, *L'Homme qui ment* (*The Man Who Lies*, 1967) and *L'Eden et après* (*Eden and After*, 1969), which followed *Trans-Europ Express*. The distinctive feature of *L'Homme qui ment* was the flow of the speech of the main character who dominates all aspects of the film. This evokes Cayrol's vision of cine-literary narrative in which the verbal, in the form of narration, dialogue or monologue, takes over the visual aspect of the film. Such a triumph of the verbal over the visual, and Robbe-Grillet's decision not to publish the script of the film, was a recognition of the value of literary cinema. Paradoxically, this view was supported by the argument regarding the relationship between literature and cinema outlined in the introduction to the cine-novel of Robbe-Grillet's next film, *Glissements progressifs du plaisir* (*Successive Slidings of Pleasure*, 1974). The cine-novel was divided into three parts: synopsis, shooting script and the transcription of the film after it was shot and edited, called *découpage* (Robbe-Grillet 1974: 9–12), and he argued that *découpage* fully conveyed the meaning of the film through form. As we have seen, Noël Burch in *Praxis du cinéma* provided support for Cayrol's vision of cine-literary narrative by identifying common narrative structures in novels and films based on the 'découpages' of the films. In their visual and textual forms, Robbe-Grillet's films continued to be the expression of the cine-literary narrative as defined by Cayrol and Burch.

For Marguerite Duras and Jacques Rivette, research into cinematic forms was associated with an exploration of the literary works which inspired them. The terms in which Rivette accounted for his experience with Duras' film *Détruire, dit-elle* (*Destroy, She Said*, 1969) and the novel of the same title were the result of the work done by critics and artists in the 1950s and 1960s and conceptualised by Cayrol. In an interview with Duras, Rivette remarked that her novel created his own cinema in his head (see Duras 1969: 45). Similarly, after having seen the film, he was not able to read the book in any other way than as a script. Duras identified with Rivette's argument because while writing the novel she had had an impression of creating a hybrid work which 'could be read, performed and filmed at the same time' (ibid.). Duras went so far as to say that, after having made the film, she understood her novel much better and gained new insight into it. In other words, this film was the perfect expression of a novel and had deepened and intensified the qualities of the novel which, without the film, would not have been apparent, even to its author. This shows that by the late 1960s, the concept of the cine-literary narrative had become common currency in the debates about cinema and the novel. Not only Duras, but also critics of her earlier film, *La Musica* (1966), emphasised the central importance of *voix* or *parole* in the film narrative (see Bontemps 1967: 42). Their argument that the speech is the film's driving force evoked Cayrol's concept of the predominance of the verbal element over the visual one in cine-literary narratives.

Duras' and Rivette's films not only showed the triumph of critical ideas developed in the 1950s and 1960s, but also offered some new developments. Rivette's *La Religieuse* (*The Nun*, 1966), like Duras' *Détruire, dit-elle*, was based on a literary work, Denis Diderot's *La Religieuse* (written in 1760, but not published until 1796). As in the time of Truffaut's 'Une Certaine tendance du cinéma français', the issue of adaptation was connected to that of authorship. For Rivette and Duras, their films were not adaptations but existed as entities independent of the novels on which they were based. It was the idea of the 'death of the author' which introduced the separation between films and their literary sources. Rivette argued that in *La Religieuse* 'the idea was not to make an adaptation, rather [the main idea] was that there was no author at all [and] film was something that has already existed [prior to shooting]' (in Aumont *et al*. 1968: 19). Such a radical view of authorship seemed to be directly inspired by Barthes's 'La Mort de l'*auteur*' (1968), which also demonstrates that, as in the past, in the late 1960s new ideas about film often came from literary criticism. Barthes was the source of a new element present in cinematic narratives; he argued that the 'death of the author' would free up the language and promote writing [*écriture*] originating in the body of the writer (1984: 61). Both Rivette and Duras struggled to grant a quasi-physical dimension to the verbal part of their films, an attempt which could become a source of new forms, a new morality and also a new politics in cinema (see Rivette in Aumont *et al*. 1968: 20; Duras 1969: 51).

In the late 1960s, developments in the concepts of adaptation, authorship and formal experimentation had an impact upon the debates regarding cinematic history which focused on avant-garde cinema made by such filmmakers as Godard, Rivette and Duras, among others. The idea of cine-literary narrative was present in the avant-garde cinema made by the new novelists and the *nouvelle vague* filmmakers who came out of *Cahiers du cinéma*. Noël Burch and Christian Metz were among the most ardent supporters of the concept of the avant-garde. For this reason, the ground for historicising cinema in terms of the avant-garde was being prepared throughout the 1960s. In their article, 'La Première Vague', Noël Burch and Jean-André Fieschi presented a new stage in the process of constructing a history of cinema as they traced the origins of the post-war avant-garde to the French avant-garde of the years between 1910 and 1930, which included such artists as Jean Epstein, Marcel L'Herbier and Abel Gance. Fieschi argued that each filmmaker should look to the history of cinema to find his/her predecessors in the same way that 'each writer invents his/her own precursors' (in Burch & Fieschi 1968: 5). Literature also set an example for cinema in matters regarding the establishment and functioning of the institution of cinema and its legal status in France. In the context of the Cinémathèque Affair, concerning the management of the archives and the museum of cinema, Georges Sadoul compared the project of burning books presented by Truffaut in *Fahrenheit 451* to the 'assault' of the French government on Henri Langlois, the founder of the Cinémathèque Française, and on his longstanding film collection; Sadoul claimed that to fail to preserve films would be the same as destroying the collections of the world's most important libraries (1966: 61).

In the late 1960s, there were two important reasons, political and economic, for film critics' focus on avant-garde cinema. Jean-Louis Comolli argued that the experience of the *nouvelle vague* had revealed that 'economic structures, work conditions, structures of employment, the mechanism of production, distribution and exploitation' were of greater importance for the final shape of a film than 'artists or aesthetic concerns' (1966: 5). Certain aspects of the impact of the industry on cinema had already been highlighted by Godard in *Le Mépris* which portrayed cinema in the context of the ferocious pursuit of profit by an American producer who was ready to rewrite *The Odyssey* in order to increase returns on his film. Godard argued that money and the movie industry corrupted cinema, but not until the 1960s did he establish the link between the auto-reflection of cinema and financial issues. The realisation that cinema was an industry took place in the context of the increasing commercialisation of France and the development of mass society. It was with films such as *Deux ou trois choses que je sais d'elle* (*Two or Three Things I Know About Her*, 1966) that, through radical formal experimentation, Godard became a critic of a society of mass consumption which encouraged housewives to engage in part-time prostitution. The critique of society, and film aesthetics, were merging into one. The ground for this had already been prepared by Cayrol's warnings regarding the stupefying effects of colour revues in *Pour un romanesque lazaréen* and of commercial features in *Le Droit du regard*.

The government's censorship of Rivette's *La Religieuse* and its attempts to remove Langlois from his post as director of the Cinémathèque Française made the critics of *Cahiers du cinéma* painfully aware of the importance of politics for their reflection upon cinema, their very existence seeming to be threatened by external forces. The level of mobilisation of the *cinéphile* community in France and abroad was unprecedented. Truffaut compared the passions accompanying 'the Cinémathèque Affair' to 'the reunion of those enthusiastic young people who, ten years earlier, had given birth, in an atmosphere of rather exceptional camaraderie, to the "new wave"' (1983: xi). Truffaut's statement was important because it pointed to the Cinémathèque Affair as the final concerted action of the *nouvelle vague* movement, and defined both politics *and* formal research as the next step in the development of avant-garde cinema. In the course of the Cinémathèque Affair, *Cahiers du cinéma* provided an impulse to defend the institution which in the past had helped to establish an equality between the arts of cinema and literature.

The Cinémathèque Affair preceded the revolutionary events of May 1968 and introduced politics into the critical debates about cinema. Some aesthetically innovative films took politics as their main subject. Resnais' vision of revolutionary strife in Spain, *La Guerre est finie*, and Godard's prophetic portrayal of the events of May 68, *La Chinoise* (1967), were examples of such cinema. However, films with political themes did not really reflect the predominant attitude towards politics and cinema. For Rivette, Duras, Godard and Robbe-Grillet, to mention just a few, experimentation with cinematic forms was a political and even a revolutionary action. They were not interested in making films about politics but rather in making aesthetics the source of politics. This idea was exercised in the most radical and uncompromising way by Godard who in the late 1960s and early 1970s found himself almost entirely outside the established circuit of cinematic production and created the Dziga-Vertov group, which was credited for his films. According to Colin McCabe, Godard was engaged in a dual struggle concerning 'on the one hand the financing of films, the methods of production and distribution and, on the other, the organisation of sounds and images which compose the films themselves' (1980: 13). His formal experiments deconstruct 'the representation of our sexuality, the grammar of advertisements' by exploring the tension between sound and image (1980: 14). His privileging of language or sounds over the image was a continuation of the investigation into the nature of cine-literary narrative proposed by Cayrol in *Le Droit du regard*.

In spite of Godard's achievement in these areas, it would be a mistake not to mention Robbe-Grillet's films from the same period. The fact is that their ideas about the link between politics and aesthetics were closely related. Robbe-Grillet believed that 'narrative forms are ways of engaging an individual or the whole society' (1972: 106). This also applies to Godard's project where 'the problems of politics and art are articulated in the same terms: the terms provided by the forms of cinema' (McCabe 1980: 51). It is clear that the origins of political engagement thus understood are in the apolitical attitude of *Cahiers du cinéma* and the *nouvelle vague* filmmakers, who argued that the only politics they had was the *politique des auteurs*, and in the new novelists' indifference towards the concept of *littérature engagée*. The background to Cayrol's theory of cinema and the novel sheds further light on the concept of aesthetics as a vehicle for politics. As we have seen, Cayrol's motivation for the development of Lazarean fiction was his experience of the concentration camps and the Algerian War. For Cayrol, as for the filmmakers and writers of the late 1960s and early 1970s, experiments with forms were tools for political action.

The political turn among French filmmakers during this period was reflected in the more intense interest in politics among the critics of *Cahiers du cinéma* and a new film journal, *Cinéthique*, an offshoot of *Tel Quel*. *Cinéthique* was a radical voice which echoed the concerns of *Cahiers* critics expressed by Jean-Luis Comolli and Jean Narboni in such critical writings as 'Cinéma/Idéologie/Critique' (1969a, 1969b). For them, films were ideological because they were part of the economic system, which in itself was ideological. The role of criticism was to determine the ways in which films challenged or were inscribed into the dominant ideology on a formal level. Comolli and Narboni focused on Jean-Daniel's Pollet's film *La Méditerranée* (1963) as an example of a film which was not explicitly political in content but which possessed a political message because of its radical take on form. *Cahiers'* and *Cinéthique's* focus on Pollet's films in a number of articles in which they attempted to analyse the way in which cinematic forms can be politicised was the next step in the reflection on narrative initiated in the 1950s and conducted in the 1960s (see Anon. 1967). *La Méditerranée* itself presented some continuity with the previous phase of French film criticism. Pollet made the film in collaboration with Philippe Sollers, whose literary career, as we know, was launched by Jean Cayrol. In the late 1960s the importance of *Cinéthique* and of the literary movement of the *nouveau roman*, associated with *Tel Quel*, grew, and critical debates focused on defining ways in which narrative forms could be politically subversive. It is clear, then, that the apparent novelty of this political reflection on cinema nevertheless had its origins in the critical debates associated with the *nouveau roman* and the *nouvelle vague* between 1951 and 1967, and the questions of the art of cinema and the art of the novel.

Notes

1 Antoine de Baecque's studies provide an in-depth study of the debates in *Cahiers du cinéma* in the period 1951–81 (de Baecque 1991a and 1991b) and of the cultural history of cinema in the 1940s, 1950s and 1960s (de Baecque 2003). For the historical overview of the debates associated with the *nouveau roman*, see chapters two and four in this volume.

2 Following the argument of John Orr in *Cinema and Modernity* (1993) it might be more effective to describe Resnais, as well as other *nouvelle vague* filmmakers, as neo-modern rather than modern given that the post-war filmmakers were essentially echoing the modernist experiments of their silent predecessors.

3 All translations in this volume are mine unless indicated otherwise.

4 For an interesting account of Bazin's work as a critic and the central importance of the idea of realism in his writings, see Chateau (1996). For an overview of Bazin's life-long critical achievement, see Andrew (1990).

5 This is not to say that American Hollywood filmmakers did not collaborate with such prominent writers as William Faulkner. However, such literary contributions did not seem to be as contentious an issue for American film critics as they were for their French counterparts.

6 The inclusion of Bresson in this group was challenged by the participants of the debate '6 personnages en quête d'*auteurs*' and Bresson's individual artistic achievement was recognised.

7 Ginette Vincendeau points out the contradictions which resulted from *Cahiers* critics' embrace of Hollywood cinema. She argues that 'in their fascination with US cinema, they were totally oblivious to Hollywood's role in the French film market. The negation of the social and industrial aspects of cinema led to interesting inconsistencies in their positions: they despised the "studio-bound" French cinema of the 1940s and 1950s but extravagantly praised products of the Hollywood studio system; they proposed to remedy

the "crisis" of French cinema while ignoring one of its major causes' (1992: 57).

8 For a very interesting account of Sarraute's critical works, see Jefferson (1996).

9 For an account of Sartre's impact on the cultural life in France see Ranwez (1981), Davies (1987) and Boschetti (1988).

10 For a different account of the complexities of the new novelists' relationship with Sartre as far as the question of *littérature engagée* is concerned, see Britton (1992).

11 For the details of Sartre's relationship with cinema, see Contat & Rybalka (1974), de Baecque & Braunschweig (1984), Clerc (1985) and Chateau (2005).

12 For the continuous impact of the *politique des auteurs* on film theory, see Caughie (1981).

13 For an informative discussion of Barthes's concept of *écriture*, see Moriarty (1991).

14 For an account of Godard's work as a critic, see Cerisuelo (1989).

15 For accounts of Rivette's critical activity, see Rosenbaum (1977), Mereghetti (1992) and Liandrat-Guigues (1998).

16 Bioy Casarès had some experience in cinema but was never a filmmaker or a film critic. Along with Borges he wrote a script for Hugo Santiago's film *Invasion* (1968–69) (see Cozarinsky 1975: 97–100).

17 Butor's 'Le roman comme recherche', Robbe-Grillet's 'La plage', Cayrol's 'Paris-Brest' and excerpts of Duras' *Moderato cantabile* were also singled out for a special issue of *Cahiers du Sud* entitled 'A la recherche du roman' published in 1956 (Anon. 1956).

18 See Jean Cayrol and Claude Durand, 'Splendeur du cinéma', *Tel Quel*, 8, 1962, 72–4.

19 Although Cayrol's theoretical writings on cinema set him apart from the new novelists, they granted him place in the community of French writers who felt obliged to voice their opinions on cinema: André Malraux, Jean-Paul Sartre and Maurice Merleau-Ponty.

20 *Dimanche à Pékin* (*Sunday in Peking*, 1955); *Description d'un combat* (*Description of a Struggle*, 1960); *Cuba si* (1961); *Le Mystère Koumiko* (*The Koumiko Mystery*, 1965); *Si j'avais quatre dromadaires* (*If I Had Four Dromedaries*, 1966); two *films imaginaires*: *L'Amérique rêve* (1959) and *Soy Mexico* (1965) (see Marker 1967a).

21 Cayrol's filmography consists of six shorts. Four of them he co-directed

with Claude Durand: *On vous parle* (1960), *La frontière* (1961), *Madame se meurt* (1961), *De tout pour faire un monde* (1963). He was solely responsible for directing the other two shorts: *La Déesse* (1966) and *Do Not Disturb = Prière de ne pas déranger* (1966). Together with Durand he also co-directed a feature film, *Le Coup de grâce* (1965).

22 Durand wrote a novel, *La Nuit zoologique* (1979). His record as a film editor is very impressive and includes nearly thirty films directed by Henri Decoin, Denys de la Patellière and Jean Meyer among others between 1950 and 1964.

23 Alain Robbe-Grillet made the following films: *L'Immortelle* (1962), *Trans-Europ Express* (1967), *L'Homme qui ment* (*The Man Who Lies*, 1967), *L'Eden et après* (*Eden and After*, 1969), *Glissements progressifs du plaisir* (*Successive Slidings of Pleasure*, 1973), *Le Jeu avec le feu* (*Playing with Fire*, 1974), *La Belle captive* (*The Beautiful Prisoner*, 1982) and *Un bruit qui rend fou* (*The Blue Villa*, 1995). Marguerite Duras also embarked on a very impressive film career. For her filmology, see Hill 1993. For Cayrol's filmography, see chapter three in this volume.

24 Phillipe Sollers was a scriptwriter for Jean-Daniel Pollet's film *Méditerranée* (1963), which was a structuralist work. This film was the object of a careful investigation in *Cinéthique* (Fargier 1971). Georges Perec embarked on his career as a filmmaker with *Un Homme qui dort* (*A Man Who Sleeps*, 1974). He wrote a commentary for Daniel Bertolino and François Floquet's *Aho! Ou les hommes de la forêt* (1975) and Michel Pamart and Claude Ventura's *La Vie filmée des Français* (1975), a script for Bernard Queysanne's *L'Oeil de l'autre* (1976), dialogue for Jean-François Adam's *Retour à la bien-aimée* (*Return of a Good Friend*, 1979) and for Alain Courneau's *Série noire* (*Thriller Story*, 1979) and the text for Robert Bober's *Récits d'Ellis Island* (1979). He also directed *Les lieux d'une fugue* (1976). See also Perec 1971.

25 Burch was an assistant on Pierre Kast's *Amour de poche* (*Vest Pocket Love*, 1957) and *Le Bel âge* (*The Wonderful Age*, 1958). He also made documentary films about Robbe-Grillet and Marcel l'Herbier in André S. Labarthe's series *Les Cinéastes de notre temps*.

26 At this stage, it is necessary to mention the role of Noël Burch in introducing the *nouvelle vague* filmmakers to the English-speaking world with his article in *Film Quarterly*, 'Qu'est-ce que la Nouvelle Vague?' (1959). It is his presence on the critical stage of the French- and English-speaking worlds which was behind the decision to single out his book for translation and

publication.

27 With Jean-André Fieschi, Burch made a two-part documentary about the first avant-garde: *La Première Vague: No.1: Delluc et Cie*; *La Première Vague: No. 2: Marcel L'Herbier*, as part of the *Cinéastes de notre temps* series (1968). He is recognised as an expert on this kind of avant-garde writer. He also wrote chapters on L'Herbier, Eisenstein, Fritz Lang and Carl Theodor Dreyer in *Cinema: A Critical Dictionary* (Roud 1980). This shows that his commitment to avant-garde cinema remained unchanged even into the 1980s.

28 Noël Burch and André S. Labarthe. *1. Alain Robbe-Grillet: Les Formes d'Eros. 2. Alain Robbe-Grillet: La Designation.* (*Cinéastes de notre temps*, 1969).

29 Burch stresses the importance of his exposure to musical theory in the development of *Praxis du cinéma*. In his 'Preface to the English-Language Edition', he explains that he borrowed the concept of 'form' from André Hodeir's lectures on musical form at the IFC (1973b: xviii). Burch became acquainted with Hodeir's ideas in the early 1960s when he translated into English Hodeir's book on modern music; the idea of comparing film structures and parameters with musical ones seems to have been inspired by Hodeir's research. David Bordwell suggests that Pierre Boulez's *Penser la musique aujourd'hui* (1963) was another source of taxonomies used by Burch (1985: 278). Burch's interest in music demonstrates the importance of music criticism for the development of film theory.

30 The concept of parameters developed by Burch in *Praxis du cinéma* continues to live in the English-language context in the work of Bordwell's *Narration in the Fiction Film* (1985) where Bordwell develops a whole concept of parametric cinema when speaking about the cinema of Godard and Bresson in particular. He remarks that parametric narration was exceptional in that its historical context is less that of filmmaking than that of film theory and criticism. Burch seemed to realise this in 1986 when *Praxis du cinéma* was re-edited. He points out that it was theory which prompted the publication of *Praxis du cinéma* in the first place and it is the end of theory which prompts its re-editing (1986a: 12). This view is mirrored in Michelson's observation that '*Theory of Film Practice*, completed in 1967, attempts to inaugurate a fresh view of cinematic history, and also marks the conclusion of a historical period' (1973: xiv).

31 Later on, a similar charge was brought against an even more graphic film by Robbe-Grillet, *Glissements progressifs du plaisir*. Robbe-Grillet had prob-

lems distributing his films and was gradually finding himself on the margins of French film production. His films were part of French intellectual cinema which was becoming increasingly pornographic. An extreme example was Walerian Borowczyk, who became notorious for his pornographic films. In 1974 with *Les Contes immoraux* (*Immoral Tales*) he became the key figure in commercial pornographic cinema.

Bibliography

Abel, R. (1984) *French Cinema: the First Wave 1915–1929*. Princeton: Princeton University Press.

_____ (1993) *French Film Theory and Criticism. A History/Anthology 1907–1939. Vols. I and II*. Princeton: Princeton University Press.

Alazraki, J. (1990) 'Borges's Modernism and the New Critical Idiom' in E. Aizenberg (ed.) *Borges and His Successors: The Borgesian Impact on Literature and the Arts*. Columbia & London: University of Missouri Press, 99–108.

d'Allones, O. Revault (1967) 'Alain Resnais, antidoctrinaire', *Revue d'esthétique* 1, 123–30.

Alpigiano, J.-L. (1994) 'Le Cinéma lazaréen', unpublished MA thesis, held in Paris III-Sorbonne nouvelle.

Andrew, D. (1990) *André Bazin*. New York: Columbia University Press.

Anon. (1956) 'A la recherche du roman', special issue, *Cahiers du Sud*, 334.

_____ (1958) 'Le Nouveau roman,' *Esprit*, July-August.

_____ (1961a) 'Introduction', *Communications* 1, 1–2.

_____ (1961b) 'Les Entretiens de Cinémonde: Alain Resnais', *Cinémonde* 14 March, 9.

_____ (1962) 'Repères chronologiques du nouveau cinema', *Cahiers du cinéma* 136, 101–2.

_____ (1965) 'Crise du cinéma français', special issue, *Cahiers du cinéma* 161/162.

_____ (1966) 'Film et roman: problèmes du récit', special issue, *Cahiers du cinéma* 185.

_____ (1967) 'La Mer intérieure. Textes sur "Méditerranée"', *Cahiers du cinéma* 187, 35–8.

_____ (1978) 'Robbe-Grillet', *Obliques* 16–17, 21–38.

_____ (n.d.) 'Jean Cayrol', fiche personnalité, http://cinema.encyclopedie.personnalites.bifi.fr/index.php?pk=9792, accessed 6 December 2007.

Antelme, Robert (1957) *L'Espèce humaine*. Paris: Gallimard.

Astruc, A. (1992a [1945]) 'Prisonniers du passé' in A. Astruc *Du Stylo à la caméra et de la caméra au stylo*. Paris: L'Archipelag, 268–70.

_____ (1992b [1948]) 'Naissance d'une nouvelle avant-garde: la caméra-stylo' in A. Astruc *Du stylo à la caméra et de la caméra au stylo*. Paris: L'Archipelag, 324–8.

Aumont, J. J.-L. Comolli, J. Narboni and S. Pierre (1968) 'Le Temps déborde', Interview with Jacques Rivette, *Cahiers du cinéma* 204, 7–21.

Babcock, A. E. (1997) *The Nouveau Roman in France: Theory and Practice of the Nouveau Roman*. London: Prentice Hall International.

Baby, I. (1957) 'Alain Resnais présentera les coulisses de la Bibliothèque Nationale', *Les Lettres françaises* 18–24, 6.

de Baecque, A. (1991a) *Les Cahiers du cinéma: histoire d'une revue. Vol. I., A l'assaut du cinéma: 1951–1959*. Paris: Cahiers du cinéma.

_____ (1991b) *Les Cahiers du cinéma: histoire d'une revue. Vol. II, Cinéma, tours détours: 1959–1981*. Paris: Cahiers du cinéma.

_____ (1998) *La Nouvelle vague. Portrait d'une jeunesse*. Paris: Flammarion.

_____ (2003) *La Cinéphilie*. Paris: Fayard.

de Baecque, A. and S. Braunschweig (eds) (1984) *Sartre et le cinéma*, special issue, *Avancées cinématographiques* 5.

Barrot, O. (1979) *L'Ecran Français 1943–1953: l'histoire d'un journal et d'une époque*. Paris: Les Editeurs français réunis.

Barthes, R. (1952) 'Jean Cayrol et ses romans', *Esprit* 3, 482–99.

_____ (1953) *Le Degré zéro de l'écriture*. Paris: Seuil.

_____ (1954) 'Jean Cayrol: L'Espace d'une nuit', *Esprit* 8, 150–2.

_____ (1957) *Mythologies*. Paris: Seuil.

_____ (1960a) 'Le Problème de la signification au cinéma', *Revue Internationale de Filmologie* 32–33, Vol. X, 83–9.

_____ (1960b) 'Les "unités traumatiques" au cinéma. Principes de recherche', *Revue Internationale de Filmologie* 34, Vol. X, 13–21.

_____ (1964a) *Essais critiques*. Paris: Seuil.

_____ (1964b [1954]) 'Littérature objective' in R. Barthes *Essais critiques*. Paris: Gallimard, 32–43.

_____ (1964c [1955]) 'Littérature littérale' in R. Barthes *Essais critiques*. Paris: Gallimard, 66–73.

_____ (1964d [1959]) 'Zazie et la literature' in R. Barthes *Essais critiques*. Paris: Seuil, 129–35.

_____ (1964e [1962]) 'Le Point sur Robbe-Grillet' in R. Barthes *Essais critiques*. Paris: Gallimard, 205–13.

_____ (1964f) 'Présentation', *Communications* 4, 1–3.

_____ (1964g) 'La Rature', postface to C. Cayrol *Les Corps étrangers*. Paris: U. Générale d'Editions, Col. 10/18, 233–47.

_____ (1964h) 'Rhétorique de l'image', *Communications* 4, 40–51.

_____ (1966) 'Intgroduction à l'analyse structurale des récits', *Communications* 8, 1–27.

_____ (1984 [1968]) 'La Mort de l'*auteur*' in R Barthes *Le Bruissement de la langue*. Paris, Seuil, 61–7.

_____ (1997 [1943]) 'Les Anges du péché' in *Robert Bresson: Eloge*. Paris: Cinémathèque Française, 15–17.

Bazin, A. (1947) 'La Technique de Citizen Kane', *Les Temps modernes* 17, 943–9.

_____ (1948) 'Roger Leenhardt a filmé le roman qu'il n'a pas écrit', *L'Ecran français* 27, 6–7.

_____ (1949) 'Le voleur de bicyclette ou l'épreuve victorieuse du néo-réalisme italien', *Esprit* 11, 820–32.

_____ (1975a [1943]) 'Rédecouvrons le cinema' in A. Bazin *Le Cinéma de l'occupation et de la résistance*. Paris: Union générale d'éditions, 35–9.

_____ (1975b [1943]) 'Pour une critique cinematographique' in A. Bazin *Le Cinéma de l'occupation et de la résistance*. Paris: Union générale d'éditions, 68–82.

_____ (1983) *Le cinéma français de la Liberation à la Nouvelle Vague (1945–1958)*. Paris: Cahiers du cinéma/Editions de l'Etoile.

_____ (1997a) *Qu'est-ce que le cinéma?* Paris: Cerf.

_____ (1997b [1946]) 'Le Mythe du cinéma total' in *Qu'est-ce que le cinéma?* Paris: Cerf, 19–24.

_____ (1997c [1948]) 'Le Réalisme cinématographique et l'école italienne de la Libération' in *Qu'est-ce que le cinéma?* Paris: Cerf, 267–93.

_____ (1997d [1951]) 'Le Journal d'un curé de campagne et la stylistique de Robert Bresson' in *Qu'est-ce que le cinéma?* Paris: Cerf, 107–27.

_____ (1997e [1958]) 'L'Evolution du langage cinématographique' in *Qu'est-ce que le cinéma?* Paris: Cerf, 63–80.

_____ (1997f [1959]) 'Peinture et cinéma' in *Qu'est-ce que le cinéma?* Paris: Cerf, 187–92.

Bazin, A. and J. Doniol-Valcroze, R. Leenhardt, J. Rivette (1957) '6 personnages en quête d'auteurs. Débat sur le cinéma français', *Cahiers du cinéma*, 71,

16–29 & 85–90.

Beaujour, M. (1965) 'Surréalisme ou cinéma' in Y. Kovacs (ed.) *Surréalisme et cinéma (1) Etudes cinématographiques* 38–39, 57–63.

Béguin, A. (1937a) *L'Ame romantique et le rêve, Vol.I*. Marseille: Edition des Cahiers du Sud.

_____ (1937b) *L'Ame romantique et le rêve, Vol. II*. Marseille: Edition des Cahiers du Sud.

_____ (1948) 'Jean Cayrol', *Cahiers du Sud* 287, 88–100.

_____ (1952) 'Giraudoux par lui-même', *Esprit* 7, 162–3.

_____ (1955a) 'Limites de l'histoire littéraire', *Esprit* 1, 166–70.

_____ (1955b) 'Notes sur la critique littéraire', *Esprit* 3, 447–51.

Belmans, J. (1968) 'Interview with Alain Resnais' in R. Prédal (ed.) *Alain Resnais, Etudes cinématographiques* 64–68, 185–91.

Benayoun, R. (1980) *Alain Resnais arpenteur de l'imaginaire: de Hiroshima à Mélo*. Paris: Stock.

Berendt, J. (1963 [1959]) *Le Jazz des origines à nos jours*, trans. C. Metz. Paris: Payot.

Beylie, C. (1964) 'Lumière de *Muriel*,' *Midi-Minuit fantastique* 8, 65–7.

Bioy Casarès, A. (1973 [1940]) *L'Invention de Morel*, trans. A. Pierhal. Paris: 10/18.

Bonnet, M. (1965) 'L'Aube du surréalisme et le cinéma: attente et rencontres' in Y. Kovacs (ed.) *Surréalisme et cinéma (1) Etudes cinématographiques* 38–39, 83–101.

Bontemps, J. (1966) 'Le cahier des autres: Film et roman: problèmes du récit', *Cahiers du cinéma*, special issue, 185, 8.

_____ (1967) 'Présentation de *La Musica*', *Cahiers du cinéma* 187, 42.

Bordwell, D. (1985) *Narration in the Fiction Film*. London: Methuen.

Borges, J.-L. (1961 [1932]) 'L'Art narratif et la magie', trans. P. Sollers. *Tel Quel* 7, 3–10.

_____ (1973 [1940]) 'Préface' in A. Bioy Casarès *L'Invention de Morel*, trans. A. Pierhal. Paris: 10/18, 7–10.

_____ (1975 [1945]) 'Au sujet du doublage' in E. Cozarinsky *Jorge Luis Borges: sur le cinema*, trans. A. Herbout. Paris: Editions Albatros, 87–9.

Borgomano, M. (1985) *Duras. Une lecture des fantasmes*. Petit Roeulx, Belgium: Cistre-Essais.

Boschetti, A. (1988) *The Intellectual Enterprise: Sartre and Les Temps moderne*, trans. R. C. McCleary. Evanston, Il: Northwestern University Press.

_____ (1997) 'Sartre and the Age of the American Novel' in J.-F. Fourny and

C. D. Minaken (eds) *Situating Sartre in Twentieth Century Thought and Culture*, trans. M.-T. Vanderboegh and D. Vanderboegh. Basingstoke: Macmillan, 71–92.

Bourin, A. (1959) 'Techniciens du roman: Interview with Jacques Rivette', *Les Nouvelles Littéraires:Lettres-Arts-Sciences-Spectacles* 1638, 1, 4.

Bremond, C. (1964) 'Le Message narratif', *Communications* 4, 4–32.

Bremond, C., E. Sullerot and S. Berton (1961) 'Les héros des films dits "de la Nouvelle Vague"', *Communications* 1, 142–77.

Dresson, R. (1957) 'Propos', *Cahiers du cinéma* 75, 3–9.

_____ (1975) *Notes sur le cinématographe*. Paris: Gallimard.

Breton, A. (1988 [1924]) *Manifeste du surréalisme* in M. Bonnet (ed.) *Oeuvres completes, Vol I*. Paris: Gallimard, 309–46.

Brion, F. (1972) 'Témoignages' in A. Gardies (ed.) *Alain Robbe-Grillet. Essai sémiocratique*. Paris: Seghers, 166–8.

Britton, C. (1992) *The Nouveau Roman: Fiction, Theory and Politics*. London: Macmillan Press.

Burch, N. (1959) 'Qu'est-ce que la Nouvelle Vague?', *Film Quarterly*, 2, 16–61.

_____ (1973a) *Marcel L'Herbier*. Paris: Seghers.

_____ (1973b) 'Preface to the English-Language Edition', N. Burch *Theory of Film Practice*, trans. H. R. Lane. London: Secker and Warburg, xvi–xx.

_____ (1986a) 'Avertissement' in N. Burch *Praxis du cinéma,* second edition. Paris: Gallimard, 11–18.

_____ (1986b) *Praxis du cinéma*, second edition. Paris: Gallimard.

_____ (1996) 'Cinéphilie et masculinité (I)', *Iris* 26, 191–6.

Burch, N. and J. Dana (1974) 'Propositions', *Afterimage* (UK) 5, 40–65.

Burch, N. and J.-A. Fieschi (1968) 'La Première Vague', *Cahiers du cinéma* 202, 20–4.

Butor, M. (1957) *La Modification*. Paris: Minuit.

_____ (1960) *Répertoire*. Paris: Minuit.

_____ (1962) 'La littérature, aujourd'hui – IV', *Tel Quel* 11, 58–65.

_____ (1964a) 'Mallarmé selon Boulez' in M. Butor *Essais sur les modernes*. Paris: Gallimard, 95–109.

_____ (1964b) 'Les Oeuvres d'art imaginaries chez Proust' in M. Butor *Répertoire II*. Paris: Minuit, 252–92.

_____ (1992a [1959]) 'Intervention à Royaumont' in M. Butor *Essais sur le roman*. Paris: Gallimard, 15–20.

(1992b [1964]) 'L'Espace du roman' in M. Butor *Essais sur le roman*. Paris: Gallimard, 48–58.

Butor, M., N. Sarraute, P. Daix, P. Gascar, C. Ollier, B. Pigaud, A. Robbe-Grillet and C. Simon (1959) 'Huit romanciers autour d'un micro aux "*Lettres françaises*"', *Les Lettres françaises*, 764, 1, 4–5.

Canudo, R. (1995 [1927] *L'Usine aux images*. Paris: Séguier/Arte.

Capdenac, M. (1967) 'Alain Robbe-Grillet, le jeu de l'aventure du mythe et de l'amour', *Lettres françaises* 26 January–1 February, 18.

Casetti, T. (1999) *Les Théories du cinéma depuis 1945*, trans. S. Soffi. Paris: Nathan.

Caughie, J. (1981) (ed) *Theories of Authorship: A Reader*. London: Routledge/ British Film Institute.

Cayrol, J. (1950a [1948]) 'Les Rêves concentrationnaires' in J. Cayrol *Lazare parmi nous*. Paris: Seuil, 15–66.

_____ (1950b) 'Chris Marker ou La Première Chance,' *Esprit* 9, 405–8.

_____ (1950c) *Lazare parmi nous*. Paris: Seuil.

_____ (1950d) *Le feu qui prend*. Paris: Seuil.

_____ (1950e) *Je vivrais l'amour des autres*. Paris: Seuil.

_____ (1951) 'Sacre et Massacre', *Esprit* 175, January, 1–8.

_____ (1953) 'Témoignage et literature,' *Esprit* 4, 575–8.

_____ (1954) *L'Espace d'une nuit*. Paris: Seuil.

_____ (1963a) 'La littérature, aujourd'hui – V', *Tel Quel* 13, 50–60.

_____ (1963b) *Muriel*. Paris: Seuil.

_____ (1964 [1950]) 'Pour un romanesque lazaréen', in J. Cayrol *Les Corps étrangers*. Paris: Union Générale d'Editions, 199–229.

_____ (1982) *Il était une fois Jean Cayrol*. Paris: Seuil.

_____ (1988) 'Jean Cayrol, la poésie au quotidian', *Magazine littéraire* 258, 114–21.

_____ (1997) *Nuit et brouillard*. Paris: Fayard.

Cayrol, J. and C. Durand (1962) 'Splendeur du cinema', *Tel Quel* 8, 72–4.

_____ (1963) *Le Droit du regard*. Paris: Seuil.

_____ (1965) *Le Coup de grâce*. Paris: Seuil.

Cerisuelo, M. (1989) *Jean-Luc Godard*. Paris: Editions de Quatre-vents.

Chateau, D. (1996) 'Bazin: le procès du film' in D. Chateau *Le Cinéma l'après guerre et le réalisme*. Paris: Jean-Michel Place, 32–57.

_____ (2005) *Sartre et le cinéma*. Biarritz: Séguier.

Clerc, J.-M. (1985) *Ecrivains et cinéma: des mots aux images*. Paris: Klincksieck.

_____ (1993) *Littérature et cinéma*. Paris: Nathan.

Cohen-Séat, G. (1946) *Essai sur les principes d'une philosophie du cinema*.

Paris: PUF.

J. Collet, M. Delahaye, J.-A. Fieschi, A. S. Labarthe and B. Tavernier (1999 [1962]) 'Interview with Jean-Luc Godard' in A. de Baecque and C. Tesson (eds) *La New Wave*. Paris: Petite bibliothèque des Cahiers du cinéma, 193–230.

Comment, B. (1993) 'Prétextes de Roland Barthes', *Magazine littéraire* 314, 59–63.

Comolli, J.-L. (1966) 'Situation I,' *Cahiers du cinéma* 176, 5.

Comolli, J.-L., J.-A. Fieschi, P. Kast, C. Ollier, J. Rivette (1963) 'Les Malheurs de Muriel', *Cahiers du cinéma* 149, 20–34.

Comolli, J.-L. and J. Narboni (1969a) 'Cinéma/Idéologie/Critique (I)', *Cahiers du cinéma* 216, 11–15.

_____ (1969b) 'Cinéma/Idéologie/Critique (II)', *Cahiers du cinéma* 217, 7–13.

Comolli, J.-L., M. Delahaye, J.-A. Fieschi and G. Guégan (1989 [1965]) 'Parlons de Pierrot' in A. Bergala (ed.) *Jean-Luc Godard par Jean-Luc Godard*. Paris: Flammarion, 263–80.

Contat M. and M. Rybalka (1974) 'Appendix on the Cinema' in *The Writings of Jean-Paul Sartre, I*. Evanston: University of Illinois Press, 601–12.

Cozarinsky, E. (1975) *Jorge Luis Borges: sur le cinema*, trans. A. Herbout. Paris: Editions Albatros.

Dauman, A. (1989) *Argos Films - Souvenir-Ecran*. Paris: Centre Georges Pompidou.

Davies, H. (1987) *Sartre and "Les Temps modernes"*. Cambridge: Cambridge University Press.

Delahaye, M. (1959) 'Un Entretien avec Alain Resnais', *Cinéma 59. Le Guide du spectacle* 38, 4–14.

_____ (1962) 'L'Idée maîtresse ou le complot sans maître', *Cahiers du cinéma* 128, 41–5.

Delahaye, M. and J. Rivette (1963) 'Entretien avec Roland Barthes', *Cahiers du cinéma* 146, 20–30.

Diderot, D. (1959 [1775]) *La Religieuse* in H. Bénac (ed.) *Oeuvres completes*. Paris: Editions Garniers Frères.

Dine, P. (1994) *Images of the Algerian War*. Oxford: Clarendon Press.

Domarchi, J., E. Rohmer, J.-L. Godard, P. Kast (1959) 'Hiroshima, notre amour', *Cahiers du cinéma* 97, 1–18.

Doniol-Valcroze, J. (1957) 'La Prisonnière Lucia', *Cahiers du cinéma* 77, 59–60.

_____ (1959) '*Les Quatre cents coups*', *Cahiers du cinéma* 96, 41–2.

_____ (1963) 'Istanbul nous appartient', *Cahiers du cinéma* 143,. 54–7.

Douchet, J. (1959) 'Avec *Hiroshima, mon amour* Alain Resnais a pris dix ans d'avance', *Arts Lettres Spectacles* 727, 4.

Durand, C. (1958) 'Le plat du jour,' *Ecrire* 6.

_____ (1979) *La Nuit zoologique*. Paris: B. Grasset.

Duras. M. (1959) 'Resnais travaille comme un romancier...', *Les Lettres nouvelles* 20, 36–8.

_____ (1960) *Hiroshima, mon amour. Scénario et dialogue*. Paris: Gallimard.

_____ (1963) *Détruire, dit-elle*. Paris: Minuit.

_____ (1969) 'La Destruction la parole: interview with Jacques Rivette', *Cahiers du cinéma* 217, 45–57.

Epstein, J. (1924) 'De quelques conditions de la photogénie', *Cinéa-ciné pour tous*, 15 August, 6–8.

_____ (1974 [1921]) 'Le Sens I bis' in J. Epstein *Ecrits sur le cinéma, Vol. 1*. Paris: Cinéma Club-Seghers, 85–93.

Fargier, J.-P. (1971) 'Vers le récit rouge (notes sur un nouveau mode de production de film)', *Cinéthique* 7–8, 9–19.

Faye, J.-P. (1957) 'Poèmes', *Ecrire* 3.

Fleischer, A. (1989) *L'Art d'Alain Resnais*. Paris: Centre Georges Pompidou.

Fouché, P. (ed.) (1998) *L'Edition française depuis 1945*. Paris: Editions du Cercle de la Librairie.

Gardies, A. (ed.) (1983) *Le Cinéma de Robbe-Grillet. Essai sémiocratique*. Paris: Editions Albatros.

Gauthier, G. (1991) 'Christiane Metz à la trace' in *CinéAction Histoire des théories du cinéma*, Corlet-Télérama, 146–53.

Genette, G. (1966 [1962]) 'Vertige fixé' in G. Genette *Figures I* (1959–1965). Paris: Seuil, 69–90.

_____ (1972) *Figures III*. Paris: Seuil.

Ghali, N. (1995) *L'Avant-garde cinématographique en France dans les années vingt. Idées, conceptions, théories*. Paris: Paris Experimental.

Gide, A. (1925) *Les Faux-monnayeurs*. Paris: Gallimard.

Godard, J.-L. (1958) 'Bergmanorama,' *Cahiers du cinéma* 85, 134–43.

_____ (1959) 'Chacun à son Tours', *Cahiers du cinéma* 92, 31–8.

_____ (1989a [1956]) 'Montage, mon beau souci' in A. Bergala *Godard par Godard*. Paris: Flammarion, 78–81.

_____ (1989b [1958]) '*Monika* d'Ingmar Bergman remporte un plein succès' in A. Bergala *Godard par Godard*. Paris: Flammarion, 146–7.

_____ (1989c [1965]) 'Pierrot mon ami' in A. Bergala (ed.) *Jean-Luc Godard par*

Jean-Luc Godard. Paris: Flammarion, 259–63.

____ (1989d [1985]) 'Commentaire de Jean-Luc Godard au disque du film *Une Femme est une femme*' in A. Bergala *Godard par Godard*. Paris: Flammarion, 210–15.

Gracq, J. (1950) *La Littérature à l'estomac*. Paris: Librairie José Corti.

Hess, J. (1974) 'La Politique des auteurs. World View as Aesthetis. Part One', *Jump Cut* 1, 19–22.

Higgins, L. A. (1996) *Nouveau Roman, New Wave, New Politics*. Lincoln: University of Nebraska Press.

Hill, L. (1993) *Duras: Apocalyptic Desires*. London: Routledge.

Hoveyda, F. (1960) 'Les Taches du soleil', *Cahiers du cinéma* 110, 33–43.

Insdorf, A. (1989) *Indelible Shadows: Film and the Holocaust*. Cambridge: Cambridge University Press.

Jefferson, A. (1996) 'Critique: notice' in N. Sarraute *Oeuvres completes*. Paris: Gallimard Bibliothèque de la Pléiade, 2034–50.

Jost, J. and D. Chateau (1979) *Nouveau cinéma, nouvelle sémiologie*. Paris: Union Générale d'Editions.

Kelly, M. (1979) *Pioneer of the Catholic Revival, the Ideas and Influence of Emmanuel Mounier*. London: Sheed and Ward.

King, J. (1986) *Sur. A Study of the Argentine Literary Journal and Its Role in the Development of a Culture, 1931–1970*. Cambridge: Cambridge University Press.

Kline, T. J. (1992) *Screening the Text: Intertextuality in New Wave French Cinema*. Baltimore: Johns Hopkins University Press.

Kyrou, A. (1963) *Le Surréalisme au cinéma*. Paris: Le Terrain Vague.

Labarthe, A. S. (1960a) 'Au Pied de la letter', *Cahiers du cinéma* 114, 58–60.

____ (1960b) *Essai sur le jeune cinéma français*. Paris: Le Terrain Vague.

____ (1961) 'La Chance d'être femme', *Cahiers du cinéma* 125, 53–6.

Labarthe, A. S. and J. Rivette (1961) 'Interview with Alain Resnais', *Cahiers du cinéma* 123, 1–18.

Larbaud, V. (1961 [1925]) 'Sur Borges', *Tel Quel* 7, 11–12.

Lawall, S. (1968) *Critics of Consciousness*. Cambridge: Harvard University Press.

Leenhardt, R. (1936) 'Le Rythme cinématographique,' *Esprit* 40, 627–32.

____ (1986) *Chroniques de cinéma*. Paris: Edition de l'Etoile/Cahiers du cinéma.

Liandrat-Guigues, S. (ed) (1998) *Jacques Rivette critique et cineaste. Etudes cinématographiques* 63. Paris: Lettres Modernes Minard.

Lowry, E. (1985) *The Filmology Movement and Film Study in France*. Ann Arbor, MI: UMI Research Press.

Magny, C.-E. (1948) *L'Age du roman américain*. Paris: Seuil.

Magny, J. (1986) *Eric Rohmer*. Paris: Rivages.

de Magny, O. (1958) 'Panorama d'une nouvelle littérature romanesque', *Esprit*, July–August, 3–17.

Malraux, A. (1996 [1946]) 'Esquisse d'une psychologie du cinéma,' *La Nouvelle Revue Française/Spécial cinéma* 520, 4–19.

Marie, M. (2002) *The French New Wave: An Artistic School*, trans. R. Neupert. Malden, Mass.: Blackwell Publishing.

Marker, C. (1950a) *Le Coeur net*. Paris: Seuil.

_____ (1950b) 'Orphée', *Esprit* 11, 694–701.

_____ (1952a) *Giraudoux par lui-même*. Paris: Seuil.

_____ (1952b) '*La Passion de Jeanne d'Arc*', *Esprit* 5, 840–3.

_____ (1953a) 'Le Cinérama', *Cahiers du cinéma* 27, 34–7.

_____ (1953b) 'Lettre de Hollywood', *Cahiers du cinéma* 25, 26–34.

_____ (1953c) 'Lettre de Mexico', *Cahiers du cinéma* 22, 33–5.

_____ (1954–81) *Collection Petite Planète*. Paris: Seuil.

_____ (1967a) *Commentaires I*. Paris: Seuil.

_____ (1967b) *Commentaires II*. Paris: Seuil.

_____ (1992) *La Jetée ciné-roman*. New York: Zone Books.

McCabe, C. (1980) *Godard: Images, Sounds, Politics*. London: British Film Institute/Macmillan Press.

Mereghetti, P. (1992) 'Jacques Rivette critique' in S. Toffetti and D. Giuffrid (eds) *Jacques Rivette: la Règle du Jeu*. Turin: Centre Culturel Français de Turin/Museo nazionale del cinema, 121–7.

Metz, C. (1964) 'Le Cinéma: langue ou langage', *Communications* 4, 52–90.

_____ (1966) 'La Grande syntagmatique du film narratif', *Communications* 8, 120–4.

_____ (1968a [1965]) 'A propos de l'impression de réalité au Cinéma' in C. Metz *Essais sur la signification au cinéma Vol. I*. Paris: Klincksieck, 13–24.

_____ (1968b [1966]) 'Le Cinéma moderne et la narrativité' in C. Metz *Essais sur la signification au cinéma Vol. I*. Paris: Klincksieck, 185–221.

_____ (1968c) *Essais sur la signification au cinéma Vol. I*. Paris: Klincksieck.

_____ (1968d) *Essais sur la signification au cinéma Vol. II*. Paris: Klincksieck.

_____ (1971) *Langage et cinéma*. Paris: Librairie Larousse.

Michelson, A. (1973) 'Introduction' in N. Burch, *Theory of Film Practice*, trans. H. R. Lane. London: Secker and Warburg, v–xv.

Molloy, S. (1972) *La Diffusion de la littérature hispano-américaine en France au XXe siècle*. Paris: Presses Universitaires de France.

Monaco, J. (1976) *The New Wave: Truffaut, Godard, Chabrol, Rohmer, Rivette*. New York: Oxford University Press.

Moriarty, M. (1991) *Roland Barthes*. Cambridge: Polity Press.

Morin, E. (1956) *Le Cinéma ou l'homme imaginaire*, trans. A. Pierhal. Paris: Minuit.

_____ (1961) 'Conditions d'apparition de la "Nouvelle Vague"', *Communications* 1, 139–41.

Mourlet, M. (1987) *La Mise-en-scène comme langage*. Paris: Editions Henri Veyrier.

Murcia, C. (1998) *Nouveau roman, nouveau cinema*. Paris: Nathan.

Narboni, J. (1967) 'La maldonne des sleepings', *Cahiers du cinéma* 188, 65–6.

Noguez, D. (1967) 'Choix bibliographique' in G. Poulet (ed.) *Les Chemins actuels de la critique*. Paris: Plon, 495–7.

Ollier, C. (1961a) 'Ce soir à *Marienbad* I', *NRF* 106, 711–19.

_____ (1961b) 'Ce soir à *Marienbad* II', *NRF* 107, 906–12.

_____ (1966) 'Présentation: Film et roman: problèmes du récit', *Cahiers du cinema*, special issue, 185, 12.

_____ (1981 [1963]) 'Muriel, qui es-tu?' in C. Ollier *Souvenirs écran*. Paris: Cahiers du cinéma/Gallimard, 140–52.

_____ (1996) *Cité de mémoire*. Paris: POL.

Orr, J. (1993) *Cinema and Modernity*. Cambridge: Polity Press.

Oster, D. (1973) *Jean Cayrol*. Paris: Seghers.

Perec, G. (1971) *L'Image: ses pouvoirs, ses limites, son role*. Paris: NRF.

_____ (1992 [1963]) 'Robert Antelme ou la vérité de la littérature' in G. Perec L.G. *Une aventure des années soixante*. Paris: Seuil, 87–114.

Pisier, M.-F. (1972) 'Témoignages" in A. Gardies (ed.) *Le Cinéma de Robbe-Grillet. Essai sémiocratique*. Paris: Seghers, 168–72.

Pleynet, M. (1957) 'Poèmes', *Ecrire* 2.

Prédal, R. (ed.) (1968) *Alain Resnais, Etudes cinématographiques* 64–68, 3–18.

_____ (1996) *L'Itinéraire d'Alain Resnais, Etudes cinématographique* 211–212, 85–110.

Propp, V. (1968) *Morphology of the Folktale*. Austin: University of Texas Press.

Queneau, Raymond (1942) *Pierrot mon ami*. Paris: Gallimard.

_____ (1959) *Zazie dans le métro*. Paris: Gallimard.

Rahv, B. T. (1974) *From Sartre to the Nouveau Roman*. London: Kenniket Press.

Ranwez, A. D. (1981) *Jean-Paul Sartre's Les Temps modernes. A Literary History 1945–1952*. Troy, NY: The Whitston Publishing Company.

Rasking, R. (1987 [1986]) 'Interview with Alain Resnais', *Nuit et brouillard*. Aarhus: Aarhus University Press, 47–63.

Resnais, A. (1948) 'Une expérience', *Ciné-Club* (*Organ de la fédération française des cinéclubs*) 3, 2.

_____ (1967) 'Pour jouer avec le temps,' interview with Bernard Pingaud, *L'Arc, Spécial Alain Resnais ou la création du cinéma*, 31, 93–102.

Resnais, A. and J. Cayrol (1963) '*Muriel* Interview'. *Lettres Françaises* 30 Septembre, microfiche.

Resnais, A. and J. Semprun (1974) *Repérages*. Paris: Chêne.

Resnais, A. and F. de Towarnicki (1962) *Les Aventures de Harry Dickson*. Unpublished script.

Ricardou, J. (1963) 'Réalités variables', *Tel Quel* 12, 31–7.

_____ (1964a) 'The God of the Labyrinth', *Jorge Luis Borges Spécial. Cahiers de L'Herne*, 125–6.

_____ (1964b) 'La Querelle de la métaphore', *Tel Quel* 18, 56–65.

_____ (1965) 'Deux livres opposes', *Tel Quel* 20, 90–2.

_____ (1966) 'Expression et fonctionnement', *Tel Quel* 24, 42–55.

_____ (1967a [1961]) 'Plume et caméra' in J. Ricardou *Problèmes du nouveau roman*. Paris: Seuil, 69–79.

_____ (1967b [1966]) 'Page, film, récit' in J. Ricardou, *Problèmes du nouveau roman*. Paris: Seuil, 80–8.

_____ (1967c) *Problèmes du nouveau roman*. Paris: Seuil.

_____ (1971a) *Pour une théorie du nouveau roman*. Paris: Seuil.

_____ (ed.) (1971b) *Nouveau Roman: hier, aujourd'hui. 1. Problèmes généraux*. Paris: UGE.

_____ (1973) *Le Nouveau Roman*. Paris: Seuil.

_____ (1976) *Robbe-Grillet: Analyse, Théorie. 1. Roman/Cinéma*. Paris: Union Générale d'Editions.

_____ (ed.) (1978) *Nouveaux problèmes du roman*. Paris: Seuil.

Rivette, J. (1953) 'Génie de Howard Hawks', *Cahiers du cinéma* 23, 16–23.

_____ (1955) 'Lettre sur Rossellini', *Cahiers du cinéma* 46, 14–24.

_____ (1957) 'La main', *Cahiers du cinéma* 76, 48–51.

Robbe-Grillet, A. (1951) 'Jean-Charles Pichon La Loutre', *Critique* 54, 1002–03.

_____ (1953a) 'Adolfo Bioy Casarès *L'Invention de Morel*', *Critique* 69, 172–4.

_____ (1953b) *Les Gommes*. Paris: Minuit.

_____ (1955) *Le Voyeur*. Paris: Minuit.

_____ (1956) 'Le Réalisme, la psychologie et l'avenir du roman', *Critique* 111–112, 695–701.

_____ (1957) *La Jalousie*. Paris: Minuit.

_____ (1959) *Dans le labyrinthe*. Paris: Minuit.

_____ (1961a) *L'Année dernière à Marienbad*. Paris: Minuit.

_____ (1961b) 'Entretien avec les deux auteurs du film *L'Année dernière à Marienbad*', *Le Monde*, 29 August, 9.

_____ (1962) *Instantanés*. Paris: Minuit.

_____ (1963a [1955]) 'A quoi servent les théories' in A. Robbe-Grillet *Pour un nouveau roman*. Paris: Minuit, 7–13.

_____ (1963b [1956]) 'Une Voie pour le roman future' in A. Robbe-Grillet *Pour un nouveau roman*. Paris: Minuit, 15–23.

_____ (1963c [1957] 'Sur quelques notions périmées' in A. Robbe-Grillet *Pour un nouveau roman*. Paris: Minuit, 25–44.

_____ (1963d [1961]) 'Nouveau roman, homme nouveau' A. Robbe-Grillet *Pour un nouveau roman*. Paris: Minuit, 113–21.

_____ (1963e [1962]) 'Temps et description dans le récit d'aujourd'hui' in A. Robbe-Grillet *Pour un nouveau roman*. Paris: Minuit, 123–34.

_____ (1963f) *L'Immortelle*. Paris: Minuit.

_____ (1963g), 'La littérature, aujourd'hui – VI', *Tel Quel* 14, 39–45.

_____ (1963h) 'Moi, un Robbe-Grillet…', *Le Figaro Littéraire*, 23 February, 3.

_____ (1965) *La Maison de rendez-vous*. Paris: Minuit.

_____ (1967) 'Brèves réflexions sur le fait de décrire une scène de cinéma. Antinomie du film et du roman', *Revue d'esthétique, nouvelle série 1*, 131–8.

_____ (1970) *Projet pour une révolution à New York*. Paris: Minuit.

_____ (1972) 'Témoignages' in A. Gardies (ed.) *Le Cinéma de Robbe-Grillet. Essai sémiocratique*. Paris: Seghers, 106.

_____ (1974) 'Introduction' A. Robbe-Grillet *Glissements progressif du plaisir ciné-roman*. Paris: Minuit, 9–19.

_____ (1978) *Trans-Europ Express* in 'Robbe-Grillet', *Obliques* 16–17, 21–38.

_____ (1987) *Angélique ou l'enchantement*. Paris: Minuit.

_____ (2001 [1956]) 'Préface' in J. Berg *L'Image* reprinted in C. Bourgois (ed.) *Le Voyageur. Textes, causeries et entretiens* (1947–2001). Paris: Christian Bourgois Editeur, 2001, 51–2.

Roger, B. (2000 [1951] 'Plan for a cinema at the bottom of a lake' in P. Hammond (ed.) *The Shadow and its Shadow: Surrealist Writings on the Cinema.* San Francisco: City Light Books, 80–1.

Rohmer, R. (1955a) 'Le Celluloïd et le marbre I. Le Bandit Philosophe', *Cahiers du cinéma* 44, 32–7.

_____ (1955b) 'Le Celluloïd et le marbre II. Le Siècle des Peintres', *Cahiers du cinéma* 49, 10–15.

_____ (1955c) 'Le Celluloïd et le marbre III. De la Métaphore', *Cahiers du cinéma* 51, 2–9.

_____ (1955d) 'Le Celluloïd et le marbre IV. Beau comme la musique', *Cahiers du cinéma* 52, 23–9.

_____ (1955e) 'Le Celluloïd et le marbre V. Architecture d'Apocalypse', *Cahiers du cinéma* 53, 22–30.

_____ (1984a [1948]) 'Le cinema, art de l'espace' in E. Rohmer *Le Goût de la beauté*. Paris: Cahiers du cinéma, 27–35.

_____ (1984b [1948]) 'Pour un cinéma parlant' in E. Rohmer *Le Goût de la beauté*. Paris: Cahiers du cinéma, 37–40.

_____ (1984c [1983]) 'Le Temps de la critique' in E. Rohmer *Le Goût de la beauté*. Paris: Cahiers du cinéma, 9–23.

Rohmer E. and C. Chabrol (1957) *Hitchcock*. Paris: Editions Universitaires.

Rosenbaum, J. (1995) 'Barthes and Film: 12 Suggestions' in J. Rosenbaum *Placing Movies. The Practice of Film Criticism*. Berkeley: University of California Press, 45–53.

_____ (ed) (1977) *Rivette: Textes and Interviews*. London: British Film Institute.

Ross, K. (1995) *Fast Cars, Clean Bodies: Decolonisation and the Reordering of the French Culture*. Cambridge, Mass: MIT Press.

Roud, R. (ed.) (1980) *Cinema: A Critical Dictionary*. London: Secker and Warburg.

_____ (1983) *A Passion for Films: Henri Langlois and the Cinémathèque française*. London: Secker & Warburg.

Roumette, S. (1961) 'Interview with Alain Resnais' in B. Pingaud (ed.) *Alain Resnais Spécial. Premier Plan* 18, 43–54.

Sadoul, G. (1966) 'Fahrenheit 1951 (Faut-il détruire tous les films anciens parce qu'ils sont inflammables?)', *Cahiers du cinéma* 184, 60–3.

Samson, P. (1967) 'Le lyrisme critique d'Alain Resnais' in *L'Arc, Spécial Alain Resnais ou la création du cinéma*, 31, 103–11.

Sarraute, N. (1939) *Tropismes*. Paris: Denoël.

_____ (1956a [1947]) 'De Dostoïevski à Kafka' in N. Sarraute *L'Ere du soupçon*.

Paris: Gallimard, 13–55.

____ (1956b [1950]) 'L'Ere du soupçon' in N Sarraute *L'Ere du soupçon*. Paris: Gallimard, 59–79.

____ (1956c) 'Conversation et sous-conversation' in N.Sarraute *L'Ere du soupçon*. Paris: Gallimard, 81–122.

____ (1956d) 'Ce qui voient les oiseaux' in N. Sarraute *L'Ere du soupçon*. Paris: Gallimard, 125–51.

____ (1956e) 'Préface' in N. Sarraute *L'Ere du soupçon*. Paris: Gallimard, 7–12.

____ (1962) 'La littérature, aujourd'hui – II', *Tel Quel* 9, 48–53.

Sartre, J.-P. (1938) *La Nausée*. Paris: Gallimard.

____ (1947a [1938]) 'Sartoris par W. Faulkner' in J. P. Sartre *Situations, I*. Paris: Gallimard, 7–13.

____ (1947b [1938)] 'A propos de John dos Passos et de 1919' in J. P. Sartre *Situations, I*. Paris: Gallimard, 14–24.

____ (1947c [1938]) 'M. François Mauriac et la liberté' in J. P. Sartre *Situations, I*. Paris: Gallimard, 33–52.

____ (1947d [1939]) 'A propos de Le Bruit et la Fureur. La temporalité chez Faulkner' in J. P. Sartre *Situations, I*. Paris: Gallimard, 65–75.

____ (1956 [1947]) 'Préface' in N. Sarraute *Portrait d'un inconnu*. Paris: Gallimard, 7–14.

____ (1964) *Les Mots*. Paris: Gallimard.

Sellier, G. (1998) 'Cinéphilie et masculinité (II)', *Iris* 26, 197–206.

Semprun, J. (1966) *La Guerre est finie. Scénario du film d'Alain Resnais*. Paris, Gallimard.

Seyrig, D. (1967) 'Délphine Seyrig', in *L'Arc, Spécial Alain Resnais ou la création du cinéma*, 31, 65–9.

Smith, R. C. (1992) 'The First Films: *Last Year at Marienbad* and *L'Immortelle*' in A. N. Fragola and R. C. Smith (eds) *The Erotic Dream Machine: Interviews with Alain Robbe-Grillet on His Films*. Carbondale and Edwardsville: Southern Illinois University Press, 23–33.

Sollers, P. (1957) 'Le défi', *Ecrire* 3.

Souriau, A. (1953a) 'Fonctions filmiques des costumes et des décors' in E. Souriau (ed.) *L'Univers filmique*. Paris: Flammarion.

____ (1953b) 'Succession et simultanéité dans le film' in E. Souriau (ed.) *L'Univers filmique*. Paris: Flammarion.

Sternberg, J. (1965) *Je t'aime, je t'aime. Scénario et dialogues pour un film d'Alain Resnais*. Paris: E. Losfeld.

_____ (1968) 'En travaillant avec Alain Resnais' in R. Prédal (ed.) *Alain Resnais, Etudes cinématographiques* 64–68, 192–9.

Sweet, F. (1981) *The Film Narratives of Alain Resnais*. Ann Arbor, MI: UMI Research Press.

Todorov, T. (1965a [1964]) 'Présentation' in T. Todorov (ed.) *Théorie de la littérature. Textes des formalistes russes*. Paris: Seuil, 15–27.

_____ (ed.) (1965b) *Théorie de la littérature. Textes des formalistes russes*. Paris: Seuil.

_____ (1971 [1966]) 'Langage et littérature' in T. Todorov *Poétique de la prose*. Paris: Seuil, 32–41.

Torok, J.-P. (1964) 'Le Surréalisme au cinéma', *Midi-Minuit Fantastique* 8, 81–2.

Tournès, L. (1999) *New Orleans sur Seine. Histoire du jazz en France*. Paris: Fayard.

de Towarnicki, F. (1967) 'Scénario' in *L'Arc, Spécial Alain Resnais ou la création du cinéma*, 31, 20–5.

Trintignant, J.-L. (1972) 'Témoignages' in A. Gardies (ed.) *Le Cinéma de Robbe-Grillet. Essai sémiocratique*. Paris: Seghers, 174–8.

Truffaut, F. (1983) 'Foreword,' in R. Roud *A Passion for Films. Henri Langlois and the Cinémathèque française*. London: Secker and Warburg, v–xv.

_____ (1987a [1954]) 'Une Certaine tendance du cinéma français' in F. Truffaut, *Le Plaisir des yeux*. Paris: Flammarion, 211–29.

_____ (1987b [1957]) 'Vous êtes tous témoins dans ce procès: le cinéma français crève sous les fausses légendes' in F. Truffaut, *Le Plaisir des yeux*. Paris: Flammarion, 234–49.

_____ (1987c [1969]) 'Le réalisateur, celui qui n'a pas le droit de se plaindre' in F. Truffaut, *Le Plaisir des yeux*. Paris: Flammarion, 9–18.

Van Wert, W. F. (1977) *The Film Career of Alain Robbe-Grillet*. Boston: G. K. Hall.

Vincendeau, G. (1992) 'France 1945–65 and Hollywood: the Policier as International Text', *Screen* 33, 1, 50–80.

de Vincenti, G. (1980) *Le Cinéma et les films des Cahiers du cinéma 1951–1969*. Venise: Massilio.

Virmaux, A. (1965) 'Une promesse mal tenue: le film surréaliste (1924–1932)' in Y. Kovacs (ed.) *Surréalisme et cinéma (1) Etudes cinématographiques* 38–39, 103–33.

Virmaux, A. and O. Virmaux (1983) *Un Genre nouveau: le ciné-roman*. Paris: Edilig.

Weyergans, F. (1961a) 'Avant les avant-premières', *Cahiers du cinéma* 116, 22–7.

____ (1961b) 'Dans le dédale', *Cahiers du cinéma* 123, 22–7.

Wilson, E. (2006) *Alain Resnais.* Manchester: Manchester University Press.

Wincock, M. (1975) *Histoire politique de la Revue Esprit 1930–1950.* Paris: Seuil.

Index